TRADE AND INVESTMENT ACROSS THE NORTHEAST BOUNDARY:

QUEBEC, THE ATLANTIC PROVINCES, AND NEW ENGLAND

TRADE AND INVESTMENT ACROSS THE NORTHEAST BOUNDARY:

QUEBEC, THE ATLANTIC PROVINCES, AND NEW ENGLAND

Edited by
WILLIAM D. SHIPMAN

The Institute for Research on Public Policy/
L'Institut de recherches politiques

Legal Deposit First Quarter
Bibliothèque nationale du Québec

Canadian Cataloguing in Publication Data

Main entry under title:
Trade and investment across the northeast boundary

Summaries in English and French.
ISBN 0-88645-031-4

1. Canada, Eastern-Commerce-New England.
2. New England-Commerce-Canada, Eastern.
I. Shipman, William D., 1925- II. Institute
for Research on Public Policy

HF3228.U5T73 1986 382'.0971 C86-090084-3

The Institute for Research on Public Policy/
L'Institut de recherches politiques
2149 Mackay Street,
Montreal, Quebec H3G 2J2

CONTENTS

FOREWORD

Canada-US economic relations are clearly one of the principal items on the public policy agenda in Canada at the present time. As the debate on the future of Canada-US economic relations unfolds at the national level, it is important that we take into account the interests and perspectives of individual regions of both countries.

For these reasons, the publication of *Trade and Investment Across the Northeast Boundary: Quebec, the Atlantic Provinces, and New England* is particularly timely. This book describes existing trade and investment links among Quebec, the Atlantic Provinces, and New England and examines the policy environment in the light of these links.

The ultimate contribution of this book lies in its attempt to document the nature and extent of economic linkages among these three regions. This contribution stands out because so little work has been done heretofore on this subject.

The Institute did not commission this work, although some of the chapters appearing here found their roots in a 1980 conference that was co-sponsored by the Institute. The Institute is pleased, however, to promote the wider dissemination of these ideas through publication of the collected papers. Although some of these papers focus on a statistical snapshot at a moment in time, and the structure is changing, the overall work adds an important dimension to our understanding of Canada-US economic relations. And it does this at a particularly important time in the history of these relations.

Rod Dobell
President

February 1986

AVANT-PROPOS

Il ne fait aucun doute que les relations économiques entre le Canada et les États-Unis constituent actuellement l'un des principaux articles à l'ordre du jour de la politique d'État canadienne. À mesure que se déroule, au plan national, le débat sur l'avenir de ces relations, il importe de tenir compte des perspectives et des intérêts régionaux au sein des deux pays.

Pour ces raisons, la publication de *Trade and Investment Across the Northeast Boundary: Quebec, the Atlantic Provinces, and New England,* vient à point nommé. Cet ouvrage décrit les rapports existant en matière de commerce et d'investissement entre le Québec, les provinces Atlantiques et la Nouvelle-Angleterre et examine, à la lumière de ces rapports, le contexte politique dans lequel ils s'inscrivent.

La principale contribution de ce livre au débat actuel réside dans la tentative de documenter la nature et l'étendue des liens économiques entre ces trois régions. Elle apparaît d'autant plus importante que ce sujet avait été encore peu traité jusqu'ici.

Cette étude n'a pas été commandée par l'Institut, bien que certains de ses chapitres aient trouvé racine dans un congrès qu'il a coparrainé en 1980. Toutefois, l'Institut est heureux de pouvoir favoriser, en publiant ce recueil des communications, une plus large diffusion des idées qui y sont exprimées. Bien que certaines des communications présentent un instantané statistique des relations économiques canado-américaines, et que la structure de ces dernières soit en train de se modifier, le présent ouvrage ajoute, dans son ensemble, une importante dimension à notre compréhension de ces relations, et ce, à un moment crucial de leur histoire.

Rod Dobell
Président

Février 1986

PREFACE

The origins of this study go back to 1979, when James D. McNiven, then executive vice-president of the Atlantic Provinces Economic Council (APEC), Alfred O. Hero, Jr., then director of the World Peace Foundation and the Greater Boston Fund for International Affairs (and a figure well known to students of Canada-US affairs), and this writer first discussed the possibility of launching a study of tri-regional trade and associated economic policy. At that time there were two compelling reasons for knowing more about trade and investment flows in the Northeast and their potential for expansion. One reason was Quebec's movement toward independence. This was thought to open up a number of new north-south trade possibilities involving both Quebec and the Atlantic Provinces, whose east-west trade connections would be fundamentally altered by an autonomous Quebec. The other principal reason was a growing awareness that regional north-south trade and investment seemed to be showing more vigour than east-west trade, quite apart from the changing political position of Quebec, and that lower tariffs emanating from the GATT (General Agreement on Tariffs and Trade) trade agreements might soon usher in a new chapter in Canada-US economic relations. The Quebec-Atlantic-New England area was and is thought to offer some interesting case studies of regional north-south trade. New York and Ontario were excluded from this study (with the exception of references in Chapters 4 and 5) primarily on grounds of manageability and their wholly inseparable economic links with the rest of their respective countries.

During an early stage of the study Canada's Institute for Research on Public Policy (IRPP) and Johns Hopkins University's Center of Canadian Studies elected, with support from the Government of Quebec, to sponsor the conference "Toward the Year 2000: Quebec in the North American Economy" at the Johns Hopkins School of Advanced International Studies in Washington, D.C. This conference was held in March 1980 and elicited three papers which, in modified form, became chapters in this volume. A paper on Quebec-US trade flows by Pierre- Paul Proulx (University of Montreal) provided a point of departure for Chapter 3 which deals with tri-regional trade. Another paper in which Hugh M. Pinchin (Colgate University) assesses the impact of free trade in manufactured goods between the United States and Canada became, with additional material on the Atlantic Provinces, Chapter 4. A paper I presented on some effects of closer economic integration among Quebec, New England, and the Maritimes, with special reference to energy policy, became, in expanded form, Chapter 5.

Not long after the Johns Hopkins conference, steps were taken to round out the study areas by adding chapters on trade and policy in the fisheries, on investment flows across the northeast boundary, and on basic demographic/economic similarities and contrasts among the three regions. Hal Mills, a marine policy consultant, undertook preparation of the fisheries chapter (Chapter 6) and was later assisted in updating it by Michael LeBlanc. Lacking sufficient volunteers, I undertook the investment (7) and introductory chapters (1 and 2), and became editor of the volume as well, which in turn led to enlarging and updating Chapter 3. In Chapter 1 on historic and demographic outlines, I benefited from the assistance and perspectives of Barry Lesser of IRPP and Dalhousie University, and of Alfred O. Hero, Jr. In Chapter 2 on labour market characteristics, I received major help from Elizabeth Beale of the Atlantic Provinces Economic Council. James McNiven, who was the original instigator of the study when he was with APEC, and who is now Deputy Minister of Development for Nova Scotia, provided the overview and agenda (Chapter 8). Our thanks go to the anonymous readers who made helpful comments on early drafts of each chapter. Barry Lesser was especially helpful in cutting out non- essential elements as the text neared publication.

The study was also assisted by numerous other people in the government, business, and academic fields. At a series of conferences organized in Boston, Halifax, and Montreal during 1981-1983 to discuss various aspects of tri-regional trade and investment, drafts of several chapters were circulated. A number of suggestions arising from those discussions have been incorporated. Professor Marcel Daneau in Quebec City, and Pierre Lortie, Roger Miller, and Bernard Bonin in Montreal, made contributions at many points in the study's now considerable history. David Dodge, Antal Deutsch, William McCarten, and Oli Havrylyshyn reacted to some of the early drafts presented at the Johns Hopkins conference. In Boston, Wayne Ayers, Edward Ladd, and Richard Wiley, among others, offered helpful criticism, and David Francis of the *Christian Science Monitor* did an astute summary of the Boston conference. Alfred Hero participated in most of these conferences and was largely responsible for keeping the whole project moving.

Some financial support for the Canadian side of the study was provided by the Donner Foundation, by APEC, and by the IRPP. Modest subsidies for the preparation of three chapters also were forthcoming from the Government of Quebec and the Nova Scotia Department of Development. On the US side, support for some of my own work was provided by the Greater Boston Fund for International Affairs and by the World Peace Foundation. In addition, a Faculty Enrichment Grant from the Canadian Embassy in 1981-1982 enabled me to devote substantial time to study of the Canadian economy. Finally, acknowledgement is due to my own institution, Bowdoin College, for support in the form of secretarial time and various overhead expenses, and to Barry Lesser and John Curtis of the Institute for Research on Public Policy, under whose research programs this volume is being published.

Much of the early typing of my own chapters and most of the next-to-final typing of all chapters were the work of Irene Hilton and Virginia Linkovich. If the truth be known, they were more tolerant than I when it came to making the repeated corrections, revisions, and updating necessitated by having to co-ordinate multiple authors working on subjects that were themselves continually changing.

None of the above acknowledgements should be construed as shedding responsibility for errors, omissions, or strong opinions occasionally expressed in the text. That responsibility remains with the primary chapter authors and, most important, with the editor, whose original knowledge of the Canadian economy was meagre and whose subsequent education has left a number of gaps which will no doubt become evident as the study is perused. But I believe I can say, on behalf of all the authors, that we think this effort at understanding regional economic relationships and prospects between friendly neighbours is at least (and at last) on the right track.

William D. Shipman
Brunswick, Maine

February 1986

THE AUTHORS

William D. Shipman is Adams-Catlin Professor of Economics at Bowdoin College in Brunswick, Maine. Born in Illinois, he received his Ph.D. from Columbia University in 1960. He has worked extensively in the field of energy economics and policy and has served as a consultant in this field to the New England Regional Commission, the Maine Public Utilities Commission, the Maine Office of Energy Resources, and the New England Governors' Conference. From 1979 to 1981, he was a member of the Northeast International Committee on Energy.

Hugh McA. Pinchin was born in London, England in 1939. He studied economics at the University of British Columbia and Yale University, receiving his Ph.D. from Yale in 1970. For a brief period he served with the Department of Regional Economic Expansion in Ottawa. He now teaches economics at Colgate University. Among his other work, he is the author of a 1979 study for the Economic Council of Canada entitled *The Regional Impact of the Canadian Tariff*.

Hal Mills, a native of Nova Scotia, was trained as a geographer specializing in coastal and marine resource management. His career has included employment with the Dalhousie Ocean Studies Programme, study of the Georges Bank boundary dispute and related fisheries management issues, and work as a free-lance marine policy consultant. Since completion of his work on this book, he has taken employment with the Canadian Department of Fisheries and Oceans.

Michael LeBlanc is a graduate of McGill University, where he took a degree in geography, concentrating in cultural ecology and environmental studies. He has been involved in a wide range of resource management studies. Most recently, he completed a review of the environmental issues and regulatory regime associated with onshore gas pipeline development for the Nova

Scotia Department of the Environment. He is currently with Aspotogan Research in Blandford, Nova Scotia.

James D. McNiven is the Deputy Minister of Development for the Province of Nova Scotia. During 1985-1986, he is on leave at the Centre for American Studies at the University of Western Ontario. He was formerly executive vice-president of the Atlantic Provinces Economic Council. He is the co-author of *The Atlantic Vision: 1990*, published by APEC in 1979.

Pierre-Paul Proulx is a graduate of Canadian and American universities (Ottawa, Toronto, Princeton). He is a university professor whose career in the past led to the public sector where he served as Assistant Deputy Minister in the Department of Regional Industrial Expansion, and to the private sector where he was a partner in Secor Inc. He is currently in the Department of Economics at the Université de Montréal. His research interests cover commercial-industrial-regional development, the determinants and socio-economic impacts of technological change, and the implications of these for domestic adjustment.

SUMMARY

The economic ties among Quebec, the Atlantic Provinces, and New England have been important to each of the three regions since the days of European colonization. They have continued to be important over time, and in recent years they have been growing in strength.

Trade across the northeast boundary has been growing more rapidly in recent years than east-west trade in Canada and is showing greater diversity. While fish and forestry products still dominate the north-to-south flow, energy and a variety of manufactured goods have become increasingly important. South-to-north trade continues to reflect New England's manufacturing strengths, now including an array of high-technology goods and services. Three-way trade in business and professional services is strong but presents unusual measurement problems (Chapter 3).

The prospect of a free trade agreement between Canada and the United States raises important issues involving trade dominance, investment, and job migration, as well as the influence of multinational firms (Chapter 4). While such an agreement would benefit consumers in both countries, effects on producers are highly uncertain. Some Canadian manufacturers should realize scale economies through improved access to the US market, and increased competition should enforce greater efficiency. But the plant location decisions of many firms will reflect both their ownership structure (Canadian, US, or other) and southward and westward shifts in the US market itself. Quebec's industry mix, moreover, may not yield scale economies to the same extent as Ontario's. Atlantic Canada's ability to obtain better access to US markets may depend on its giving up those governmental transfers that help to lower production costs.

The increasing flow of Canadian-generated electricity to New England (and New York) is highly advantageous to both seller and buyer (Chapter 5). Such flows are capable of substantial further growth, but some impediments exist on both sides of the boundary. New England in particular needs to reexamine these impediments (e.g., private company preference for domestic, base-load generating capacity, fragmentation of ownership and regulation) to insure that regional interests take precedence over private motives. Natural gas from offshore Nova Scotia could be readily absorbed into New England-Middle Atlantic markets. In view of competing sources (e.g., Alberta), however, effecting this result depends upon a border price that (1) reflects Canadian producer and provincial willingness to accept less than maximum returns, and (2) recognizes the nature of an increasingly decontrolled US gas market. Petroleum product exports from eastern Canada to New England may revive in the context of trade liberalization and the working off of excess capacity in Middle Atlantic refineries.

Trade in fish products – most of it southward – has been strongly influenced by gains in efficiency in the Canadian offshore fleet, by various Canadian government measures to rationalize the fishery, and by low US tariffs on unprocessed as compared with processed fish (Chapter 6). The latter has led Canadian processors to locate plants in New England where they have access to both low-cost Canadian suppliers and the very important Boston market and distribution centre. Settlement of the international boundary has not resolved the issue of "subsidization," which US fishermen are convinced explains much of the Canadian ability to export. It is urgent that the issue be resolved. It will probably require agreement as to what constitutes a "subsidy" (on either side) and might best be pursued at the regional level where government policies applicable to specific industries (even firms) can be examined.

Interregional investment flows, while more difficult to identify, are believed to be increasing and without question are helping to shape current account flows (Chapter 7). This would seem to be as applicable to services (computer, financial, engineering, tourist) as to physical goods (fish, forest products, electronic equipment). In recent years the northward flow of US investment has been importantly (and adversely) influenced by Canadian federal policy. The eastern provinces have good reason to criticize such policy in view of their greater need to attract and hold US investment. At the same time some US reaction to the Canadian desire to control foreign investment is unwarranted and fails to recognize the unique, and in some respects overbearing, influence of US firms in Canadian affairs.

A more detailed summary of the study, together with suggestions for future policy, is found in Chapter 8.

ABRÉGÉ

Les liens économiques qu'entretiennent le Québec, les provinces Atlantiques et la Nouvelle-Angleterre ont eu une grande importance pour chacune de ces trois régions depuis la colonisation européenne. Ils sont restés importants au cours des années et connaissent depuis quelque temps une intensité croissante.

Au cours des dernières années, les échanges commerciaux canado-américains passant par la frontière du Nord-Est se sont accrus plus rapidement que le commerce entre l'est et l'ouest du Canada et sont également plus diversifiés. Si les produits de la pêche et de la forêt jouent encore un rôle prépondérant dans le commerce nord-sud, l'énergie et une variété de produits manufacturés ont acquis une importance croissante. Quant aux échanges sud-nord, ils continuent de refléter les secteurs forts de l'industrie manufacturière de la Nouvelle-Angleterre, qui comptent à présent tout un éventail de biens et de services de haute technologie. Les échanges trilatéraux de services professionnels et de services aux entreprises sont très intenses, mais posent des problèmes de mesure inhabituels (chapitre 3).

La perspective d'un accord de libre-échange entre le Canada et les États-Unis soulève d'importantes questions quant à la prédominance commerciale, l'investissement, la migration de l'emploi ainsi que l'influence des entreprises multinationales (chapitre 4). Si un tel accord bénéficierait aux consommateurs des deux pays, ses effets sur les producteurs paraissent, au contraire, très aléatoires. En principe, certains producteurs canadiens devraient, grâce à un meilleur accès au marché américain, réaliser des économies d'échelle, de même que l'accroissement de la concurrence devrait entraîner une amélioration de l'efficacité. Toutefois, les décisions de nombreuses entreprises en matière d'implantation d'usines refléteront à la fois leur structure d'appartenance (canadienne, américaine ou autre) et les déplacements vers le sud et vers l'ouest du marché américain lui-même. En outre, il est possible que la composition des industries du Québec ne produise pas autant d'économies d'échelle que celle de l'Ontario. Quant à la capacité du Canada Atlantique d'accroître ses débouchés sur les marchés américains, elle pourrait bien exiger qu'il renonce aux transferts gouvernementaux qui favorisent la réduction des coûts de production.

Les exportations croissantes d'électricité canadienne vers la Nouvelle-Angleterre (et New York) se révèlent extrêmement avantageuses tant pour le vendeur que pour l'acheteur. Il est possible qu'elles continuent à s'intensifier, mais certains obstacles s'y opposent des deux côtés de la frontière. La Nouvelle-Angleterre, en particulier, devra réexaminer ces obstacles (tels que la préférence des entreprises privées pour la capacité de production de charge minimale américaine, le morcellement de l'appartenance et la réglementation) afin d'assurer que les intérêts régionaux prendront le pas sur les intérêts privés. Il est également possible que le gaz naturel provenant des puits situés au large de la Nouvelle-Écosse trouve facilement des débouchés sur les marchés de la Nouvelle-Angleterre et du Centre-Est. Mais étant donné l'existence de sources compétitives (telle que l'Alberta), il faudra pour cela établir un prix de frontière. Un tel prix devra 1) refléter le fait que le producteur canadien et le gouvernement provincial sont prêts à ne pas réaliser les rendements maximaux et 2) tenir compte de la nature de moins en moins contrôlée du marché du gaz naturel aux États-Unis. Les exportations de produits pétroliers de l'est du Canada vers la Nouvelle-Angleterre pourraient reprendre dans le contexte d'une libéralisation du commerce et de l'absorption de l'excédent de capacité par les raffineries du Centre-Est américain.

Le commerce des produits de la pêche – dirigé principalement vers le Sud – a été fortement influencé par les gains d'efficacité réalisés dans la flotte côtière du Canada, par diverses mesures du gouvernement canadien destinées à favoriser une gestion rationnelle du secteur des pêches et par les bas tarifs américains s'appliquant au poisson non conditionné par opposition au poisson conditionné (chapitre 6). Ces derniers ont conduit les entreprises de conditionnement canadiennes à implanter des établissements en Nouvelle-Angleterre, ce qui leur permet à la fois de bénéficier des prix peu élevés des fournisseurs canadiens et d'accéder à l'important marché et centre de distribution de Boston. Le règlement du différend concernant la frontière internationale n'a pas apporté de solution au problème du "subventionnement", dans lequel les pêcheurs américains voient la principale raison de la capacité d'exportation du Canada. Il est urgent que cette question soit résolue. Il faudra vraisemblablement que l'on se mette d'accord sur ce qu'est une "subvention" (des deux côtés) et que la recherche d'une solution s'effectue au niveau régional, où il est plus facile d'examiner les politiques gouvernementales applicables à des industries (voire à des entreprises) spécifiques.

S'il est vrai que les flux d'investissement interrégionaux sont plus difficiles à identifier, on pense qu'ils sont en train de s'intensifier et aident sans aucun doute à déterminer les flux du compte courant (chapitre 7). Il semble que cela s'applique tant aux services (informatique, finances, ingénierie, tourisme) qu'aux biens matériels (produits de la pêche, produits forestiers, équipement électronique). Au cours des dernières années, le flux d'investissement américain vers le Nord a été fortement (et défavorablement) influencé par la politique du gouvernement fédéral. Les provinces de l'Est ont tout lieu de critiquer une telle politique du fait qu'elles ont un plus grand besoin d'attirer et de retenir l'investissement américain. En même temps, la réaction de certains milieux américains au désir des Canadiens de contrôler l'investissement étranger est injustifiée et dénote un défaut de prise de conscience de l'influence unique, et à bien des égards dominatrice, qu'exercent les entreprises américaines sur les affaires canadiennes.

Un résumé plus détaillé de cette étude, accompagné de suggestions quant aux orientations futures de la politique d'État, est présenté au chapitre 8.

1:   REGIONAL CHARACTERISTICS AND INTERREGIONAL RELATIONS

W.D. Shipman

History

Relations between the northeastern United States and the eastern Canadian provinces* have traditionally reflected their common, yet different, colonial backgrounds and their similar resource bases. Founded and subsequently fought over by competing European powers in the seventeenth century, these regions had an early history of gradual British ascendency followed by a successful independence movement which imposed an international boundary between the regions. One effect of this boundary was that it ultimately prevented interregional trade from developing in ways or to the extent that would have occurred in its absence, or that did in fact occur south of the border and across Canada. Even north of that boundary the geographic separation of the Maritime Provinces from the St. Lawrence Valley, together with differences in national origin of most of their populations, led to quite different patterns of economic, social, and cultural development.[1]

In the decades immediately following the American Revolution, these separations may have had only minor effects on interregional trade since all three regions were primarily producers of raw materials and relied heavily on exports of fish and lumber to Europe and the Caribbean. (The fur trade had by that time mostly relocated to the interior of each country.) Furthermore, the international boundary was apparently not a major impediment to trade, much of it illegal, during the Napoleonic Wars.[2] By the 1820s, however, New England was becoming an important centre of textile manufacture, and from

---

*For purposes of this discussion, Canada refers here to the area now known as Canada, which historically formed part of British North America.

that point on the international boundary had a major inhibiting influence on northeast resource flows and markets.

The post-Revolution separation was not only political and economic; linguistic, cultural, and religious differences also worked against communication and exacerbated both perceptions and suspicions. One region, Quebec, was a predominantly French-speaking, Roman Catholic society with conservative religious and social values and institutions. While most of the lay Catholic leaders had been supplanted (after the Seven Years War) by a mixture of English and Scottish elites, the general character of the colony remained strongly French. The northeastern United States, on the other hand, was English-speaking, and largely Calvinist, with strong rationalist and commercial inclinations. During the American Revolution and for some decades thereafter, thousands of British loyalists — often from property-owning and otherwise privileged and influential walks of life — fled to the Maritimes, to the eastern townships of Quebec, to Montreal, and to the southern and southeastern Gaspé coasts. They and their descendents for several generations continued to harbour and communicate their pro-British and anti-American views. Successive but unsuccessful American military invasions and threats of invasion served mainly to fuel these sentiments. An influx of northeastern US farmers into what is now southern Ontario from about 1815 onward did nothing to relax the separative effect of the boundary east of that province.

From roughly the mid-nineteenth century to World War I interregional relations were marked by two distinct phases. The first phase consisted of a brief period of essentially free trade in raw materials and foodstuffs between Canada and the United States as a result of the adoption of "reciprocity" from 1854 to 1866. (Tariffs on manufactured goods were variable, but trended downward — on the Canadian side — until 1858.) During this period trade expanded rapidly in the Northeast as well as farther west. In 1849, just previous to this downward trend, there had been a serious, if short-lived, movement toward political union with the United States. "Reciprocity" was to some extent a substitute for union, with much wider political support.[3]

The second phase, following the American Civil War, witnessed movement in the opposite direction. Ascendancy of the Republican Party led to sharp increases in US tariffs, evidenced by a doubling of nominal rates. At first, Canadian tariffs were lowered consequent to the Confederation agreement of 1867, thus reconciling the interests of the Maritime Provinces with those of Quebec and Ontario. But Canadian fears of growing US industrialization and tariff barriers, together with a desire for unification of the country and for building its own industrial base, resulted in the adoption of high import duties on the Canadian side as well by 1879.

The other major interregional "event" during this period was the wave of Quebec and, to a lesser degree, Maritime immigration into the northeastern United States. In Quebec a combination of very high birth rates and a static agrarian economy resulted in nearly one million francophones seeking work in the textile mills, shoe factories, and other industries of New England, upstate New York, and other states north of Delaware and along the Great Lakes. This migration had actually begun somewhat earlier, but it accelerated after the Civil War as the industrial sector in the US Northeast expanded very rapidly. Moreover, the movement continued at a fairly strong pace, with waves of migrants more or less coinciding with the US business cycle, until the 1929 crash and ensuing Great Depression. By that time there were more people of Quebec origin in the northeastern part of the United States than there were in Canada outside of Quebec itself.[4]

Until well after World War II, most of these migrants and their descendants formed a blue-collar underclass regarded with condescension by the Yankees and with some antagonism by competing blue-collar, English-speaking groups in the Northeast. Since these migrants had had little education in Quebec, their children seldom went on to college. In fact, most of them dropped out to work in mills and factories well before completing high school. For a long while, these migrants lived in ghetto-type communities that included bilingual schools and churches made up of people with similar Quebec origins. After a generation or two, however, they became Americanized and many lost their ancestors' language. Particularly after the 1920s, the influx of new French speakers declined and links with distant relatives in Quebec were progressively weakened.

Along with the massive Quebec migration, a good many Maritimers, similarly pushed by a static economy and a very low standard of living, also migrated south. Emigration from the Maritimes took two different forms. One group consisted of Acadians of French ancestry coming primarily from New Brunswick and Nova Scotia. Most of these people migrated from the farms, timberlands, and fishing villages of the Maritimes and ended up in New England and New York occupations similar to those of the incoming Quebec immigrants. The other group was primarily of Scottish and English descent. Their educational backgrounds were generally superior, and their migratory pattern was in fact much broader. Many of them eschewed opportunities in the United States in favor of Montreal, Toronto, and points farther west in Canada. Those who went to the States frequently started in New England, but within a few years they moved on to other northeastern and north central states. While some of these latter migrants ended up in mill towns, a surprising number sought out and succeeded to an extraordinary degree in careers in commercial, financial, and transportation enterprises.

Economic linkages between the American Northeast and eastern Canadian provinces entered a new phase during the 1920s, when American companies began to develop or expand investment in Canadian forest products, minerals, and other resources, largely for export to the United States. (Actually, some of these ventures had been started earlier.) This expansion was centred in Quebec and Ontario; most of the (limited) foreign capital invested in the Maritimes came from Great Britain until after the Depression, and most of the foreign trade of these provinces was with Britain. British investment also figured in the early twentieth-century development of Quebec, frequently through anglophone firms based in Montreal and through enterprises controlled by them. Manufacturing activity increasingly reflected the "branch plant" economy of Canada, fostered, if not wholly determined, by the high tariff wall. Since the latter severely dampened cross-boundary trade in manufactures, northeast trade flows during this period consisted largely of the southward movement of raw materials and semi-finished goods.[5]

In the years following World War II, many of the investment and trade linkages mentioned above were further strengthened. The volume of trade among the three regions* increased at a fairly steady pace, both because of imports and exports normally associated with the growth of regional economies and because foreign trade policy was being liberalized generally throughout the Western world. But while manufactured goods increasingly flowed across the boundary, the bulk of north-south trade continued to consist of raw materials and, more recently, energy (oil, gas, electricity) flowing from eastern Canada to the northeastern United States. (Chapters 3,

---

*What is now the Atlantic Region consisted of only the three Maritime Provinces prior to 1949, when Newfoundland and Labrador became part of Canada. Economic relations with the United States were nevertheless essentially those described here.

5, and 6 examine these trade flows in detail.)

During much of this period the southern and western parts of the United States were growing more rapidly than the Northeast. Consequently, it is not surprising that Canadian trade with New England was no longer as important, proportionately, as it had been in earlier years. Much the same thing was true of Canada itself; the westward movement of economic activity had become more pronounced after World War II. Thus, New England exports were finding their way increasingly into central and western Canada, although trade with the eastern provinces continued to be very important (see Chapter 3). Investment relationships between the northeastern United States and eastern Canada were altered to some extent during the 1960s by the advent of publicly owned, province-wide utility systems which took over foreign — including US-owned — companies. They were altered substantially during the 1970s by the extension of public ownership into a number of other sectors of the Quebec economy (Chapter 7). Nevertheless, as will be seen in Chapter 3, the volume of trade among the three regions increased very rapidly during the 1970s. There is reason to believe that new complementarities — in both physical goods and services — are being found every year which provide opportunities for investment and new trade. Moreover, the volume of tourist trade among the three regions, which has long been an important source of income for specific areas, continues to increase.[6] This basic flow of tourists has been augmented recently by the even more rapid growth in cross-boundary trips to business and professional conferences.

Demographic Outlines

Preliminary data from the 1981 Canadian census show the Atlantic Provinces having a population of about 2.2 million persons and Quebec having approximately 6.3 million. These figures compare with a total estimated 1980 population in New England of 12.3 million persons (see Table 1.1). While the combined Quebec and Atlantic Provinces figures represent more than a third of the total population of Canada (approximately 24.3 million in 1981), New England accounts for only about 5.5 per cent of the US total. Thus, while New England's population is twice that of Quebec and half again as large as the combined total of Quebec and the Atlantic Provinces, its proportionate weight in the United States is much less than that of its Canadian neighbours in their own country. The inclusion of New York with New England would not greatly change this picture.

Table 1.1:   Area and Population of Quebec, Atlantic Provinces, and New England, 1980-1981

	Area (sq. mi.)[a]	Population (thousands)[b]	Population/ Sq. Mile
Newfoundland: Island	43,359	568	3.6
Labrador	112,825		
Prince Edward Island	2,184	123	56.3
Nova Scotia	21,425	847	39.5
New Brunswick	28,354	696	24.3
Atlantic Provinces	208,147	2,234	10.7
Quebec	594,857	6,438	10.8
Quebec and Atl. Prov.	803,004	8,672	10.8
Canada	3,831,012	24,342	6.4
Atl. Prov./Canada	.054	.092	
Quebec/Canada	.155	.264	
Quebec and Atl. Prov./ Canada	.210	.356	
Maine	33,215	1,125	33.9
New Hampshire	9,304	921	99.0
Vermont	9,609	511	53.2
Massachusetts	8,257	5,737	694.8
Rhode Island	1,214	947	780.1
Connecticut	5,009	3,108	620.5
New England	66,608	12,348	185.4
New York	49,576	17,557	354.1
United States	3,618,467	226,505	62.6
New England/US	.018	.055	
N.E. and N.Y./US	.032	.132	

a   Includes freshwater areas.
b   1981 Canadian population; 1980 US population.

Sources: Statistics Canada, Cat. No. 92-901.
US Bureau of the Census, *Statistical Abstract of the United States*, 1982-1983.

Data showing population density reveal even more striking contrasts (Table 1.1). In general it may be said that southern New England is one of the more densely settled parts of the United States, while northern Quebec and Newfoundland are among the least densely populated areas in all of North America. These extremes tend to make regional — even provincial — averages deceptive. Maine and Vermont, for example, have population densities quite similar to those of New Brunswick and Nova Scotia, but New England's *average* population density is seventeen times that of the Atlantic Provinces. At the same time, while the average population density of Quebec is very low, density figures for that area lying between Montreal and Quebec City probably approximate those for southern New England.

Some additional features of the distribution of population are brought out in Table 1.2. The three major metropolitan areas in the Atlantic Provinces account for only 24 per cent of that region's population (1976 data), thus confirming views as to its essentially rural-seacoast character. In Quebec, on the other hand, the Greater Montreal and Quebec City areas account for over half the province's population. Moreover, when the St. Lawrence Valley is defined to include the cities of Hull, Sherbrooke, and Chicoutimi, (that is, by a zone extending roughly seventy-five miles on either side of the river), it appears that nearly 95 per cent of Quebec's total population is included therein.[7] In New England, the three southern tier states have about 22 per cent of the land area but 80 per cent of the population. Within this southern tier, the metropolitan areas of Boston, Providence, and Hartford account for 47 per cent of the New England total.

These somewhat unusual distributions of population reflect a combination of topographic, climatic, and historic influences. The St. Lawrence Valley, in addition to being the traditional route to the interior, contains most of Quebec's best arable land. The Connecticut River played — on a much smaller scale — a somewhat similar role in early New England. The granitic shield north of the St. Lawrence Valley, with its severe climate and unworkable land, has remained hostile to settlement for several hundred years, and will probably continue to do so. On the other hand, the historically important but geographically awkward location of the Atlantic Provinces (relative to continental Canada — even to the St. Lawrence Valley) has, together with a meagre resource base, enforced limits on the growth of cities and hence on population generally in that region.

Table 1.2: Distribution of Population within Regions, 1976 (Canada) and 1978 (New England)

Region		Population of Metropolitan Area (thousands)[a]	Per cent of Region
Atlantic Provinces			
Metropolitan	Halifax	268	12.3
	St. John's	143	6.5
	Saint John	113	5.2
Total		524	24.0
Quebec			
Metropolitan	Montreal	2,802	44.9
	Quebec City	542	8.7
Subtotal		3,344	53.6
St. Lawrence Valley[b]		5,900 [c]	94.6
New England			
Metropolitan	Boston	3,888	31.7
	Providence	853	7.0
	Hartford	1,045	8.5
Subtotal		5,786	47.2
Mass., R.I., Conn.		9,819	80.0

a Definitions of "metropolitan area" vary between Canada and the United States.
b Valley defined as area within seventy-five miles of the river.
c Estimated.

Sources: Statistics Canada, *Canada Year Book*, 1980-1981.
US Bureau of the Census, *Statistical Abstract of the United States*, 1980.

When the regions are considered together, however, several significant facts emerge. First, while most New Englanders think of their region as one in which civilization peters out as one moves from south to north (witness the everlasting tales concerning life in the "north woods"), in reality northern New England lies *between* two highly developed, highly urbanized subregions or belts. Were it not for the purely political circumstance of the international boundary, much stronger ties would almost certainly have developed to the north as well as to the south. (Such ties would have taken somewhat longer to develop even in a unified political framework due to the topography of watersheds: most rivers in this in-between region flow southward.) One aim of this study, therefore, is to examine regional resource endowments with a view to trade potential given the possibility (some would say probability) of lower political and economic barriers in the future. In such a context, it can be presumed that southern New England and the St. Lawrence Valley would continue to be the primary generators of economic activity, with northern New England increasingly a "bridge" area and both it and the Atlantic Provinces benefiting from their ability to furnish resources and services to *either* of the two urbanized regions.

A second fact of some importance is the rough similarity of climate and certain other resource endowments. Mean January temperatures (Celsius) in Montreal, Halifax, and Boston are respectively -9, -3, and -2; corresponding July means are 22, 18, and 23. Not surprisingly, such things as recreational activities and electric loads follow similar seasonal patterns in all three regions. There is, moreover, a common urge on the part of habitants to escape the entire northeast for at least brief periods during the winter months — an urge whose satisfaction is largely determined by levels of income.

Perhaps more significant, among regions there has been a traditional emphasis on forest products and fish as sources of regional "export earnings." To a considerable extent the regions have thus been in competition with one another. Given their basic resource positions, it would be unwise to anticipate a major change in this regard, although this study does attempt to identify new areas of complementarity and mutually beneficial trade.

A third fact of great importance to all three regions is that, notwithstanding their historical roles, they have seen, and probably will continue to see, the population — read markets — of North America continue to shift southward and westward. Their role and weight in their respective national economies are thus going to shrink further. Indeed, they have much in common in this respect. It may well be true that each of these northeastern regions can legitimately lay claim to cultural traditions and advantages unmatched by its southern and western counterparts. They may also benefit intermittently from the operation of "back to the land" or "back to the roots" movements. They may even see some periodic resurgence of industrial activity following new techniques. But it is clear nevertheless that the more basic influence of resources and markets will continue to draw the national economic centres of gravity away from the northeast.

This movement is not unrelated to the climate factor already discussed. Without question, the combination of rising real incomes, a relative increase in the number of retired persons, and the search for more moderate temperatures ("liveability" as it is called) has greatly strengthened the basic investment and market shifts already under way. Even the much-discussed growth of Canadian investment in Alberta has in all probability been outstripped by Canadian investment growth (direct and indirect) in the southern and western United States. The obvious fact of rising investment in energy resources in remote regions should not be allowed to obscure the more basic movements away from the northeast.

Data showing population growth over recent decades reflect this shifting center of gravity as well as highlighting different patterns within and among the three regions (Table 1.3). In general it may be said that Canada's population has been growing more rapidly than that of the United States, although the *difference* in growth rates has narrowed considerably in recent years. While the rate of population growth has fallen in both countries since 1950, the decline has been more dramatic in two of the three northeastern regions. (The growth rates of the Atlantic Provinces, while low by national standards, have declined less in a relative sense.) Quebec's population grew only 5 per cent between 1971 and 1981, as compared to a 30 per cent increase between 1951 and 1961.[8] Within the Atlantic Provinces, growth rates have been better maintained in New Brunswick and Prince Edward Island. Indeed, the Island's rate of growth has increased moderately in contrast to regional and national trends. In Newfoundland, on the other hand, the rate of growth has decreased almost as dramatically as in Quebec. Data for five-year intervals, moreover, show that in the Atlantic Provinces growth between 1971 and 1981 comprised two quite different segments: fairly rapid growth in the early 1970s, followed by very slow growth from 1975 on.[9]

Table 1.3: Population Growth in Three Regions, 1950/51-1980/81

	1951	Per cent Increase 1951-61	1961	Per cent Increase 1961-71	1971	Per cent Increase 1971-81	1981[a]
Newfoundland: Island & Labrador	361	(26.8)	458	(14.0)	522	(8.8)	568
Prince Edward Is.	98	(6.7)	105	(6.7)	112	(9.8)	123
Nova Scotia	643	(14.8)	738	(7.0)	789	(7.3)	847
New Brunswick	516	(15.9)	598	(6.1)	635	(9.6)	696
Atl. Provinces	1,618	(17.3)	1,898	(8.4)	2,057	(8.6)	2,234
Quebec	4,056	(29.6)	5,259	(14.6)	6,028	(6.8)	6,438
Quebec & Atl. Prov.	5,674	(26.1)	7,157	(13.0)	8,086	(7.2)	8,672
Canada	14,009	(30.2)	18,238	(18.3)	21,568	(12.9)	24,342

	1950	Per cent Increase 1950-60	1960	Per cent Increase 1960-70	1970	Per cent Increase 1970-80	1980
Maine	914	(6.0)	969	(2.5)	994	(13.2)	1,125
New Hampshire	533	(13.9)	607	(21.5)	738	(24.8)	921
Vermont	378	(3.2)	390	(14.1)	445	(15.0)	511
Massachusetts	4,691	(9.8)	5,149	(10.5)	5,689	(0.8)	5,737
Rhode Island	792	(8.5)	859	(10.5)	949	(-0.3)	947
Connecticut	2,007	(26.3)	2,535	(19.6)	3,032	(2.5)	3,108
New England	9,314	(12.8)	10,509	(12.7)	11,847	(4.2)	12,348
New York	14,830	(13.2)	16,782	(8.7)	18,241	(-3.8)	17,557
United States	151,326	(18.5)	179,311	(13.4)	203,302	(11.4)	226,505

[a] Preliminary.

Sources: Statistics Canada, *Canada Year Book*, various dates.
US Bureau of the Census, *Statistical Abstract of the United States*, various dates.

In New England, intraregional differences are even more marked. The southern tier states experienced virtually no growth during the 1970s. Connecticut has changed over the past thirty years from being one of the fastest-growing to one of the slowest-growing states in the entire United States. (But not the slowest: New York and Rhode Island actually experienced negative growth during the 1970s.) Northern New England's population, on the other hand, has grown quite rapidly in recent years, with New Hampshire turning in a phenomenal — for New England — gain of almost 25 per cent between 1970 and 1980. Given the much greater numbers, and hence weight, of the southern tier in New England, total growth of the region as a whole was only about 4 per cent during the 1970s, which compares with over 11 per cent for the United States generally.

The reasons for these various trends are numerous, and reflect to a considerable degree some long-run patterns already mentioned. The dramatic slow-down in Quebec's population growth is without question attributable to cultural and age distribution influences as well as to changes in migratory patterns. These have also been at work in the Atlantic Provinces where economic opportunity has been limited. The divergent showings in the New England states reflect both the problems of an older, mature economy facing new competition from the Sun Belt, and the increasing tendency for firms and families to partake of New England's cultural, educational, research, and other amenities while escaping the taxes, congestion, and other costs associated with locating in the southern tier. New Hampshire in particular seems to have gained ground at the expense of Massachusetts, which is not surprising when one considers that low-cost locations (i.e., lower taxes, land values, labour costs) in southern New Hampshire are virtually within the Boston metropolitan area. These and other influences — as well as migration patterns themselves — are discussed in some detail in Chapter 2 which deals with demographic and labour force characteristics.

Income and Output

Economic characteristics of the three regions can best be summarized by a few tables showing approximate levels of living and output per capita. In Table 1.4, personal income per capita in US dollars is given for each state, province, and region over a period extending from 1965 to 1981. Starting with the most recent data (1981), personal income per capita in New England was $11,056. The corresponding figures in Quebec and the Atlantic Provinces, respectively, were $8,893 and $6,985 or

Table 1.4: Personal Income per Capita in Three Regions, 1965-1981

	Current Dollars					Constant Dollars			Annual Rate of Growth	
	1965	1969	1973	1977	1981	1965	1973	1981	1965-73	1973-81
							(Canada: 1971 $)			
Canada ($ Canadian)	2,091	2,943	4,438	7,356	11,520	2,598	3,938	4,863	5.34	2.67
Quebec	1,880	2,601	3,959	6,837	10,661	2,335	3,513	4,500	5.24	3.14
Atlantic Provinces	1,424	2,065	3,252	5,533	8,374	1,769	2,886	3,535	6.31	2.57
Newfoundland	1,238	1,796	2,842	5,077	7,528	1,538	2,522	3,178	6.38	2.93
Prince Edward Island	1,257	1,847	3,114	4,983	7,829	1,561	2,763	3,305	7.40	2.26
Nova Scotia	1,562	2,279	3,545	5,898	9,041	1,940	3,146	3,816	6.23	2.44
New Brunswick	1,421	2,062	3,253	5,531	8,272	1,778	2,886	3,492	6.25	2.41
Canada ($ US)	1,940	2,733	4,438	7,086	9,609					
Quebec	1,744	2,415	3,959	6,429	8,893					
Atlantic Provinces	1,321	1,918	3,252	5,203	6,985					
Newfoundland	1,148	1,668	2,842	4,774	6,280					
Prince Edward Island	1,166	1,713	3,114	4,685	6,531					
Nova Scotia	1,449	2,116	3,545	5,546	7,542					
New Brunswick	1,327	1,915	3,253	5,201	6,900					
United States ($ US)	2,770	3,708	5,041	6,984	10,495	2,931	(US: 1967 $) 3,787	3,853	3.25	0.22
New England	2,969	3,998	5,216	7,221	11,056	3,142	3,919	4,059	2.80	0.44
Maine	2,269	3,010	4,040	5,768	8,530	2,401	3,035	3,131	2.97	0.39
New Hampshire	2,556	3,418	4,615	6,539	10,013	2,705	3,467	3,676	3.15	0.73
Vermont	2,365	3,262	4,185	5,752	8,726	2,503	3,144	3,203	2.89	0.23
Massachusetts	2,985	4,058	5,268	7,298	11,127	3,159	3,958	4,085	2.86	0.40
Rhode Island	2,804	3,705	4,869	6,718	10,156	2,967	3,658	3,728	2.65	0.24
Connecticut	3,418	4,606	5,931	8,180	12,806	3,617	4,456	4,701	2.64	0.67
$ Conversion rate[a]	107.80	107.68	100.01	106.35	119.88					
Price indices: Canada (1971 = 100)						80.5	112.7	236.9		
US (1967 = 100)						94.5	133.1	272.4		

a $ Canadian/ $ US.

Sources: Statistics Canada, Cat. No. 13-201; Bank of Canada; Bureau of Economic Analysis, US Department of Commerce.

approximately 80 and 63 per cent of the New England average (Canadian dollars were converted to US dollars using the average exchange rate for the year). Such comparisons may be an inaccurate index of real income to the extent that differences in living costs are not reflected by the exchange rate and due to the exclusion, particularly in Canada, of numerous in-kind social services such as housing subsidies and medical care. The figures do, however, include cash transfer payments.

It can be seen that, within the regions, substantial differences exist among states and provinces. Income levels in Massachusetts and Connecticut are well above the regional average, and the same is true of Nova Scotia within the Atlantic Provinces. Per capita income in New Brunswick, on the other hand, is much closer to that of Maine than would be suggested by the regional averages. Once again, the interregional differences may overstate real differences; otherwise, migration from, say, Maine and Vermont to southern New England would be more pronounced.

As a broad generalization it may be said that New England's advantage over eastern Canada with respect to income level has been attributable primarily to the nineteenth-century growth of its commercial and manufacturing sectors and to its ability to maintain its position in the twentieth century through the furnishing of capital and services to other parts of the country. Most recently, the latter has included the development of new technologies, products, and services for both national and international markets.

It appears, however, that real income levels in recent years — at least before 1981 — have been rising more rapidly in eastern Canada than in the northeastern United States (Table 1.4). Between 1973 and 1981 growth rates in New England were only about 14 per cent of those in Quebec and 17 per cent of the Atlantic Provinces average. Indeed, only New Hampshire and Connecticut showed any significant growth during these years; New England real incomes on average were essentially stagnant between 1973 and 1981. These differential rates of growth thus have narrowed regional per capita income differences considerably. For example, while Quebec's per capita income was 58 per cent of New England's in 1965, by 1981 the Quebec figure had risen to approximately 80 per cent.

It is also true that regional incomes have been moving toward their respective national averages (Table 1.5). Between 1965 and 1979, New England personal income per capita decreased from 1.08 times the US average to 1.02 times that average. During the same period, Quebec personal income rose

Table 1.5: **Personal Income and Gross Product per Capita Relative to the National Average: 1965, 1973, 1979**

	Personal Income per Capita			Gross Product per Capita		
	1965	1973	1979	1965	1973	1979
Newfoundland	0.592	0.640	0.659	0.515	0.526	0.564
Prince Edward Island	0.601	0.702	0.681	0.502	0.574	0.525
Nova Scotia	0.747	0.799	0.796	0.635	0.693	0.671
New Brunswick	0.684	0.733	0.727	0.621	0.665	0.637
Atlantic Provinces	0.681	0.733	0.733	0.593	0.635	0.625
Quebec	0.899	0.892	0.937	0.917	0.881	0.897
Northern Tier:	0.872	0.865	0.869	0.796	0.772	0.752
Maine	0.821	0.815	0.809	0.769	0.731	0.699
New Hampshire	0.952	0.931	0.959	0.832	0.813	0.813
Vermont	0.861	0.856	0.842	0.805	0.793	0.759
Southern Tier:	1.130	1.078	1.062	1.073	1.008	0.981
Massachusetts	1.084	1.045	1.021	1.051	0.983	0.943
Rhode Island	1.012	0.957	0.977	0.942	0.872	0.828
Connecticut	1.255	1.179	1.163	1.157	1.094	1.098
New England	1.083	1.037	1.023	1.023	0.963	0.935

Sources: Statistics Canada, Cat. Nos. 13-201, 13-213, 62-002, and 91-201.
US Bureau of the Census, *Statistical Abstract of the United States*, various dates.
Federal Reserve Bank of Boston, *Gross State Product New England*, various dates.
US Department of Commerce, *Survey of Current Business*, various dates.

(This table was compiled by P.-P. Proulx.)

from 90 to 94 per cent of the Canadian average, while income in the Atlantic Provinces grew from 68 to 73 per cent of that average. The tendency for regional income levels to converge over time is not unusual, reflecting in part the mobility of labour and capital seeking higher returns. The movements in the above data are notable, however, given the relatively brief time span under consideration.

Part of the improvement — and perhaps a major part — in levels of per capita income in eastern Canada is clearly attributable to the growth of transfer payments from Ottawa. Federal transfers to persons in the Atlantic Region grew from $462 million to $1,491 million between 1970 and 1976.[10] By 1978, the overall equalization component per capita exceeded $1,200 or roughly one-fifth of personal money income.[11] In Quebec the corresponding figure was somewhat under $800 per capita, or about 10 per cent of personal money income.[12]

New England also has benefited from rising transfer payments during recent years. But such transfers are far more closely related in the United States to demographic factors than to regional equalization policies. Not only has regional equalization been a much feebler effort in the United States (some would say not even an explicit objective), but also New England's income levels, at least in the southern tier, would not qualify it for such treatment, "development" agencies such as the New England Regional Commission notwithstanding.

An indirect method of determining the role of transfer payments is to compare levels or rates of growth in output (gross state or provincial product), which excludes transfers, with income received by persons. Indeed, output itself is an important indicator of economic performance. Unfortunately, measurement of state or provincial product is beset by problems stemming from the interrelatedness among state and/or provincial economies. While value-added data can be assembled for local and regional economies (Table 1.9), the effort involves strenuous assumptions once one moves beyond wages and salaries. Because many regional exports and imports are, moreover, of raw materials and semi-finished goods, "final" product measurement at the state or provincial level involves conceptual difficulties as well. Nevertheless, some efforts have been made to estimate gross product by state and province. A summary of data for the years 1965, 1973, and 1979 is given in Table 1.6.

The table reveals, once again, that per capita value of output was highest in New England (due largely to the influence of Connecticut and Massachusetts) at $10,063 in 1979. This equals about 93 per cent of the US average. The corresponding

Table 1.6: Real and Current Dollar Gross Product per Capita and Growth Rates: 1965-1973, 1973-1979, 1965-1979

| | Nominal GP per Capita ($US) | | | Real GP per Capita (1971 Canadian figures in $ Can, US figures in $US) | | | Average Annual Growth Rate (per cent) | | | | | |
| | | | | | | | Real GNP | | | Real GNP per Capita | | |
	1965	1973	1979	1965	1973	1979	1965-73	1973-79	1965-79[a]	1965-73	1973-79	1965-79[a]
Canada	2,614	5,605	9,391	3,563	4,891	5,479	5.5	3.1	4.5	4.0	1.9	3.2
Atlantic Prov.	1,551	3,561	5,870	2,114	3,107	3,425	5.8	2.8	4.4	4.9	1.6	3.4
Newfoundland	1,345	2,951	5,298	1,833	2,575	3,091	5.6	4.2		4.3	3.1	
P.E.I.	1,312	3,216	4,933	1,788	2,806	2,878	6.4	1.7		5.8	0.4	
Nova Scotia	1,660	3,886	6,304	2,262	3,391	3,678	6.0	2.2		5.2	1.4	
New Brunswick	1,623	3,725	5,982	2,212	3,250	3,490	5.6	2.6		4.9	1.2	
Quebec	2,397	4,936	8,423	3,267	4,307	4,915	4.4	2.8	3.7	3.5	2.2	3.0
United States	3,556	6,226	10,763	4,594	5,650	6,243	3.7	2.5	2.8	2.6	1.7	1.9
New England	3,637	5,995	10,063	4,699	5,440	5,837	2.7	1.4	1.5	1.8	1.2	0.8
Northern Tier:	2,832	4,807	8,092	3,656	4,362	4,694	3.5	2.5	3.0	2.2	1.2	1.1
Maine	2,736	4,554	7,526	3,535	4,132	4,365	2.5	1.9		2.0	0.9	
New Hampshire	2,957	5,059	8,754	3,820	4,591	5,078	4.4	3.6		2.3	1.7	
Vermont	2,861	4,940	8,166	3,696	4,483	4,737	4.2	1.9		2.4	0.9	
Southern Tier:	3,817	6,273	10,561	4,932	5,692	6,126	2.6	1.2	1.3	1.8	1.2	0.8
Massachusetts	3,739	6,122	10,148	4,831	5,555	5,886	2.4	0.9		1.8	1.0	
Rhode Island	3,351	5,430	8,915	4,329	4,927	5,171	2.7	0.1		1.6	0.8	
Connecticut	4,114	6,814	11,817	5,315	6,183	6,854	2.9	1.9		1.9	1.7	

[a] Computed by regression analysis (log Y = Bo - BiT).

Sources: Statistics Canada, Cat. No. 91-201, 1979.
US Bureau of the Census, *Statistical Abstract of the United States*, various dates.
Revue du Ministere des Finances du Canada, April 1981.
Rate of exchange: Revue mensuelle de la Banque du Canada (average daily rate at midday).
Gross state product, New England: Federal Reserve Bank of Boston.

(This table was compiled by P.-P. Proulx.)

figure (in US dollars) for Quebec was $8,423 and for the Atlantic Provinces $5,870, which amount to 84 and 58 per cent, respectively, of the Canadian average. The New England and eastern Canada relationships are thus similar to those mentioned above for personal income per capita. (The higher absolute figures for gross product are mainly attributable to the fact that not all income generated by production accrues to "persons.") As before, the rate of growth of gross product appears on average to be significantly higher in the eastern Canadian provinces than in New England. There were exceptions to this generalization during the 1970s, however, in the case of Prince Edward Island (low growth) and New Hampshire and Connecticut (high growth).

The more interesting information to be inferred from gross product data lies in their relationship to their respective national averages. Table 1.5 shows the relative data for product as well as for personal income. Both the Atlantic Provinces and New England demonstrate a better relative standing in terms of persohal income than of gross product. Quebec, on the other hand, shows a rough correspondence between the two. It may be tentatively concluded, therefore, that transfer payments (of all kinds) are of considerably greater importance in the Atlantic Provinces and New England than in Quebec. Furthermore, while the figures for any specific year do not provide an adequate basis for generalization, it does appear that transfers may be of increasing importance in northern New England as well as in the Atlantic Provinces.[13] Southern New England, on the other hand, presents a mixed picture, perhaps reflecting its larger manufacturing and financial services base.

Along with the level and rate of growth of personal income (or product), it is instructive to consider the distribution of income. One approach to the subject is to consider proportions of families in each of several dollar income brackets. Interestingly, while there do not appear to be wide divergencies between Quebec and New England in this respect (Table 1.7), the Atlantic Provinces present a different picture. Admittedly, comparisons using dollar income brackets are rendered doubtful here by differences in currency values (it is not possible to make adequate adjustments without having access to the underlying data) as well as by differences in median income levels, in non-cash income, and in the cost of living. Ignoring these problems for the moment, it appears that in 1978 the Atlantic Provinces had only a slightly larger proportion of very low-income (under $5,000) families than Quebec. If the definition of "low income" is broadened to include family incomes up to $12,000, then the Atlantic group has a much larger proportion of low-income families (38.1 per cent) than either Quebec (26.0 per cent) or the northeastern United States (28.8 per cent). Since we are measuring income groups in terms of dollars rather than, say, deciles, it can be assumed that the larger proportion of poor families and the smaller proportion of well-off families in the Atlantic Region reflect the lower incomes generally prevailing in that area as well as the distribution of those incomes. What is a bit surprising, given this general picture, is that the 42 per cent of Atlantic Provinces families having incomes in the $12,000-$25,000 range is so close to the corresponding percentages for Quebec and New England. The median family income levels shown in Table 1.7, when adjusted by the exchange rate, are generally consistent with the per capita data shown in Table 1.4.

Table 1.7: **Distribution of Families by Income Group (Per cent) and Median Family Income, 1978**

Income Group	Under $5,000	$5,000-11,999	$12,000-25,000	Over $25,000	Median Income ($)
Atlantic Provinces	6.6	31.5	42.1	19.8	15,304
Quebec	5.1	20.9	45.5	28.5	18,592
Canada	5.0	19.4	43.8	31.8	19,717
Northeast Region[a]	6.8	22.0	41.8	29.3	18,200
United States	8.2	22.5	41.3	27.9	17,640

Note: Income groups and medians are measured in their respective currencies. In 1978, the US dollar sold at an average premium of 1.140 Canadian dollars.

a Includes New York.

Sources: Statistics Canada, *Canada Year Book*, 1980-1981.
US Bureau of the Census, *Statistical Abstract of the United States*, 1980.

While per capita or family incomes in any given year can be compared (imperfectly) across the international boundary by use of the going exchange rate, comparisons of internal real rates of growth require the use of constant dollars in each currency. In Table 1.4 current dollar income was converted to constant dollars using the respective country's *national* consumer price index. The relevant indices and inflation rates are shown in Table 1.8.

It can be seen at once that rates of inflation in Canada and the United States have been closely comparable in recent years. The Canadian rate, however, has slightly exceeded that of the United States in roughly two-thirds of the years shown. Thus, it can be concluded that inflation has been an equally important problem in both countries — and all three regions — but with marginally higher long-term rates north of the boundary. A primary reason for the close relationship is, without question, the impact of imported US goods and services on the Canadian economy.

It is probable that the modest differential in inflation rates contributed to the decline in the value of the Canadian dollar in US markets over the period (i.e., appreciation of the US dollar in Canada). That decline was particularly evident after 1977. Thus, the two currencies, which were of roughly equivalent value in 1973, had diverged substantially by 1983, with the US dollar then selling at a 23 per cent premium (Table 1.9). Apart from differential inflation rates, cross-boundary investment flows have probably been of major importance in determining movements in exchange rates; the premium rose substantially in 1981 and 1982 as US investment in Canada decreased following implementation of the Canadian energy program.

Economic Structure

New England and Quebec have a broadly similar economic structure when measured by industrial sector employment. The Atlantic Provinces, with their considerably lower emphasis on manufacturing, are the exception, however. As might be expected, none of these regions has an agricultural sector proportionately as large as their respective national averages; the proportion of the labour force engaged in agriculture is less than 4 per cent everywhere, except on Prince Edward Island where it reaches 12-13 per cent.[14] In the other Atlantic Provinces and in northern New England, the importance of other "primary" industry (forestry, fishing, mining) tends to more than compensate for the lesser role of agriculture, the result being that the primary sectors overall account for a somewhat *greater* proportion of the total labour force than is true of the respective national economies. (At the national level, however, Canada's primary sector is about half again as large as that of the United States — roughly 7.5 per cent versus 4.6 per cent of the labour force).[15]

Table 1.8: Canadian and US Consumer Price Indices and Inflation Rates, 1960-1983

	Canada (1971 = 100)	Rate of Increase (per cent)	United States (1967 = 100)	Rate of Increase (per cent)
1960	74.3		88.7	
1961	75.0	0.9	89.6	1.0
1962	75.9	1.2	90.6	1.1
1963	77.2	1.8	91.7	1.2
1964	78.6	1.7	92.9	1.3
1965	80.5	2.4	94.5	1.7
1966	83.5	3.7	97.2	2.9
1967	86.5	3.6	100.0	2.9
1968	90.0	4.0	104.2	4.2
1969	94.1	4.6	109.8	5.4
1970	97.2	3.3	116.3	5.9
1971	100.0	2.8	121.3	4.3
1972	104.8	4.8	125.3	3.3
1973	112.7	7.5	133.1	6.2
1974	125.0	10.9	147.7	11.0
1975	138.5	10.8	161.2	9.1
1976	148.9	7.5	170.5	5.8
1977	160.8	8.0	181.5	6.5
1978	175.2	9.0	195.4	7.7
1979	191.2	9.1	217.4	11.3
1980	210.6	10.1	246.8	13.5
1981	236.9	12.5	272.4	10.4
1982	262.5	10.8	289.1	6.1
1983	277.7	5.8	298.4	3.2

Sources: Statistics Canada, Cat. No. 62-010.
US Bureau of Labor Statistics, *Handbook of Labor Statistics*, various dates.

Data covering distribution of the *non-agricultural* labour force (Table 1.10) gain in reliability to the extent that they are less influenced by strong seasonal and part-time components. It can be seen, for example, that manufacturing or "secondary"

Table 1.9:   **Annual Average Dollar Exchange Rate, 1965-1983**

	Price of US Dollar in Canada (cents)	Price of Canadian Dollar in US (cents)
1965	107.80	92.76
1966	107.73	92.82
1967	107.87	92.70
1968	107.75	92.81
1969	107.68	92.87
1970	104.40	95.79
1971	100.98	99.03
1972	99.05	100.96
1973	100.01	99.99
1974	97.80	102.25
1975	101.73	98.30
1976	98.61	101.41
1977	106.35	94.03
1978	114.02	87.70
1979	117.15	85.36
1980	116.90	85.54
1981	119.88	83.42
1982	123.40	81.04
1983	123.20	81.17

Source: Bank of Canada.

activity is of somewhat greater importance to the economies of Quebec (24 per cent) and both northern and southern New England (28 per cent) than it is to either of the national economies (22-23 per cent). Such data, of course, hide significant variations *within* the manufacturing sector, which will be discussed shortly. In both countries, and in two of the three regions, this secondary sector has declined moderately in importance (as measured by employment) over recent decades due to a combination of rising labour productivity in manufacturing and the increased demand for services characteristic of most developed economies. The Atlantic Provinces once again provide the exception, with a manufacturing sector which, while smaller than those in the other regions, has expanded somewhat since the 1950s.

The services or "tertiary" sector has been expanding in all three regions as it has in the national economies. This sector is conventionally broken down into five or six subsectors as shown in Table 1.10. Unfortunately, definitions of some of these subcategories are not consistent across the international boundary, and comparisons must be made with caution. It is probably safe to say that wholesale and retail trade account for a somewhat larger proportion of the labour force in New England than in eastern Canada. Transportation, communications, and utilities show the reverse tendency, which is no doubt attributable in part to the much greater physical size of the Canadian provinces. Southern New England, not surprisingly, shows a relatively heavy emphasis on the financial (including insurance) subsector.

The "other services" category is a catchall, including business and personal services, health care, education, welfare, recreation, and public administration, among other things. Overall, the proportion of the labour force occupied in these activities does not vary greatly among the regions (or nations). Differences among public sector service activities are camouflaged by the typical inclusion in US data of primary and secondary school teachers in "government," while they are excluded in the Canadian "public administration" category. This measurement inconsistency reflects a more basic — perhaps ideological — difference: while the distinction between public and private sector activities (in this case employment) has been traditionally emphasized in US thinking, in Canada the distinction has been blurred in the context of a more "mixed" economy. Thus, no important distinctions of a statistical sort are drawn in Canada between employees of publicly and privately owned institutions or firms in fields such as transportation, manufacturing, or education. In the United States, by way of contrast, "public" employees, like their employers, are considered a breed apart.

Table 1.11 shows a cross-section of the more important types of manufacturing activity in each region as measured by value added (roughly, final sales minus purchases of raw

Table 1.10: Distribution of Non-agricultural Labour Force by Industrial Sector (Per Cent), 1979-1980

	Canada	Atlantic Provinces	Quebec	New England Northern	New England Southern	New England Total	US
Forestry	0.8	1.7	0.8				1.2
Mining	1.7	2.2	1.1				
Manufacturing	21.6	15.4	24.1	28.4	28.1	28.2	23.4
Services							
Trade and commerce	17.4	17.9	16.6	21.7	21.5	21.5	22.5
Transport and public utilities	9.4	10.9	9.5	4.2	4.4	4.4	5.8
Finance, insurance, real estate	5.8	4.3	5.7	4.3	6.1	5.8	5.5
Construction	5.4	6.2	4.4	5.0	3.2	3.6	5.2
Other services	37.8	41.3	37.9	36.6	36.6	36.6	36.4
(Public admin.) ("Government")	(7.2)	(9.7)	(6.8)	(17.7)	(15.0)	(15.5)	(17.4)

Sources: Statistics Canada, Cat. No. 71-001, 1980.
US Bureau of Labor Statistics, *Employment and Economics, States and Areas, 1981.*

Table 1.11: Leading Manufacturing Industries in the Three Regions, 1978

	Atlantic Provinces		Quebec		New England[a]	
	$ Mill.	% Region	$ Mill.	% Region	$ Mill.	% Region
Pulp and paper mills	428	20.6	1,272	9.1	2,006	5.6
Fish products	279	13.4				
Lumber mills			377	2.7	569	1.6
Primary metals			1,124	8.0	1,333	3.7
Fabricated metals	31	1.5	602	4.3	3,178	8.9
Clothing and shoes			749	5.4		
Machinery, excl. elec.					5,482	15.4
Electrical equipment			387	2.8	4,080	11.5
Instruments and controls						6.7[b]
Transportation equipment			882[b]	6.3		7.8[b]
Printing and publishing	57	2.8	335	2.4	2,059	5.8
Total	2,079	100.0	13,995	100.0	35,587	100.0

Note: Some data withheld to avoid disclosure. Canadian and US industrial classifications may vary slightly.

a   1977 data.
b   Estimated.

Sources: Statistics Canada, Cat. No. 31-203.
US Bureau of the Census, *Census of Manufactures, 1977*, Vol. 111.

materials and semi-finished goods). As before, value-added data should be interpreted with caution, particularly at the state and provincial level. Analysis of the composition of manufacturing activity across regions, like that of the labour force, is further complicated by inconsistencies in the definition of particular industries or industry groups. The categories in Table 1.11 are, therefore, only approximate.

Not surprisingly, patterns of manufacturing in most states and provinces tend in some degree to reflect their natural resource endowments. Thus, lumber and wood products, paper making, and primary metals have traditionally been of great importance in Quebec, New Brunswick, and (except for metals) northern New England. Textile manufacturing and the apparel industries were traditionally important in both Quebec and New England; the latter region, however, has seen much of this activity (except for leather products) move to other areas. Electrical and other types of machinery, on the other hand, remain strong in southern New England, and both this region and Quebec continue to benefit from substantial activity in transportation equipment, particularly aircraft engines and automobile assembly (both regions), snowmobiles and vehicles used in public transportation (Quebec), and shipbuilding (New England). A number of the so-called high-technology industries have flourished in New England — especially Massachusetts and Connecticut — since the 1960s and have helped the region adjust to the loss of textile manufacturing. Quebec also has an incipient high-technology sector, although it does not as yet play a comparable role in that province. Manufacturing in the Atlantic Provinces, while expanding in recent decades, appears to be much more closely tied to the region's natural resource base.

General Comments
The authors of following chapters delve into some of the characteristics reviewed above in greater detail as they explore the bases for trade, present and future. It remains to be emphasized that none of the three regions is homogeneous: all are made up of subregions having some characteristics in common but many that are contrasting. Reference has already been made to the substantial differences between northern and southern New England. The same applies to the Atlantic Provinces: Newfoundland and Prince Edward Island each show interesting contrasts with New Brunswick and Nova Scotia, and even the latter two, with their respective orientation to forests and to the sea, are far from homogeneous. In Quebec, neither the industrialized section of the St. Lawrence Valley nor Eastern

Townships agriculture has much in common with the vast Laurentian highlands undergoing mineral and hydroelectric development. It follows that any generalization about "the economy" of any of the three regions is probably a good deal more hazardous than similar generalizations about their history or culture.

Another fact of great importance in thinking about the future of the two Canadian regions is their relation to the United States in general. US influence has traditionally been very powerful in the economic sphere. The United States has, since the mid-nineteenth century, provided the primary market for goods exported from both Quebec and the Atlantic Provinces. A large proportion of Quebec's manufacturing sector, probably 25-30 per cent, is owned or controlled by US firms.[16] The same would be true of its mining and utility sectors had it not been for "nationalization" efforts undertaken in recent years. While new US investment in eastern Canada was dampened by a number of factors up to 1984 – including Canadian policies aimed at restricting such investment – the fact remains that these regions, like all of Canada, are heavily dependent on both the economic health and economic policies of the United States for their own prosperity. When the future of northeast interregional trade and investment is discussed in later chapters, therefore, one should not lose sight of the importance of this basic relationship, both in its capacity to shape Canadian views toward New England and in its potential for communicating US problems northward.

Finally, an important theme underlying both Quebec and Atlantic Provinces development strategies is the desirability of diversifying exports to the United States – and, of course, to other areas as well. Over at least the past century, both regions have been primarily suppliers of raw materials and semi-finished goods and consumers of finished manufactures. (This role, to a considerable extent, has been shared by northern New England.) Given their conviction that more emphasis on finished goods would help to raise incomes, and that greater diversification would render them less vulnerable to cyclical disturbances, it is not surprising that strenuous efforts are being made by Quebec and the Atlantic Provinces to reshape north-south trade by expanding indigenous manufactures, especially high-technology industries, and specific types of services exports, e.g., engineering services. It remains to be seen whether or to what extent demographic, resource, and market factors will continue to work against achievement of the diversification objective.

Notes

1.   Useful surveys of the early economic development of New England and eastern Canada include (1) on New England, Curtis P. Nettels, *The Roots of American Civilization* (New York: Appleton-Century, 1938) Chs. 5-10, 14; Samuel E. Morison, *The Maritime History of Massachusetts* (Boston: Houghton Mifflin, 1921); Bernard Bailyn, *The New England Merchants in the Seventeenth Century* (New York: Harper, 1955); Douglas McManis, *Colonial New England: A Historical Geography* (New York: Oxford, 1975); and (2) on eastern Canada, Harold A. Innis, *The Cod Fisheries* (Toronto: University of Toronto Press, 1940); Harold A. Innis, *The Fur Trade in Canada* (New Haven: Yale University Press, 1930); J.B. Brebner, *New England's Outpost: Acadia Before the British Conquest of Canada* (New York: Columbia University Press, 1927); W.T. Easterbrook and Hugh G.J. Aitken, *Canadian Economic History* (Toronto: Macmillan, 1956) Part I; William L. Marr and Donald G. Paterson, *Canada: An Economic History* (Toronto: Macmillan, 1980) Ch. 3 and early sections of Chs. 4-7. Probably the best treatment of US-Canada economic relations during the early years can be found in Harold A. Innis, *Essays in Canadian Economic History*, edited by Mary Q. Innis (Toronto: University of Toronto Press, 1956).

2.   Robert G. Albion, and Jenny B. Pope, *Sea Lanes in Wartime* (New York: Norton, 1942) Ch. IV.

3.   Canada's pursuit of "reciprocity" with the United States followed the loss of colonial preference in British markets in 1846. The expansion of trade after 1854, however, may have reflected trade diversion (e.g., via the Erie Canal and other US waterways) more than a lowering of tariffs. A good overview of mid-century economic policy is provided by Easterbrook and Aitken, *Canadian Economic History*, Chs. 16 and 17. A somewhat broader discussion of mid- and late nineteenth-century developments may be found in J.B. Brebner, *Canada: A Modern History* (Ann Arbor: University of Michigan Press, 1960) Chs. 18-21.

4.   By 1930, 264,261 or 71 per cent of the 370,852 persons in the United States who were French-Canadian born were in New England. These and similar data on immigration

patterns are summarized in Hugh L. Keenleyside and Gerald S. Brown, *Canada and the United States*, revised edition (New York: Knopf, 1952) Ch. IX.

5.   See Easterbrook and Aitken, *Canadian Economic History*, Chs. 17 and 21. Also see Marr and Paterson, *Canada: An Economic History*, Chs. 9 and 12. A good discussion of the Canadian tariff and its consequences is found in J.H. Dales, *The Protective Tariff in Canada's Development* (Toronto: University of Toronto Press, 1966).

6.   See US Department of Commerce, US Travel Service, *Vacation Travel by Canadians in United States*, Washington, D.C., various issues from 1974 on. Also, Statistics Canada, Financial Flows and Multinational Enterprises Division, *Travel Between Canada and Other Countries*, Ottawa, various dates.

7.   Author's estimate.

8.   Information from Statistics Canada, Cat. No. 92-901.

9.   For an interesting discussion of these trends and some of their consequences, see Atlantic Provinces Economic Council, *APEC Newsletter*, February 1982, pp. 2-3.

10.   Atlantic Development Council, *The Atlantic Region of Canada: Economic Development Strategy for the Eighties* (St. John's, Newfoundland: ADC, 1978) Tables 11 and 13 and pp. 19-26.

11.   Atlantic Development Council, *The Atlantic Region of Canada*, Tables 12 and 13.

12.   Statistics Canada, *Canada Yearbook 1980-81*, Table 22.20. See also Quebec, Department of Economic Development, *Challenges for Quebec*, Quebec City, 1979, p. 12.

13.   The index of transfer payments as a proportion of personal income in New England (US = 100) in 1978 varied from 84 in Connecticut to 133 in Maine. See US Bureau of Census, *Statistical Abstract of the United States*, 1980, Table 741.

14.   See Statistics Canada, Cat. No. 71-001 (*The Labour Force*), 1980.

15.   See Statistics Canada, Cat. No. 71-001. Also, see US Bureau of the Census, *Statistical Abstract,* 1980, Table 679.

16.   See Chapter 7, Table 7.3. The comparable 1980 proportions for the Atlantic Provinces, Ontario, and Canada as a whole were 16 per cent, 46 per cent, and 35 per cent, respectively.

2: SELECTED DEMOGRAPHIC AND LABOUR MARKET CHARACTERISTICS

W.D. Shipman with E. Beale

Introduction

The brief review in Chapter 1 of the respective histories of Quebec, New England, and the Atlantic Provinces showed that there have been many linkages among the populations of the three regions, both in terms of migration between regions and in terms of shared patterns of growth and transformation. During the early part of the twentieth century (prior to World War II) when the economy of the Atlantic Region was frequently in a slump, it was common for workers from the Maritimes and Newfoundland to migrate to New England, either to work on a seasonal or short-term basis, or to establish permanent residence there. The folklore and songs of the Atlantic Region are full of stories of uncles who made fortunes in the "Boston States." As noted in Chapter 1, migration from Quebec to New England was important during the late nineteenth and early twentieth centuries.

After World War II and up to the 1970s, migration from the Atlantic Region to New England waned. Ontario then became the primary recipient of expatriates from the Atlantic Provinces. New England, particularly the northern tier states, also witnessed a considerable outflow of population to the western and southern states after the war. This represented the continuation of a long-term movement westward, but, unlike that of the nineteenth century, this movement was not compensated for by an influx of settlers from overseas or Canada. Hence, population in several New England states grew very slowly between 1945 and 1970.

As Table 2.1 shows, the 1970s witnessed a continuation of net outmigration from most parts of the three regions to the west and south, but also a surprising reversal of that trend in northern New England. Migrants from the Atlantic Region tended to go farther west than before, primarily to Alberta and British Columbia, where they were joined by substantial numbers of

Table 2.1: Components of Population Change (Thousands), 1971-1981 (Canada) and 1970-1980 (United States)

	Population Change	%	Births[a]	Deaths[a]	Net Migration[b]
Newfoundland	53	+ 10.1	111	32	-26
Prince Edward Is.	10	+ 9.4	19	10	+ 1
Nova Scotia	58	+ 7.4	129	68	- 3
New Brunswick	60	+ 9.4	115	51	- 4
Atlantic Prov.	181	+ 8.8	374	161	-32
Quebec	372	+ 6.2	925	427	-125
Maine	131	+ 13.2	161	107	+ 76
New Hampshire	183	+ 24.8	122	75	+136
Vermont	67	+ 15.0	72	44	+ 38
Massachusetts	48	+ 0.8	737	553	-136
Rhode Island	- 3	- 0.3	123	93	- 33
Connecticut	75	+ 2.5	391	263	- 52
New England	501	+ 4.2	1,607	1,135	+ 29

a   Approximate data.
b   Net migration = observed number increase - births + deaths.

Sources: Statistics Canada, Cat. Nos. 92-901 and 84-204.
US Bureau of the Census, Statistical Abstract of the United States, 1982-1983.

Quebecers. New England's three northern tier states benefited from an influx of firms and individuals attempting to escape the high costs of northeastern urban centres, and New Hampshire attracted increasing numbers of Massachusetts people into its own southern counties, from which Boston was easily accessible. Large numbers of migrating individuals to these states were either retired or had independent incomes, and they brought with them to states such as Maine and Vermont a deep commitment to environmental values which did not always sit well with the "natives," most of whom were trying to increase their low wage incomes through whatever development strategies were available. But, these states aside, the main thrust of migration was nevertheless in a westward and southerly direction as it had been in earlier decades. In absolute numbers, net outmigration during the 1970s was especially notable in Quebec and Massachusetts.

Cultural Comparisons: The French Language

Table 2.2 brings out an important cultural fact of life in eastern Canada – namely, the continuing dominance of French-speaking persons in Quebec and a strong minority French group in New Brunswick. About 60 per cent of the Quebec population speaks only French, while another 30 per cent is bilingual – but presumably with a preference for French outside of a few traditional business and professional occupations and anglophone districts in Montreal. In New Brunswick, the proportion that is bilingual has increased enough to offset the decrease in people speaking only French, so that the combined group continues to account for close to 40 per cent of the total population. The other Atlantic Provinces are predominatly English-speaking.

In recent years Quebec has moved to re-emphasize the French language. The population speaking only English has decreased from more than 12 per cent in the 1950s to 6.5 per cent in the early 1980s, while the bilingual percentage has increased commensurately. Such figures, of course, reflect the combination of outmigrating English-only speakers and the efforts of the Quebec government to promote French as the language of business in Quebec. More will be said about the impact of such programs on Quebec-New England economic relations, including US investment north of the boundary, in later chapters.

New England's cultural life is based almost wholly on the English language, and more so today than a generation ago. While the region continues to have pockets of minority language groups – for example, Italian in Connecticut, Portugese in southeastern Massachusetts, French in northern Maine – the homogenizing influence of technology and the media (and of most educational institutions) has drastically limited their extent. The once strong position of French in the region's many textile towns has thus been severely weakened. Only among the older generation in these towns does French remain the customary "home" language, and even that seems to be passing today.

Table 2.2:   **Distribution of English- and French-Speaking Populations in Quebec and Atlantic Provinces (Per cent): 1961, 1971, 1981**

		English Only	French Only	English & French
Quebec	1961	11.6	61.9	25.5
	1971	10.5	60.9	27.6
	1981	6.6	59.4	32.3
Newfoundland	1961	98.5	0.1	1.2
	1971	98.0	0.1	1.8
	1981	96.9	0.2	2.3
P.E.I.	1961	91.1	1.2	7.6
	1971	91.2	0.6	8.2
	1981	90.8	0.2	8.0
Nova Scotia	1961	92.9	0.8	6.1
	1971	92.6	0.5	6.7
	1981	91.4	0.2	7.4
New Brunswick	1961	62.0	18.7	19.0
	1971	62.5	15.9	21.5
	1981	59.9	12.8	26.2

Source: Statistics Canada, Cat. No. 92-910.

Indeed, Quebec's language policies can, from one point of view, be fully justified by looking at the New England experience. Between 1900 and 1940 a number of New England towns and cities had a social and cultural structure resembling that of Quebec as of 1960, with French- speaking residents occupying most of the lower-rung positions. An elite group of English-speaking owners, managers, and professionals constituted the upper class. The combined influence of national media (exclusively English) and a stratified educational system, dominated outside the Church by anglophones, relegated French to a status identified with inferior position. Thus, it was a language to be avoided by upwardly mobile young people. In retrospect, the trend in favour of an "American English" culture probably could have been avoided only by official policies and laws aimed at elevating French at the expense of English. In New England, however, the dominance of English as a medium for both technological and business pursuits, not to mention entertainment, would have defeated any such move. Even in Quebec, direct legislative action was ultimately required.

As for New England-Quebec economic relations, connecting linkages, trade, communications, and the like continue to be based mainly on English. The key players on the Quebec side are almost certain to be bilingual, while language versatility on the US side continues to be a rare occurrence. While there are business and professional conferences conducted in both languages, US participation is likely to be conditioned on English being the common denominator. The alternative — insistence by Quebec on communication in French — simply raises barriers to trade in information (as well as commodities and investment) that benefit neither party.

Educational Levels

The educational level of the adult population of New England is higher than that of the United States as a whole, with relatively more people educated at the university level and relatively fewer who have only a primary school education. As Table 2.3 indicates, 34 per cent of New England's population had at least some university background in 1976 compared with 30.6 per cent for all of the United States. Within the region, however, there is some variation. Both Maine and Rhode Island have a below-average percentage of population with some university training. In all the New England states except Rhode Island, however, the proportion of the adult population with education at or above the high school level is greater than the national average. In all New England states, again except for Rhode Island, the percentage of

Table 2.3: Education Attained by Persons Fifteen Years and Over (Canada) or Eighteen Years and Over (United States) in Selected Provinces and States (Per cent), 1976

	Elementary, 0-8	Secondary, 9-13	Post-secondary Degree/Certificate	University Degree	Post-secondary and University
Canada	28.4	42.5	14.5	8.5	4.4
Newfoundland	39.8	39.2	12.9	6.5	2.9
P.E.I.	32.6	39.1	14.6	8.4	5.2
Nova Scotia	27.3	42.6	16.5	7.7	4.5
New Brunswick	29.7	38.8	13.7	6.5	4.3
Quebec	36.6	36.6	12.8	7.8	6.2

	Elementary, 0-8 Years	High School, 1-4 Years	College, 1-4 Years	High School Graduate and Above	College Graduate and Above
United States	17.4	52.0	30.6	66.6	13.9
New England	14.9	51.1	34.0	70.3	16.6
Connecticut	15.3	49.4	35.2	70.2	18.3
Maine	15.5	55.6	29.0	67.8	13.6
Massachusetts	13.6	51.3	35.1	72.3	16.8
New Hampshire	14.6	51.2	34.0	70.3	15.3
Rhode Island	19.8	51.2	28.8	61.7	14.9
Vermont	16.6	50.0	33.1	69.7	15.6

Sources: Statistics Canada, Census, 1976.
US Bureau of the Census, *Demographic, Social and Economic Profile of States, Spring 1976*, Current Population Reports Series P-20, No. 334.

the population with eight years of schooling or less is below the national average.

The profile of educational levels in Quebec and the Atlantic Region is a rather different picture. While the data are not strictly comparable, Table 2.3 shows that the level of educational attainment is generally lower in Quebec and each of the Atlantic Provinces, with the exception of Nova Scotia, than in Canada as a whole. In all provinces except Nova Scotia, the proportion with only an elementary school education is larger than in Canada as a whole. Newfoundland, in particular, has the largest proportion in all of Canada of its population fifteen years and older with only an elementary school education, 11.4 percentage points above the Canadian average. A similar pattern holds true at the other end of the educational scale; a smaller than (national) average percentage of the population fifteen years and over in three of the provinces (Newfoundland, Quebec, and New Brunswick) recorded some post-secondary education. The proportion of those who have some university training is also lower in three of the provinces (Nova Scotia, Newfoundland, and New Brunswick) in comparison with all of Canada.

The general level of education in the three regions has risen over the years, as it has for both the United States and Canada. While New England has retained an absolute edge when compared with the rest of the United States, the rest of the United States is gaining just as rapidly in educational levels. In 1960, for example, 44.5 per cent of New England's population twenty-five years and older had completed high school compared to 41 per cent in the United States. The respective figures in 1976 were 68 per cent and 64 per cent. A comparable differential has been maintained into the 1980s.

Data for Quebec and the Atlantic Provinces again, however, tell a different story. While in terms of educational attainment these regions have been catching up to the rest of Canada in an absolute sense, the educational level in the rest of Canada by most measures is still equal to or greater than that in each of these regions. In 1961, 58 per cent of those fifteen years and over in Newfoundland had an elementary school education while only 3.2 per cent had some university education. In 1976, the percentage with some university attendance had tripled and the percentage with an elementary education alone had fallen to 39.8 per cent. A similar pattern holds true for the other provinces, although growth rates for the different levels of educational achievements differ. For example, in 1961 Quebec had a below (Canadian) average percentage of its population with some university education (5.6 per cent), while in 1976 this group had increased to 14 per cent of the population fifteen years and over, or 1.1 percentage points *above* the Canadian average. Nova Scotia, of all these provinces, most closely mirrors the Canadian average.

Labour Force Participation and Unemployment Rates

Table 2.4 shows participation rates for selected years in the three regions. Perhaps the most notable feature of the table is the lower male participation rates in the Atlantic Provinces than in either Quebec or New England, and the lower female participation rates in the eastern Canadian provinces generally. The latter is to some extent a cultural phenomenon having to do with customary attitudes toward the role of women. (Female participation rates have risen in all three regions, as in the two nations generally.) While New England women are *more* apt to be in the job market than US women generally, the opposite is true in Quebec and the Atlantic Provinces, where female participation rates of 47 per cent and 44 per cent, respectively, contrast with the all- Canadian average of 52 per cent. Since participation rates reflect to some extent the problem (or fear) of unemployment, it is likely that lower participation in the Atlantic Provinces is partly the result of a more slowly growing economy, as well as cultural factors and age distribution.

Unemployment rates in the Atlantic Provinces have averaged several points higher than in New England in recent years, with Quebec frequently occupying an in-between position. Interestingly, Quebec weathered the recession of the mid-1970s somewhat better than her immediate neighbours. But, following expansion in the late 1970s, the recession of 1980-1981 brought substantial rises in unemployment in both Quebec and the Atlantic Provinces, more so than in New England where growth of some high-technology industries helped to offset declines in more traditional areas. After 1981, the situation deteriorated in all three regions as the tight money policies followed by the US government drove up interest rates in both countries. In general, it can be said that Quebec and the Atlantic Provinces have trailed the Canadian economy regarding employment over the past decade, while New England, after a weak showing in the mid-1970s, has been able to outperform much of the United States – or at least those sections of the country most dependent on the traditional "smokestack" industries.

Table 2.4: Selected Labour Force Characteristics: 1971, 1976, 1981

		Participation Rate [a]			Unemployment Rate [b]		
		1971	1976	1981	1971	1976	1981
Newfoundland	Male		66.6	67.0			
	Female		31.8	38.2	8.4	13.4	14.1
P.E.I.	Male		72.4	71.2			
	Female		41.7	41.7	-	9.6	11.4
Nova Scotia	Male		71.9	70.5			
	Female		39.4	45.0	7.0	9.5	10.2
New Brunswick	Male		69.7	69.3			
	Female		38.0	43.7	6.1	11.0	11.7
Atl. Provinces	Male		69.9	69.5			
	Female		37.4	43.5		11.0	11.6
Quebec	Male	76.4	76.4	76.1			
	Female	36.4	41.1	47.4	7.3	8.7	10.4
Maine	Male		78.2	72.8			
	Female		47.8	50.0	7.4	8.9	7.2
New Hampshire	Male		80.8	80.9			
	Female		52.1	57.5	5.1	6.4	5.0
Vermont	Male		81.0	80.1			
	Female		48.1	56.1	6.3	8.7	5.7
Massachusetts	Male		79.9	78.5			
	Female		51.1	56.1	6.6	9.5	6.4
Rhode Island	Male		78.3	78.7			
	Female		49.7	54.1	5.4	8.1	7.6
Connecticut	Male		78.8	79.2			
	Female		51.5	55.1	8.4	9.5	6.2
New England	Male		79.5	78.5			
	Female		50.8	55.7	6.9	9.1	6.4
Canada	Male	77.3	77.6	78.3			
	Female	39.4	45.2	51.6	6.2	7.1	7.6
United States	Male	78.5	77.5	77.0			
	Female	42.9	47.3	52.1	5.9	7.7	7.6

[a] Per cent of civilian population sixteen years and older in the United States, fifteen years and older in Canada, in civilian labour force.
[b] Per cent of civilian labour force unemployed.

Sources: Statistics Canada, Cat. No. 71-201.
US Bureau of the Census, *Statistical Abstract of the United States, 1982-1983*.
Federal Reserve Bank of Boston, *New England Economic Almanac, 1982*.

Relative Wages in the Three Regions

Tables 2.5 and 2.6 extend the comparisons of income presented in Chapter 1. One such comparison is average earnings in manufacturing, a series that has been collected in both countries for many years and is believed to be relatively complete as far as coverage. Table 2.5 shows the relevant data for 1965, 1973, and 1981, all expressed in US dollars using the average exchange rate prevailing in each year. (Questions concerning the validity of the exchange rate for obtaining comparable data are ignored here.)

Table 2.5:   Average Hourly Earnings in Manufacturing (US Dollars): 1965, 1973, 1981

	1965	1973	1981
Canada	1.97	3.85	7.65
Quebec	1.74	3.35	7.07
Atlantic Provinces	1.62	3.25	6.92
Newfoundland	1.62	3.29	7.17
Prince Edward Island			
Nova Scotia	1.64	3.30	6.81
New Brunswick	1.62	3.23	7.06
United States	2.61	4.09	7.98
New England	2.44	3.82	7.04
Maine	2.06	3.23	6.66
New Hampshire	2.06	3.39	6.40
Vermont	2.17	3.50	6.80
Massachusetts	2.45	3.89	7.01
Rhode Island	2.18	3.37	6.10
Connecticut	2.69	4.14	7.67

Sources: US Bureau of Labor Statistics, *Employment and Economics*, various dates.
Federal Reserve Bank of Boston, *New England Economic Almanac*, 1982.
Statistics Canada, Cat. Nos. 72-002 and 72-003.

In general it can be seen that the Canadian provinces have shown notable advances over these years relative to the American experience. By 1981, average hourly earnings in Quebec, Atlantic Provinces, and New England manufacturing establishments, measured in US dollars, were within a few percentage points of one another, yet all three lagged behind their respective national averages by a considerable margin. But the rate of improvement since 1965, again measured in US dollars, was dramatically better in Canada, the ratio 1981/1965 being 4.06 in Quebec, 4.27 in the Atlantic Region, and only 2.89 in New England. Most of the relative improvement occurred between 1965 and 1973, years when the exchange rate varied only moderately (Table 1.9). The achievement of approximate parity by the early 1980s, however, may have been assisted by a much weakened Canadian dollar after 1977.

Some significant variations within the regional averages are worth noting. While the manufacturing sectors of the Atlantic Provinces showed close wage comparability in 1965 and 1973, differences had emerged by 1981, with Newfoundland wages perhaps 4 per cent above the regional average and 5 per cent above those in Nova Scotia. Given the probability of year-to-year variations among the provinces, however, and the effects of severe post-1981 unemployment in the fisheries, the 1981 differentials may not be characteristic of the 1980s as a whole.

Within New England, on the other hand, there is no question about the significance of wage variation among the six states. Connecticut has long been the leader in this respect (despite its manufacturing wages having now fallen behind the US average), and its roughly 8-10 per cent advantage over the regional average has been maintained since the 1960s. (The difference has been variously attributed to differences in industry mix, occupational skills, degree of unionization, and the cost of living.) The northern tier states traditionally have had lower manufacturing wages than the southern. Recent years have witnessed considerable improvement in this respect in Vermont and, to a lesser extent, Maine and New Hampshire, while Rhode Island has suffered a relative decline, to the point where its manufacturing wages are presently the lowest in New England.

One cross-border comparison frequently encountered in the business community involves the wages paid to public sector employees in the two countries. It is widely believed that public sector employees in Canada, particularly at the provincial level, fare relatively better than do their counterparts in the United States. One approach to measuring this differential is afforded by recent studies of the International Monetary Fund. A

Table 2.6: Public Sector Wage Relationships in Canada and the United States, 1981

	Canada	United States
Average wage of central government employees ($ US)	17,862	18,540
Ratio of central government wage to per capita income[a]	1.51	1.64
Ratio of state and local government wage to central government wage	0.97	0.75
Ratio of average public sector wage to average private sector wage	1.35	0.88
Distribution of government employees (%):		
Central government employees	19.1	23.2
State and local employees	60.6	73.2
Public enterprise employees	20.3	3.6
	100.0	100.0
Distribution of government wages (%):		
Central government employees	19.0	27.9
State and local employees	58.7	66.4
Public enterprise employees	22.3	5.6
	100.0	100.0

[a] The measure of per capita personal income implied here is different than that shown in Table 1.4.

Source: International Monetary Fund, *Government Employment and Pay: Some International Comparisons*, 1983.

summary of results applicable to Canada and the United States (1981) is given in Table 2.6.

While federal government employees receive a slightly higher average salary in the United States than in Canada (measured, once again, in US dollars), employees of states and municipalities show the opposite tendency. Indeed, Canada's provincial and municipal employees receive wages that, on average, are within 5 per cent of those of Canadian federal employees. In the United States, the comparable figure is only about three-fourths. Moreover, when all public employees are lumped together, the Canadian figure is 35 per cent *above* the average private sector wage, whereas in the United States, public employees earn, on average, 12 per cent *less* than their counterparts in the private sector. Thus, the perceived contrast is borne out by national data, at least insofar as non-federal employees are concerned.

The fact that the Canadian public sector is larger in a relative sense, contains a substantial number of public enterprises in a variety of fields (whose employees typically receive better-than-average public wages in both countries), and has undergone a more thorough unionization than is true in the United States, all contribute to the observed differential. While the implications of this differential for trade and other economic relations among the regions are not entirely clear, it is understandable that Canadian private sector employers complain about the tax burden resulting from the high wages paid public service employees and the possible impact of public sector wages on those of the private sector. On the US side, employers fear that closer international ties might possibly lead to US adoption of what they consider the Canadian brand of "socialism."

Union Membership and Work Stoppages

The degree of unionization in the three regions—not just in the public sector—is shown in Table 2.7. The Canadian work force contains a larger proportion of organized workers than does the US work force—33 per cent versus 25 per cent—and Quebec and several of the Atlantic Provinces have higher proportions than even the Canadian average. Only Nova Scotia and Prince Edward Island fall below that average, and then only by two or three percentage points, which is interesting in view of the Island's agricultural character. Thus, the labour force of both the Atlantic Region and Quebec must be considered to be at least as "organized" as that of any region of North America.

Table 2.7: Extent of Union Membership in Three Regions (Thousands), 1980-1981

	No. of Paid Workers	No. in Unions	Per cent in Unions
Canada	9,599	3,160.1	32.9
Newfoundland	153	76.0	49.6
Prince Edward Island	31	9.3	30.0
Nova Scotia	294	86.6	29.5
New Brunswick	223	72.1	32.3
Atlantic Provinces	701	244.0	34.8
Quebec	2,300	871.4	37.9
United States	90,520[a]	22,811.0	25.2
Maine	417	101.0	24.2
New Hampshire	386	61.0	15.8
Vermont	200	36.0	18.0
Massachusetts	2,651	660.0	24.9
Rhode Island	398	113.0	28.4
Connecticut	1,428	327.0	22.9
New England	5,480	1,298.0	23.7

[a] Total non-agricultural employment in United States.

Sources: Statistics Canada, Cat. No. 71-202 and unpublished data.
US Bureau of Labor Statistics, *Directory of National Unions and Employee Associations*.

New England, on the other hand, contains two states — New Hampshire and Vermont — whose degree of unionization is well below the US average. (Only Rhode Island is above that average.) Massachusetts, Maine, and Connecticut have proportions of organized workers fairly close to the national average, which is surprising in view of the industrial character of southern New England. Maine differs notably from Vermont and New Hampshire, probably because of the important position in Maine of the paper industry and shipbuilding, both of which have been organized for many years.

On the whole, it can be said that the extent of unionization is considerably greater in eastern Canada than in New England. Explanations for the difference would likely be found in differences in industry mix, in the size and degree of unionization of the respective public sectors, and probably in historical factors such as the socio- linguistic stratification of Quebec.

An expected consequence of more effective worker organization is a greater ability to withhold labour to achieve union objectives. Strikes and slow-downs are thus usually associated with strong unions. Table 2.8, which contains information on work stoppages from 1978 through 1981, shows that the percentage of working time lost was considerably greater in Canada than in the United States. It was also greater, though not to the same degree, in most of the Atlantic Provinces than in New England. Quebec, in particular, has been the scene of frequent and costly labour disputes; the percentage of time lost in that province has been well above the Canadian average and several times the US average in recent years. On the other hand, while the overall effect of unions has been debated at length by economists and others, it would take a feat of imagination to argue that recent gains in wages in eastern Canada were not at least in part the result of effective labour organization, both in the workplace and at the polls.

Table 2.8: Work Stoppages in Three Regions (Person-days Not Worked as Per cent of Estimated Working Time), 1978-1981

	1978	1979	1980	1981
Canada	0.34	0.34	0.38	0.37
Newfoundland	1.01	0.15	2.20	0.11
Prince Edward Island	0.17	0.04	0.02	0.20
Nova Scotia	0.11	0.07	0.34	0.17
New Brunswick	0.23	0.19	0.50	0.14
Quebec	0.35	0.61	0.71	0.25
United States	0.17	0.15	0.14	0.11
Maine	0.21	0.06	0.11	0.01
New Hampshire	0.07	0.05	0.06	0.08
Vermont	0.02	0.05	0.06	0.08
Massachusetts	0.05	0.08	0.06	0.10
Rhode Island	0.08	0.15	0.13	0.20
Connecticut	0.07	0.32	0.14	0.05

Sources: Labour Canada, *Strikes and Lockouts in Canada,* various dates.
US Bureau of Labor Statistics, *Handbook of Labor Statistics*, 1983.

3: TRADE RELATIONS AMONG QUEBEC, THE ATLANTIC PROVINCES, AND NEW ENGLAND

P.-P. Proulx* and W.D. Shipman

Trade flows among the northeastern regions of North America reflect both their basic differences in regional endowments and the evolution of national development and trade policies. Following an examination of merchandise trade flows, an attempt can be made to identify specific regional policies that have had or will have a bearing on future cross-border trade, both volume and composition. Trade in certain services is discussed later in this chapter. Energy flows and policies, while introduced here, are covered in detail in Chapter 5.

With the above in mind, the following tables and discussion proceed from the national to the regional level. That is, Canada-US trade is summarized first, followed by trade between each region and the other country, and finally trade among the three regions themselves.

Canada-US Trade

It has frequently been observed that Canada and the United States are each other's most important trading partner. Table 3.1 summarizes Canada-US trade decennially back to 1950 and annually for the decade 1973-1983. While the volume of trade has grown rapidly in the years since World War II, the relative stability in proportionate shares is notable. Throughout the thirty-three-year period, the United States took approximately 60-70 per cent of Canadian exports, while Canada obtained from the United States about the same proportion of its imports. On the US side, Canada accounted for between 16 and 22 per cent of US exports, and between 17 and 28 per cent of US imports.

---

*Proulx's contribution to this chapter was completed prior to service with the Canadian government from 1982 to 1984.

Table 3.1: Canada-US Trade and Balances (Million $ Canadian), 1950-1983

Year	Can. Imports from US[a]	Per cent of Total Can. Imports	Per cent of Total US Exports[b]	Can. Exports to US[a]	Per cent of Total Can. Exports	Per cent of Total US Imports[b]	Canadian Balance
1950	$2,130	67.1	19.6	$2,050	64.9	22.1	$-80
1960	3,687	67.2	18.5	3,036	56.4	19.8	-651
1970	9,917	71.1	21.0	10,900	64.8	27.8	983
1973	16,502	70.0	21.2	17,129	67.4	25.5	627
1974	21,387	67.4	20.2	21,399	66.0	22.1	12
1975	23,641	68.1	20.2	21,697	65.1	22.9	-1,944
1976	25,801	68.8	21.0	25,901	67.3	21.7	100
1977	29,815	70.4	21.3	30,404	69.8	20.0	589
1978	35,437	70.7	19.8	36,651	70.4	19.5	1,214
1979	45,571	72.5	18.2	43,521	67.8	18.4	-2,050
1980	48,614	70.2	16.0	46,941	63.3	17.2	-1,673
1981	54,538	68.6	16.9	53,900	66.3	17.7	-638
1982	47,866	70.5	15.9	55,847	68.2	19.1	7,981
1983	54,103	71.6	19.1	64,528	72.9	20.0	10,425

Note: Data refer to "merchandise trade" in US terminology.

a   Canadian data; data from US sources differ slightly.
b   US share data are from US Bureau of the Census, *Foreign Commerce and Navigation of the US; Highlights of US Export and Import Trade*.

Sources: Statistics Canada, Cat. Nos. 65-003, 65-006.   US Bureau of the Census.

There has been some fluctuation in recent years in the relative export and import dependence of the two countries. Between 1970 and 1980, for example, the share of total US exports going to Canada declined moderately, from slightly over 20 per cent to about 16 per cent, but it then recovered in the early 1980s. At the same time, the share of US imports coming from Canada (following a rise in the 1960s) also declined, from 27-28 per cent in 1970 to 17 per cent in 1980. But it too rose somewhat in the early 1980s. Finally, Canada's dependence on the US market for its exports, after showing little or no trend during the 1970s, increased substantially in the early 1980s. Thus, Canadian exports to the United States held up better than imports in the face of recession in both countries after 1980. This may have been due in part to the altered exchange rate, to rising electricity exports, and to revived US demand for large automobiles, many of which were assembled in Canadian plants.[1]

Region-Country Trade

Table 3.2 summarizes for five recent years the relevant data applicable to Quebec-US trade, Atlantic Provinces-US trade, and New England- Canada trade. (All data are from Canadian sources and are expressed in Canadian dollars.) Over this period Quebec has enjoyed a net favourable balance (exports to the United States over imports from the United States) of between $1.5 and $3.6 billion annually, with a strong upward trend in evidence since 1980. In the case of Atlantic Provinces-US trade, the dollar balance has remained between $1.2 and $1.8 billion, although here the *ratio* of Atlantic Provinces exports to imports is about three to one, as compared with a Quebec ratio of three to two.

Quebec provides a much larger volume of exports — four to five times the Atlantic Provinces total — but also accounts for a proportionately large volume of imports, on the order of eight to ten times that of the Atlantic Provinces. About 57 per cent of Quebec's total exports went to the United States in 1983, with no clear trend in evidence after 1978. At the same time, Quebec's imports from the United States ranged between 45 per cent and 52 per cent of its total imports over the same period. While the United States took about half of Atlantic Provinces exports in 1981 (and close to 60 per cent in 1983), it was the direct source of only 12-20 per cent of their total imports (until 1983). This low percentage undoubtedly reflects the importance of oil imports, the transhipment of US manufactured goods via central Canada, and perhaps the traditionally closer ties with Europe.[2]

Table 3.2: Trade Between Northeast Regions and Countries (Million $ Canadian), 1979-1983

	1979	1980	1981	1982	1983
Quebec-US trade					
Quebec exports to US	7,573	8,671	10,072	9,172	10,368
% of total Quebec exports	56.4	50.5	55.8	52.6	56.7
% of Can. exports to US	17.4	18.5	18.7	16.4	16.1
Quebec imports from US	6,247	7,059	7,521	5,704	6,713
% of total Quebec imports	51.3	51.5	46.4	44.7	48.5
% of Can. imports from US	13.7	14.5	13.8	11.9	12.4
Quebec balance	1,326	1,612	2,551	3,468	3,655
Atlantic Provinces-US trade					
AP exports to US	1,928	2,018	2,491	2,035	2,319
% of total AP exports	48.2	43.5	50.8	51.2	58.8
% of Can. exports to US	4.3	4.6	4.6	3.6	3.6
AP imports from US	660	621	684	778	938
% of total AP imports	17.1	11.9	12.6	21.3	27.5
% of Can. imports from US	1.5	1.3	1.3	1.6	1.7
AP balance	1,268	1,397	1,807	1,257	1,381
New England-Canada trade					
N.E. exports to Canada[a]	2,282	2,697			3,270
% of US exports to Can.	5.0	5.5			6.0
N.E. imports from Canada	2,833	2,764	3,629	4,242	4,889
% of US imports from Can.	6.4	5.9	6.7	7.6	7.6
N.E. balance	-551	-67			-1,619

a   Special runoffs.

Source: Statistics Canada, Cat. Nos. 65-003, 65-006, 65-202, 65-203.

New England's exports to Canada are more closely in balance with its imports. While it is not possible, given data limitations, to generalize about trends in either an export or import surplus, it may be noted that New England's apparent deficit in 1983 was well above that registered in 1979 and 1980. The recent data on trade volume show New England's proportionate weight in Canada-US trade to be only about 5-7 per cent.

Thus, Quebec appears to be more thoroughly integrated with the United States than are the Atlantic Provinces, or than is New England with Canada. It is possibly significant, however, that New England's share of both US imports from and exports to Canada is increasing moderately.

When the principal Quebec exports to the United States are broken down by commodity (Table 3.3), it can be seen that printing paper (mainly newsprint), aluminum and alloys, and automobiles account for over 40 per cent of the total. (In 1974 and 1979, other metals and alloys were also quite important; they had dropped out of the top ten by 1983, however.) Aside from automobiles, the only manufactured export of primary importance is aircraft components. The General Motors plant, located in St. Therese, Quebec, which assembles cars for the North American market, together with the large Pratt & Whitney (United Technologies) subsidiary near Montreal, have thus considerably reduced Quebec's export dependence on those primary and semi-finished materials which clearly reflect its natural resource base. Moreover, if the variety of smaller-volume finished goods, many of them in the high- technology area, were added to the above, it could be seen that finished manufactures now account for roughly one-third of Quebec's total exports to the United States.[3] Exports of technical and professional services have also assumed some importance in recent years, as will be seen shortly.

A substantially different picture emerges from examining the exports of the Atlantic Provinces (Table 3.4). Seven out of ten leading exports to the United States are in the primary or semi-finished goods categories. Unlike Quebec, there is no single manufacturing activity that accounts for more than 6-7 per cent of total export value, and inspection of miscellaneous categories not shown in the table suggests that manufactures probably account for no more than 15 per cent of that total. ("Manufacturing" here excludes refined petroleum products and electricity as well as newsprint.) The role of supplier of primary goods and semi-finished materials is a traditional one for the Atlantic Provinces. Thus, while there is today considerable

Table 3.3: Quebec Exports to the United States (Thousand $ Canadian), Ten Leading Products: 1974, 1979, 1983

Product	1974	1979	1983
Printing paper	643,705	1,410,879	1,830,556
	(19.5)	(18.1)	(17.6)
Automobiles and chassis	268,921	807,059	1,343,209
	(8.1)	(10.4)	(12.9)
Aluminum and alloys	201,519	366,731	929,674
	(6.1)	(4.7)	(8.9)
Lumber	79,184	243,251	418,798
	(2.4)	(3.1)	(4.0)
Electricity	10,356	104,007	332,995
	(0.3)	(1.3)	(3.2)
Airplane motors and parts	77,905	309,415	316,796
	(2.4)	(4.0)	(3.0)
Airplanes with motors		8,074	253,089
			(2.4)
Airplane assemblies and equipment			236,435
			(2.3)
Fresh and refrig. meat		96,215	208,818
		(1.2)	(2.0)
Electronic tubes and semi-conductors			193,011
			(1.9)
Total, ten principal products[a]	1,939,691	4,682,252	6,063,383
	(58.6)	(60.1)	(58.2)
Total exports to the US[b]	3,308,316	7,786,543	10,423,668
	(100.0)	(100.0)	(100.0)

Note: Based on 1983 rank.

[a]   Refers to ten leading products in the indicated year.
[b]   BSQ data differ slightly from Statistics Canada data shown in Table 3.2.

Source: Bureau de la Statistique du Québec, *Exportations Internationales du Québec*, various dates.

Table 3.4: **Atlantic Provinces Exports to the United States (Thousand $ Canadian), Ten Leading Products: 1974, 1979, 1983a**

Product	1974	1979	1983
Fresh and frozen fish blocks and fillets	83,225 (8.7)	295,441 (15.3)	403,127 (17.4)
Fresh and frozen fish	12,403 (1.3)	26,233 (1.4)	50,317 (2.2)
Other fish products	a	139,976 (7.3)	281,390 (12.1)
Wood pulp and similar pulp	220,885 (23.2)	297,440 (15.4)	289,393 (12.5)
Electricity	29,673 (3.1)	125,097 (6.5)	266,257 (11.5)
Newsprint	164,664 (17.3)	243,821 (12.6)	246,706 (10.6)
Petroleum derivatives and coal	137,003 (14.4)	291,131 (15.1)	155,460 (6.7)
Other (non-whisky) beverages		4,838 (0.3)	39,788 (1.7)
Automobiles and chassis	2,056 (0.2)	14,718 (0.8)	34,652 (1.5)
Other transport equipment	36,080 (3.8)	122,063 (6.3)	184,291 (7.9)
Total, ten principal products	503,541 (52.9)	b	1,951,381 (84.2)
Total, all products	951,138 (100.0)	1,928,049 (100.0)	2,318,889 (100.0)

Note: Based on 1983 rank.

a Not shown separately.
b 1974 total includes $17,522 for "preserved fish" which was not in top ten in 1983.

Source: Statistics Canada, Cat. No. 65-202.

diversity of economic activity within the Atlantic Region, its exports continue to reflect the resource base traditionally associated with a forested, maritime location.

New England's exports to Canada reflect a broad mix of finished and semi-finished manufactures (Table 3.5). Electronic and telecommunications goods and aircraft components (with Pratt & Whitney again a major actor) stand out in this mix, as do — to a much lesser degree — processed wood products. But, aside from computers, no single category of manufacturing accounts for significantly more than 5 per cent of the total. The trend of New England-Canada exports over the period 1979-1983 has clearly been upward (Table 3.2). But, unfortunately, the product data are either more limited or more difficult to extract for region-to-country flows northward than southward. Thus, it is not possible to generalize about "leading product" trends.

Although Tables 3.3-3.5 do not show data for the leading *imports* into each of the three regions from the other country, that information can be inferred in a general way from the export data, and Table 3.6 gives a specific "leading import" breakdown for Quebec. Clearly automobiles and aircraft — both whole and components — are moving in both directions across the border. In 1979, Quebec and the Atlantic Region accounted for about two-thirds of New England's total imports from Canada, with fish and newsprint by far the largest items. Ontario was the source of an additional 20 per cent or so.[4]

Quebec's imports from the United States, like those from New England, are concentrated heavily in semi-finished materials and finished manufactures (Table 3.6). Of particular importance are automobiles and parts traded under the 1965 automobile pact. More generally, Quebec's numerous branch plants of (mostly) US manufacturers, which assemble goods primarily for the Canadian market, are responsible for the very large number of parts and accessories imported.[5]

The Atlantic Provinces, as indicated earlier, import about a third as much from the United States as they sell to the United States. Of the import total, 20 per cent comes from the New England states. As might be expected, imports to the Atlantic Provinces from the United States consist of a very broad range of (mostly) finished goods, including food and beverages. The Atlantic Region is thus a net recipient of manufactures from both the northeastern United States and central Canada.

Interregional Trade

Turning to trade among the three regions, Figure 3.1 and Tables 3.7- 3.12 present information concerning purely interregional

Table 3.5: **New England Exports to Canada (Thousand $ Canadian), Ten Leading Products, 1979**

Product	1979
Electronic computers	$172,271
	(7.5)
Electronic tubes and semi-conductors	125,690
	(5.5)
Aircraft engines and parts	98,655
	(4.3)
Mineral concentrates and reduced metals	90,967
	(4.0)
Paper and paperboard	68,075
	(3.0)
Raw wood materials	59,143
	(2.6)
Telecommunications and related equipment	51,810
	(2.3)
Misc. finished goods, non-edible	47,401
	(2.1)
Misc. tools and materials	45,358
	(2.0)
Other laboratory instruments	41,754
	(1.8)
Total, ten leading products	801,134
	(35.1)
Total, all products	$2,282,477
	(100.0)

Source: Statistics Canada, unpublished data.

Table 3.6: **Quebec Imports from the United States (Million $ Canadian), Leading Products, 1979 and 1983**

Product	1979	1983
Automobiles and chassis	328.5	1,221.1
Parts and accessories, and other vehicles	456.1	586.1
Electronic tubes and semi-conductors	139.6	359.7
Office equipment and supplies	99.1	285.8
Aircraft motors and parts	144.9	264.1
Aircraft with motors		217.0
Aircraft assemblies, equipment, and parts	135.1	182.6
Automobile motors and parts	132.5	144.8
Crude oil	244.2	
Subtotal		3,261.2
Total imports from US	6,247.1	7,749.6
Total imports, all countries	12,177.4	15,390.1

Note: Based on 1983 rank.

Sources: BSQ, *Importations Internationales du Québec*, 1980.
Commerce International du Québec, 1984.

product flows. Figure 3.1 summarizes these flows for the year 1979. (Flows shown between Quebec and the Atlantic Provinces are limited to manufactured goods; raw materials data are spotty.) One glance shows that trade flows *within* eastern Canada were quite substantial – $1.3 billion in manufactured products alone moving from Quebec. The reverse flow may also have been over $1 billion from the Atlantic Provinces when account is taken of raw materials and energy as well as manufactured goods. Exports from each Canadian region across the international boundary to New England were also approaching the $1 billion mark. Indeed, the only flow of an entirely different magnitude is that from New England to the Atlantic Provinces – about $140 million in 1979. With this one exception, the north-south product flows were surprisingly even, ranging from $800 to $954 million. Table 3.7 shows changes in north-to-south trade volume since 1979.

Quebec and Atlantic Provinces Exports to New England

In considering the exports of Quebec and the Atlantic Provinces to New England, it is possible to gain an impression of specific content by using the commodity breakdown employed by Statistics Canada to identify major trade categories (Table 3.7). Clearly fish products (43 per cent) and semi-finished fabricated materials (50 per cent) constitute the bulk of Atlantic exports to New England – $889 of $954 million in 1979. Within the "fabricated" materials category, wood pulp, petroleum products, and electricity are easily the most important items – as indeed they are (along with newsprint) for Atlantic Provinces exports to the United States generally (Table 3.4). While New England accounts for roughly half of Atlantic Provinces exports to the United States, its proximity to the Atlantic Region accounts for its much larger share of electricity and wood pulp. The fact that the boundary state, Maine, receives all of the electricity and most of the wood pulp is attributable to both power and paper company interconnections at the border; the electricity is subsequently transmitted throughout New England (see Chapter 5). Within the end products category, the largest item appears to be "other transport equipment," mainly reflecting the export of more than $6 million in automobile tires from Nova Scotia.

Quebec is also primarily an exporter of semi-finished goods to New England (63 per cent), with newsprint (16 per cent) and lumber (11 per cent) the largest constituents of the category. Moreover, food (mainly fish and feeds) and beverages (mainly whisky and beer) accounted for $85 million (9 per cent) of the

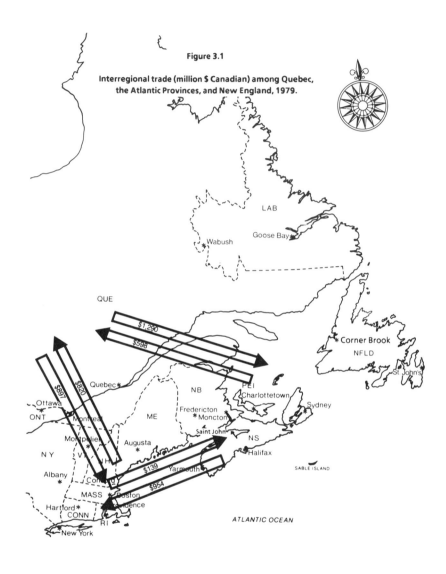

Figure 3.1

Interregional trade (million $ Canadian) among Quebec,
the Atlantic Provinces, and New England, 1979.

Table 3.7: Quebec and Atlantic Provinces Exports to New England States (Million $ Canadian), 1979

Type of Product	Maine		New Hampshire		Vermont		Massachusetts		Rhode Island		Connecticut		New England	
To: From:	AP	Q	AP	Q	AP	Q	AP	Q	AP	Q	AP	Q	AP	Q
Live animals	1.2	8.6	--	0.2	--	1.3	0.1	0.5	--	--	--	0.5	1.3	11.1
Food, feed, beverages, and tobacco	51.7	5.5	14.4	7.6	0.2	18.9	338.2	43.1	13.7	2.3	3.1	7.9	421.3	85.3
Fish and fish products	44.6	1.1	14.2	3.8	--	--	334.4	13.8	13.4	--	2.3	0.4	409.0	19.1
Animal feeds	1.4	0.7	--	0.6	--	11.6	0.2	1.4	--	--	0.1	1.6	1.7	16.0
Crude materials, inedible	19.7	2.4	0.7	2.6	--	3.1	4.2	10.5	0.2	0.6	0.7	6.3	25.5	25.5
Pulpwood, chips	14.2	0.8	--	--	--	0.2	--	--	--	--	--	--	14.2	1.0
Non-ferrous ores, scrap	--	--	--	--	--	--	0.3	0.3	--	0.4	0.1	3.7	--	4.4
Fabricated materials, inedible	315.8	72.1	10.5	48.3	6.5	64.6	79.3	219.1	5.5	67.6	62.7	96.0	480.3	567.7
Lumber and other mill prod.	7.8	10.5	4.8	11.9	2.3	18.2	10.6	47.2	0.5	3.2	1.8	9.7	27.9	100.7
Wood pulp	152.4	27.2	4.4	6.4	3.8	3.2	9.2	15.8	0.1	--	1.6	2.3	171.5	54.9
Newsprint	2.8	2.2	0.8	7.4	0.1	4.8	8.9	59.3	2.1	25.7	10.4	46.3	25.2	145.8
Other paper	0.2	3.7	--	2.5	0.1	2.2	2.7	12.8	--	1.4	0.8	7.7	3.8	30.4
Chemicals and fertilizer	4.9	8.5	--	5.8	0.1	3.1	--	7.7	--	--	0.1	3.0	5.1	28.5
Iron and steel products	4.2	5.4	0.4	6.0	0.1	5.7	2.4	11.2	--	0.4	0.1	5.0	7.1	34.6
Petroleum and coal products	15.5	0.2	--	2.7	--	4.0	43.8	4.7	2.4	1.3	46.5	0.1	108.2	11.7
Electricity	125.1	3.5	--	--	--	2.9	--	--	--	--	--	--	125.1	6.4
Precious metals	--	--	--	--	--	--	--	18.9	--	30.9	--	--	--	49.8

Table 3.7:   Continued

Type of Product	Maine		New Hampshire		Vermont		Massachusetts		Rhode Island		Connecticut		New England	
To: / From: AP	AP	Q	AP	Q	AP	Q	AP	Q	AP	Q	AP	Q	AP	Q
End products, inedible	7.9	15.8	1.7	38.9	0.7	33.9	11.1	45.4	0.5	8.6	3.5	64.5	25.4	207.1
Machinery and related equip.	1.5	8.0	0.4	4.9	0.2	4.0	0.8	5.3	0.1	0.3	0.2	6.2	3.2	28.7
Motor vehicles and parts	0.8	1.3	0.7	8.6	--	0.6	0.2	5.4	0.1	0.3	0.5	12.5	1.9	16.7
Aircraft and parts	0.4	0.2	--	8.1	--	9.7	--	1.1	--	--	0.2	11.7	0.3	31.7
Other transport equip.	0.5	0.8	--	--	--	0.6	4.6	1.2	0.1	5.0	1.9	2.9	7.0	19.3
Telecommunication equip.	--	0.3	--	4.8	--	3.2	--	6.2	--	0.2	--	0.3	0.6	17.7
Apparel and footwear	--	1.7	--	1.1	--	2.1	--	3.4	--	0.1	--	0.3	0.1	8.7
Sporting and recreation equip.	--	--	--	6.0	--	4.4	--	2.8	--	--	--	--	0.1	13.8
Printed matter	--	--	--	0.2	--	0.8	--	4.0	--	0.5	--	20.6	0.1	26.1
Special transactions, trade	0.3	0.3	--	--	--	--	--	--	--	--	--	0.1	0.3	0.4
Total	396.6	104.6	27.3	97.6	7.4	121.8	432.9	318.6	20.0	79.1	70.1	175.3	954.3	897.0

To: / From:	Northern New England		Southern New England		New England	
	AP	Quebec	AP	Quebec	AP	Quebec
All Products						
1979	431.3	323.8	523.0	573.0	954.3	897.0
1980	466.1	387.7	548.6	639.7	1,014.7	1,027.4
1981	555.5	548.9	863.7	778.3	1,419.2	1,327.2
1982	493.5	525.9	668.4	975.6	1,161.9	1,501.5
1983	566.6	613.0	791.4	990.7	1,358.0	1,603.7

Source: Statistics Canada, Cat. No. 65-202 and special compilations.

total going to New England in 1979. But the province exports finished manufactures in substantial quantities (23 per cent) as well, and enjoys a fairly broad diversification within that category (Tables 3.7 and 3.8). Telecommunications equipment, machinery, aircraft and parts, and printed matter all play significant roles. Thus, Quebec's broader export base mentioned earlier (Table 3.3) is reflected in shipments to New England as well as to the United States generally. The chief differences in this respect appear to be the somewhat lower proportion of newsprint (most of which goes to the Mid-Atlantic region), and the much lower proportion of motor vehicles and parts and metals and ores (going for the most part to the Great Lakes states) in exports to New England. This is balanced in part by greater-than-proportionate shares of feed, wood, and wood products exported to New England than to the United States as a whole.

Table 3.7 shows that Quebec exports to New England increased more rapidly than those from the Atlantic Region between 1979 and 1983 — roughly 79 per cent versus 42 per cent — reflecting mainly post-1981 stagnation in Atlantic exports. Examination of individual product flows after 1979 suggests that the difference is accounted for in part by a doubling of end product shipments. Thus, such products grew from 23 per cent of total Quebec-New England shipments in 1979 to about 28 per cent in 1983.

Table 3.8 presents much the same information as Table 3.7, but it employs a slightly different product breakdown which excludes energy and indicates the province of origin within the Atlantic Region. Data in both tables have been collected and edited by Statistics Canada in such a way as to net out most of those transactions whose true origin was not the Canadian province in question. This "transhipment" problem is obviously a major one in analysing trade among subnational regions. While the data in Tables 3.7 and 3.8 can be viewed as an improvement over those depicting aggregate cross-boundary flows, they are not wholly free of ambiguity. It is especially likely that "destinations" in New England are in some cases intermediate, not final.[6]

Within the Atlantic Provinces, Newfoundland's shipments to New England are wholly dominated by fish and fish products, with a large proportion destined for Massachusetts processing plants, some of which are owned by Newfoundland- and Nova Scotia-based firms (see Chapter 7). Prince Edward Island is also primarily a supplier of fish products, but contributes a number of other food products as well, reflecting its broader agricultural base. Nova Scotia depends on the sea for about 80-85 per cent of

Table 3.8: New England Imports, Excluding Energy, from Quebec and Atlantic Provinces (Thousand $ Canadian), 1979

Commodity	Que.	Nfld.	N.S.	P.E.I.	N.B.	Atl. Prov. Total	Eastern Canada Total
Meat, eggs, dairy prod., cereals	32,552	7	607	244	912	1,770	34,322
Fish, marine animals	19,131	170,150	174,467	13,036	51,350	409,003	428,134
Fruits, vegetables, & preparations	2,345	54	1,235	2,432	5,566	9,287	11,632
Sugar products, coffee, tea, miscellaneous	12,680	--	62	20	277	359	13,039
Fodder, animal feeds	15,980	387	669	68	584	1,708	17,688
Beverages, tobacco	13,619	--	36	--	583	619	14,238
Hides, fur, rubber, soybeans	7,132	--	979	306	2,648	3,933	11,065
Trees, logs, pulpwood	1,701	4	744	23	14,911	15,682	17,383
Cotton, wood, other fibres	473	--	--	--	8	8	481
Metal ores, scrap	5,482	--	--	--	471	471	5,953
Stone, clay, other crude minerals	10,657	--	1,980	148	3,323	5,451	16,108
Leather, rubber fabric products	640	--	6	--	5	11	651
Lumber, plywood, veneer	100,738	45	764	79	27,020	27,908	128,646
Wood pulp, other pulp	54,932	51	3,452	164	167,804	171,471	226,403
Paper, newsprint, paperboard	176,214	5,257	9,094	125	14,597	29,073	205,287
Textiles & other fabrics	3,538	--	177	--	272	449	3,987
Vegetable oils, other oils, fats	661	541	84	--	149	774	1,435
Chemicals & related products	34,967	5	329	11	6,185	6,530	41,497
Iron & steel products	34,636	--	1,514	--	5,594	7,108	41,744
Non-ferrous metal products	72,988	--	8	--	370	378	73,366
Finished metal products, hardware	36,437	5	479	8	979	1,471	37,908
Glass, other non-metallic materials	33,821	--	71	3	1,622	1,696	35,517
Machinery & equipment, incl. agricultural	28,779	176	1,386	126	3,145	4,833	33,612
Machinery & equipment & parts (excl. aircraft)	35,638	128	6,964	15	2,043	9,150	44,788
Aircraft, parts, engines	31,690	1	19	25	212	257	31,947
Communication, electronic & related equipment	17,192	17	521	--	31	569	17,761
Heating, cooking equip., electric fix., controls	11,402	10	2,141	214	910	3,275	14,677
Furniture, fixtures, tools, cutlery	412	--	8	11	131	150	562
Electronic computers & related	--	12	23	1	--	36	36
Office equipment & miscellaneous	11,408	--	3	--	7	10	11,418
Apparel, accessories, footware	8,670	--	53	63	24	140	8,810
Watches, clocks, jewelry, misc. household	4,140	--	360	7	5	372	4,512
Sports & recreation equip., toys, games	13,822	--	56	--	8	64	13,886
Medical, medicinal, pharmaceutical products	699	18	--	131	28	177	876
Books, printed matter	26,083	--	18	2	63	83	26,166
Office supplies, photographic material	1,386	--	7	--	39	46	1,432
Miscellaneous end products	15,180	2	471	58	5,714	6,245	21,425
"Special transactions, trade"	467	1	16	27	299	343	810
Total	878,292	176,871	208,803	17,347	317,889	720,910	1,599,202

Source: Statistics Canada, special compilations.

its exports to New England. But manufacturing activities also ocntribute to exports more than is true of the other Atlantic Provinces. These activities are mostly centred around machinery, heating equipment, and motor vehicle components (especially tires). Modest quantities of fruit and related food preparations and a substantial volume of newsprint and wood pulp also figure in these exports. New Brunswick is, not surprisingly, much less dependent on fish, and much more dependent on wood products for its exports. It will be seen later how important this province is to New England as a source of electric power and petroleum products.

This study of imports and exports reveals a strong upward trend over the past decade. Table 3.9 indicates the overall pace of growth in Quebec and Atlantic Provinces exports to New England in real as well as in current dollar values. It suggests that export growth rates were very similar for the two Canadian regions through 1981. The years 1975, 1980, and 1982 represent the only breaks in the upward trend (in real terms), attributable to the US recessions in those years. Underlying US data suggest that the dollar value of Canadian goods entering the Portland customs district, for example, more than doubled between 1974 and 1979. These authors estimate that between 40 and 50 per cent of that increase was accounted for by real growth. Rates of growth were particularly high in the late 1970s, with the dollar volume of imports passing through the St. Albans district, for example, increasing 54 per cent between 1976 and 1978 and 100 per cent through Boston during the same years.

Exports from New England to Eastern Canada

In 1983, trade flowing from New England to Quebec and the Atlantic Provinces constituted about 40 per cent of all exports from New England to Canada. On the Canadian side, about 17 per cent of Quebec and 18 per cent of Atlantic Provinces imports from the United States came from New England (Table 3.10), even though the dollar volume of exports to Quebec in 1983 was considerably larger than that of exports to the Atlantic Provinces – $1,158 million versus $170 million. Not surprisingly, southern New England with its manufacturing centres is the primary source of goods moving to Quebec (60 per cent), whereas Massachusetts (manufacturing) and Maine (resources plus proximity) account for the bulk of New England goods moving to the Atlantic Provinces (84 per cent). Overall, New England accounts for only 6 per cent of total Canadian imports from the United States.

Table 3.9: Exports to New England from Quebec and Atlantic Provinces (Million Current and Constant $ Canadian), 1972-1983

Year	Quebec	Atlantic Provinces	Total	Export Price Index[a] (1971 = 100)	Total Exports in 1971 ($)	Per cent Change from Previous Year
1972	320.2	269.5	589.7			
1973	386.6	366.5	753.0			
1974	433.9	430.9	863.8	156.5	551.9	-21.5
1975	373.2	377.9	751.1	173.4	433.2	11.1
1976	414.3	440.4	854.7	177.5	481.5	21.0
1977	532.5	567.0	1,099.6	188.8	582.4	17.4
1978	721.2	678.8	1,400.0	204.8	683.4	9.2
1979	897.0	954.3	1,841.3	248.0	746.5	-6.0
1980	1,027.4	1,014.7	2,042.1	291.1	701.5	27.4
1981	1,327.2	1,419.2	2,746.4	307.4	893.4	-3.9
1982	1,501.5	1,161.9	2,663.4	310.1	858.9	12.7
1983	1,603.7	1,358.0	2,961.7	306.0	967.9	

a   Weighted index of prices in five broad categories applicable to all Canadian exports.

Source: Statistics Canada Cat. No. 65-202.

Table 3.10: Quebec and Atlantic Provinces Imports from New England (Million $ Canadian), 1979 and 1983

Imports from:	Quebec		Atlantic Provinces		Canada	
	1979	1983	1979	1983	1979	1983
Maine	93.6	125.3	60.7	68.3		261.9
New Hampshire	49.8	56.2	5.1	7.7		176.9
Vermont	145.9	281.6	0.9	1.7		350.6
Northern New England	289.3	463.1	66.7	77.7	518.1	789.4
Massachusetts	285.5	364.0	58.1	74.9		1,502.5
Rhode Island	46.8	62.6	6.9	2.9		186.9
Connecticut	198.3	268.7	6.8	14.5		791.0
Southern New England	530.6	695.3	71.8	92.3	1,764.4	2,480.4
Total New England	819.9	1,158.4	138.6	170.0	2,282.5	3,269.8
Total US	6,247.1	6,713.0	659.8	938.0	45,571.0	54,103.0
% No. N.E./N.E.	35.3	40.0	48.1	45.7	22.7	24.1
No. N.E./US	4.6	6.9	10.1	8.3	1.1	1.5
% So. N.E./N.E.	64.7	60.0	51.9	54.3	77.3	75.9
So. N.E./US	8.5	10.4	10.9	9.8	3.9	4.6
% N.E./US	13.1	17.3	21.0	18.1	5.0	6.0

Source: Statistics Canada, special compilations.

Quebec-Atlantic Provinces Trade

Information concerning shipments between Quebec and the Atlantic Provinces is difficult to obtain since there is no international boundary involved and hence no customs documents. Much of this movement takes place within firms, although it is not possible to say that intrafirm movement is more important within Canada than between Canada and the United States. However, Statistics Canada and other agencies do undertake periodic surveys of interprovincial trade from which manufactured goods moving in interprovincial distribution channels can frequently be identified. Estimates of interprovincial shipments of manufactures in 1979 are shown in Table 3.11.

Ontario and Quebec are, of course, the source of most Canadian manufactured goods, accounting for 50 per cent and 26 per cent, respectively, of total manufacturing shipments to the Atlantic Region. Estimated shipments from Quebec to the Atlantic Provinces were $1,290 million in 1979, or about 10 per cent of Quebec's interregional manufacturing exports. (Exports to overseas destinations via Halifax and Saint John are excluded.) Shipments from the Atlantic Provinces to Quebec, on the other hand, were $598 million (95 per cent from New Brunswick and Nova Scotia), or approximately 40 per cent of shipments to provinces outside the Atlantic Region.

There is no readily available breakdown of these trade flows by commodity. However, information from an earlier study of Quebec's exports suggests that the leading products moving from Quebec to the Atlantic Provinces (1974 data) would include transport equipment (including both automobiles and trucks), dairy products, textiles and clothing, tobacco, pulp and paper, and a variety of machinery and metal products.[7] Electricity, some of which Quebec imports from Labrador, has since that time also become a major export to New Brunswick (see Chapter 5).

The chief products moving from the Atlantic Region to Quebec, aside from general imports in transit from Halifax and Saint John, include seafood of various sorts, forest products, vehicle components (especially tires), and petroleum products.

Table 3.12 shows information gleaned from a special study of interprovincial rail shipments. The rail data (expressed in tonnes) are broken down here into five categories, two of which overlap (manufacturing and piggyback). In general, these data confirm the uneven flow of manufactures shown in Table 3.11. They also suggest that, at least in tonnage terms, forest products are a major commodity of trade within eastern Canada, and that

Table 3.11: Interprovincial Shipments of Goods of Own Manufacture ($ Millions), by Province, 1979

Province	Delivery Destination						
	Newfoundland	Prince Edward Island	Nova Scotia	New Brunswick	Quebec	Ontario	Manitoba
Newfoundland	321.4	**	49.5	18.9	19.1	15.5	**
Prince Edward Island	8.9	68.6	29.1	17.5	12.6	17.4	**
Nova Scotia	122.2	**	1,347.5	137.4	276.9	341.0	56.5
New Brunswick	90.8	55.6	194.6	894.5	289.7	246.3	14.7
Quebec	320.4	84.5	410.5	474.6	19,228.5	6,696.5	560.1
Ontario	434.5	150.1	804.7	772.2	7,997.8	37,524.6	1,428.4
Manitoba	19.6	7.2	37.0	24.8	267.6	515.4	1,626.0
Saskatchewan	1.6	0.8	8.2	3.8	101.2	82.7	127.8
Alberta	9.2	0.7	24.0	19.7	536.7	867.8	195.1
British Columbia	14.0	4.6	28.4	44.3	244.7	467.6	151.1
Yukon and N.W.T.	--	--	--	--	--	--	--
Canada	1,342.5	430.2	2,933.6	2,407.8	28,974.7	46,775.0	4,160.9

Province	Delivery Destination						
	Saskatchewan	Alberta	British Columbia	Yukon and N.W.T.	Outside Canada	Not specified	Total
Newfoundland	**	1.5	**	--	534.8	**	1,028.0
Prince Edward Island	**	--	**	**	37.5	**	212.5
Nova Scotia	13.7	31.5	51.6	**	671.3	110.1	3,212.5
New Brunswick	9.3	43.7	33.4	**	1,048.7	**	2,970.5
Quebec	311.6	873.3	821.0	23.6	7,331.3	1,981.4	39,117.3
Ontario	887.6	2,739.6	2,321.4	42.2	17,320.0	3,797.1	76,220.2
Manitoba	299.8	335.4	188.4	3.8	407.9	181.8	3,914.7
Saskatchewan	901.5	150.5	64.2	**	230.2	**	1,863.3
Alberta	316.7	4,912.6	735.9	29.9	833.4	398.3	9,940.0
British Columbia	167.6	863.4	5,827.8	68.8	5,963.6	781.9	14,627.8
Yukon and N.W.T.	--	--	--	**	--	**	26.3
Canada	2,908.9	10,015.5	10,044.4	191.5	34,378.6	7,533.4	152,133.1

-- Nil
** Confidential.

Source: *Statistics Canada Daily*, October 26, 1984.

Table 3.12: Interprovincial Rail Shipments from Eastern Canada (Thousand Tonnes), 1979

	From Maritime Provinces[a]		From Quebec	
	To Quebec	To Other Canada	To Maritimes[a]	To Other Canada
Agricultural and animal products	68	88	45	19
Forest products	352	136	357	681
Mine products	23	9	41	427
Manufacturing and misc.	561	688	763	3,538
Piggyback[b]	89	152	148	571
Total	1,092	1,074	1,354	5,235

Note: Carload and piggyback traffic moving on all-rail routes. Excluded are rail-water combinations, rail traffic involving two or more railroads, container shipments, and freight moving on Canada-US routes.

[a] Excluding Newfoundland.
[b] Piggyback plan 1 only (trailers of highway transport common carriers).

Source: Canadian Transport Commission, *Commodity Flow Analysis, 1978-80*, Reference Paper No. 16.

the flow is roughly balanced, as between Quebec and the Atlantic Provinces.

It is of some interest to note that interregional trade between Quebec and the Atlantic Provinces appears to have been growing more slowly than the trade of either of these regions with the northeastern United States. Quebec shipments of manufactured products to the Atlantic Provinces, for example, grew by only 46 per cent between 1974 and 1979, as compared with a 107 per cent increase in total exports to New England (both estimates are in current Canadian dollars — see Table 3.9). Similarly, the very rapid growth in Atlantic Provinces exports of fish products and electric power to New England has given north-south trade a more dynamic aspect than east-west trade. The contrast is especially interesting in light of the substantial transport subsidies enjoyed by the Atlantic Region for westward shipments within Canada.

Trade in Business and Professional Services

This section discusses some attributes of cross-boundary trade in business and professional services. Since the general category of "services" is very broad, ranging from small-scale, strictly personal services (medical, household, and personal consulting) to those provided by large organizations found, for example, in the banking, insurance, wholesale and retail trade, tourist, and transportation sectors, it is necessary to narrow the focus at the outset. As a first step in this process, Table 3.13 shows in summary form the basic elements of the Canada-US balance of trade in current items (i.e., neglecting capital flows) for the years 1977-1981.[8]

When "services" are defined to exclude travel, transportation, and income from investments, the residual ("fees and royalties" plus "other private services") makes up a small but significant category ranging from about $1.2 billion in US receipts in 1977 to $1.7 billion in 1981, and from $0.5 billion to $0.8 billion in Canadian receipts (US payments) in the same years. It should be noted, however, that these data do not include net income earned by foreign corporate affiliates engaged in the provision of services. This distinction is important enough to warrant a brief discussion.

Business and professional services of the kind of interest here can be provided across international boundaries by a number of means, including (1) directly from a headquarters or regional office in the home country, (2) through an independent agent in the host country, (3) through a joint venture with a local concern in the host country, or (4) through a wholly owned subsidiary operating in the host country. These different forms of organization most likely entail varying degrees of control by the head office; their sequence may also reflect a maturation process. The wholly owned affiliate requires the greatest investment but affords substantial control and the closest continuing relationship with clients.

Cross-boundary trade in business and professional services undoubtedly utilizes all of the above methods, though perhaps fewer of the agency form (2) than is true in most manufacturing industries. Payments to providers of services utilizing methods (3) and (4) above are excluded from the "services" category appearing in the US balance- of-payments tables. Instead, services trade carried out through foreign affiliates (aside from intracorporate royalty and rental fees) enters the payments tables only indirectly and partially through remission of interest and dividends to the parent organization (and via "net earnings" as a whole in the case of unincorporated affiliates). Thus, to obtain an idea of the overall importance of trade in business and professional services, it is necessary to combine some of the direct payments appearing in Table 3.13 with that part of investment income representing enterprises in this particular sector. Even this combination, while it satisfies accounting criteria for balance of payments, understates the gross dollar value of such services. As indicated, data on the US side are collected for balance-of-payments purposes on a "net" basis — that is, one in which expenses incurred in the host country to produce the income are deducted from gross receipts. Canada, on the other hand, asks for "gross" figures in some of its surveys as a means of approximating the actual value of service transactions. An attempt will be made here to pursue this necessary distinction in the macro data, starting with business services payments other than parent-affiliate net income flows.

The relevant lines in Table 3.13 are labelled "fees and royalties" and "other private services." A tentative breakdown of each category is given in Table 3.14, again based on US data sources. It can be seen that "fees and royalties" are largely intracorporate in nature, and arise primarily in the manufacturing sector. While "service charges and rentals" and "contractor fees" contain but are not limited to the kinds of services that are of immediate interest, there appears to be no way of breaking the finer components out of the subtotals, even at the national level. Thus, while Table 3.14 sheds light on the composition of these private services, the breakdown is neither fine nor consistent enough to show the extent of cross-boundary trade in business and professional services. All that can be said

Table 3.13: Summary of Canadian-US Current Account Transactions (Million $ US), 1977- 1981

	1977	1978	1979	1980	1981
US receipts					
Merchandise exports	28,533	31,229	38,690	41,389	45,217
Travel	2,150	2,248	2,092	2,428	2,628
Other transportation	527	544	637	685	808
Fees and royalties	715	858	924	984	1,050
Other private services	498	533	537	590	652
Receipts of income on US assets:					
Interest, dividends, unincorporated earnings	1,455	1,695	2,514	2,243	2,182
Reinvested earnings of corporate affiliate	1,707	1,821	3,003	3,490	1,770
Other private receipts	2,497	3,130	4,179	4,715	6,214
Total[a]	38,082	42,058	52,576	56,524	60,521
US payments					
Merchandise imports	29,645	33,552	39,020	42,434	47,316
Direct defense expenditures	213	179	143	137	173
Travel	1,433	1,407	1,599	1,817	2,022
Other transportation	455	474	557	636	651
Fees and royalties	126	142	176	240	283
Private payments for other services	344	373	401	418	471
Payments of income on Canadian assets:					
Interest, dividends, unincorporated earnings	68	123	200	228	199
Reinvested earnings of corporate affiliate	247	231	399	1,567	317
Other private payments	421	685	1,042	1,439	2,050
Total[a]	32,952	37,166	43,537	48,916	53,482
Unilateral transfers, net	-102	-127	-148	-201	-203
US balance on current account	+5,028	+4,765	+8,891	+7,407	+6,836

a   Minor amounts of government payments and receipts are omitted from the totals.

Source: Bureau of Economic Analysis, US Department of Commerce.

Table 3.14: Breakdown of "Fees and Royalties" and "Other Private Services" in Trade Between the United States and Canada (Million $ US), 1980

	Petroleum	Manu-facturing	Other	Total
"Fees and royalties"				
Receipts by US				
From affiliated firms				
Royalties and licence fees	2	334	30	367
Service charges and rentals	64	379	94	536
Film and television tape rentals	0	0	28	28
Subtotal	67	713	151	931
From non-affiliated firms				131 a
Total				1,062
Payments by US				
To foreign parents by domestic affiliates	-9	43	131	166
To non-affiliated firms				10 a
Total				176

	Receipts	Payments
"Other private services"		
(Unpublished estimates)		
Film and television rentals	49	
Contractor fees	112	n.a.
Communications settlements	258	246
Reinsurance	27	27
Wages of US residents in Canada and vice versa	43	80
Canadian government expenditures in US private sector (embassies, etc.)	94	b
Receipts/payments of trade unions	85	52
Residual	20 d	10 c
Total	688	415

a   1978 data.
b   Included under government expenditures on payments side.
c   Includes film rental and expenditures of US workers in Canada.
d   Commissions.

Source: Bureau of Economic Analysis, US Department of Commerce.

from Table 3.14 is that the services components shown here have been growing roughly in line with the growth of merchandise imports and exports.

A somewhat better indication of the extent and growth of trade in particular services is given by Canadian data. Table 3.15 shows the results of a series of special surveys of business service transactions between Canada and the United States in 1969, 1973, 1977, and 1981, undertaken by the Balance of Payments Division of Statistics Canada. These survey results are believed to account for roughly one-half to two-thirds of all business services and related transactions. The latter component, along with government transactions and miscellaneous items, makes up the "other service transactions" figures shown in the overall Canadian balance of payments.[9] Table 3.16 shows the 1981 transactions between Canada and all foreign countries, as well as the Canada-US data from Table 3.15. The figures are broken down to separate out cross-boundary, parent-affiliate transactions.

The data in Tables 3.15 and 3.16 show the very important role of the consulting and management services provided to Canadians by US firms, largely through parent-affiliate relations. In 1981, for example, payments to the United States for management, administrative, consulting, and other professional services were approximately $795 million, of which $722 million (91 per cent) was paid to or through affiliates. The $795 million figure, moreover, represents a 73 per cent increase over 1977. It is, however, only 66 per cent of Canadian payments to all foreigners for such services, which is considerably less than the 90+ per cent figure evident in 1977 and earlier. Thus, there has been a more rapid growth of payments for consulting/ professional services to other countries.

On the receipts side, the comparable figure is even lower (about $175 million), as is the affiliate proportion, indicating that Canada relies relatively less on the United States in selling consulting services than in buying them. This is not surprising in view of (1) the extensive parent-affiliate relationships in the manufacturing and extractive sectors, and (2) the recognized position of a few "high-finance" and "high-technology" centres in the United States which provide both business and professional services on a world-wide basis.

Table 3.15 brings out the remarkable growth that has been affecting certain business and professional services. A number of categories show increases of five or six times for the twelve-year period, and a few, such as Canadian receipts for professional, management, and administrative services, and the category

Table 3.15: Business Services and Related Transactions Between Canada and the United States (Million $ Canadian): 1969, 1973, 1977, 1981

	1969	1973	1977	1981
Business service receipts (Canada)				
Consulting and other professional services	13	25	40	96
Management and administrative services	11	32	58	89
Commissions	8	17	29	29
Insurance premiums and other insurance transactions	9	16	25	56
Scientific research and product development	14	7	27	78
Royalties, copyrights, trademarks, film rentals	2	3	24	18
Advertising and sales promotion	12	13	19	30
Equipment rentals	3	3	13	4
Computer services				17
Other services	75	105	289	700
Totals, survey results	147	222	524	1,107
Business service payments (Canada)				
Royalties, copyrights, trademarks, film rentals	152	234	409	670
Management and administrative services	102	180	355	565
Special tooling and other automotive charges	135	118	319	638
Scientific research and product development	52	101	170	255
Insurance premiums and other insurance transactions	18	31	72	91
Consulting and other professional services	92	81	105	229
Commissions	24	32	56	80
Advertising and sales promotion	30	29	35	39
Equipment rentals	14	23	22	52
Franchises and similar rights	9	7	11	12
Computer services				56
Other services	17	31	89	151
Totals, survey results	645	867	1,643	2,838
Canadian: Deficit	498	645	1,119	1,731
Receipts/payments	.23	.26	.32	.39

Source: Balance of Payments Division, Statistics Canada.

Table 3.16: Business Service Receipts and Payments ($ Millions), by Affiliation and Area, 1981

	All Countries			United States		
	Affiliates	Non-affiliates	Total	Affiliates	Non-affiliates	Total
Receipts						
Consulting and other professional services	98	589	687	65	21	86
Insurance transactions	65	68	133	16	40	56
Management and administrative services	121	5	126	85	4	89
Scientific research and product development	78	1	79	77	1	78
Commissions	50	14	64	26	3	29
Royalties, patents, trademarks, and film rentals	19	22	41	8	10	18
Advertising and sales promotion	8	32	40	1	29	30
Computer services	22		22	17		17
Equipment rentals	5	3	8	4		4
Franchises and similar rights	1	4	5	1		1
Other services	700	106	806	660	39	699
Totals, survey results	1,167	844	2,011	960	147	1,107
Payments						
Royalties, patents, trademarks, and film rentals	672	97	769	599	71	670
Special tooling and other automotive charges	638		638	638		638
Consulting and other professional services	184	419	603	170	59	229
Management and administrative services	584	19	603	552	13	565
Scientific research and product development	272	9	280	249	6	255
Insurance transactions	100	103	203	32	59	91
Commissions	126	42	168	64	16	80
Computer services	59	4	63	52	4	56
Equipment rentals	21	31	52	21	31	52
Advertising and sales promotion	24	18	42	23	16	39
Franchises and similar rights	6	9	12	6	6	12
Other services	135	54	189	101	50	151
Totals, survey results	2,820	802	3,622	2,507	331	2,838

Source: Statistics Canada *Daily*, Aug. 11, 1983.

containing royalties, trademarks, etc., are higher yet. Even allowing for the influence of inflation, the data imply impressive rates of growth in, for example, computer services in recent years. While the traditional Canadian deficit in these types of services has been increasing in absolute terms, there has been a notable improvement (from Canada's standpoint) in relative terms; receipts as a proportion of payments increased from 23 per cent in 1969 to 39 per cent in 1981.

Our earlier discussion pointed out the partial nature of explicit services payments entering into the balance of payments, even when such payments are made by affiliated companies (as in Tables 3.15 and 3.16). To obtain an adequate idea of the extent of business and professional service relationships between US and Canadian firms it is necessary to consider as well the business carried on by affiliates within their host countries. Unfortunately, the business services surveys undertaken in both Washington and Ottawa, being balance of payments oriented, do not relate much about this. It is probably safe to say that many, perhaps most, of the services of concern here are of this kind. If a corporate affiliate, once established, pays no interest or dividends back to its home country, nothing is registered in the balance-of-payments accounts.[10] Indeed, the fact that direct Canadian payments to the United States for consulting and professional services show only moderate growth between 1969 and 1981 (Table 3.15) suggests that much of the activity is taking place *within* countries via the affiliate route.

In view of this problem, it would be desirable to look at *income* generated by foreign affiliates in these fields, regardless of its disposition toward the home country. US data do not lend themselves to a satisfactory breakdown for these purposes, and Canadian data permit only a glimpse of income generated by foreign-owned firms in the very general area of "services," excluding utilities and wholesale and retail trade. By referring ahead to Table 7.6, it can be seen that, while income generated in eastern Canada by the US-controlled corporate services sector is small relative to the whole, it has been growing very rapidly, more than tripling in both Quebec and the Atlantic Provinces between 1972 (1971 in Quebec) and 1978. How much of that growth is attributable to business and professional services as compared to, say, tourist, entertainment, and other services it is not possible to say. (Financial services, whose growth has also been rapid, are not included in Table 7.6.) But it is plausible, given the data in earlier tables, to believe that consulting services carried on through affiliates are responsible for a significant part of the observed growth.

Up to this point, discussion of trade in business and professional services (corporate income aside) has been based on overall Canada-US transactions. It is only at this level that the macro data collected by federal agencies can be used. As the focus is narrowed to north-south regional relationships, the problem of measurement becomes more difficult; to the best knowledge of these authors, no data are collected specifically to highlight such flows. Even more than in the case of investment (Chapter 7), it is difficult, using standard data collection sources, to identify regional groupings of buyers and sellers in the general area of services, much less in particular subcategories.

For example, it is well known that New England is a major provider of business and professional services to other regions of the United States and also abroad. A survey undertaken by David Ashton and Branch Sternal for the Federal Reserve Bank of Boston showed that over a third of a selected group of New England business services firms made more than 10 per cent of their sales to states outside of New England, and about 8 per cent of these firms made more than 10 per cent of their sales outside the United States (Table 3.17).[11] Interestingly, while firms in the engineering, research and development, and management consulting groups were most apt to have overseas sales, there was no consistent relationship between firm size (in the overall sample) and export position. Apparently it is quite possible for some relatively small firms to sell effectively abroad.[12] Unfortunately, the study referred to did not produce information as to destination of overseas sales. These authors know of no comparable study of these kinds of services — on either side of the boundary — which would shed light on the eastern Canada-New England connection.

Examination of specific cases, however, suggests that for New England services firms doing any considerable amount of business outside the United States, the Canadian market is an important one. Indeed, it is unusual to find any such company, if it has overseas affiliates at all, that does not have an affiliate in Canada. While this same examination leads one to believe that most such affiliates are located in Ontario (either in the Ottawa or Toronto metropolitan areas), it is also reasonable to assume that these affiliates service clients in Quebec and the Atlantic Provinces. Moreover, New England's strong position as a provider of business services makes it likely that a substantial part of the amounts recorded as Canadian payments in Tables 3.15 and 3.16 represent sales by New England firms. If the flow is unbalanced, this may simply reflect a mismatch between Montreal's strong position in hydro and high-voltage engineering

Table 3.17: Interregional and International Sales of New England Business Services Firms, by SIC Group

SIC Group	Firms in Group	Per cent of Total Sales Made to US Outside New England			Per cent of Total Sales Made Outside US		
		>10%	>50%	>90%	>10%	>50%	>90%
7311- Advertising agencies							
Number of firms	25	7	5	2	0	0	0
% of firms	100.0	28.0	20.0	8.0	0	0	0
7391- Research and development							
Number of firms	31	23	20	6	5	1	1
% of firms	100.0	74.2	64.5	19.4	16.1	3.2	3.2
7392- Mgmt. consultants and P.R.							
Number of firms	91	70	43	6	8	0	0
% of firms	100.0	76.9	47.2	6.6	8.8	0	0
7394- Equip. rental and leasing							
Number of firms	29	10	4	0	3	0	0
% of firms	100.0	34.5	13.8	0	10.3	0	0
8911- Eng., arch., and surv.							
Number of firms	177	47	16	0	16	1	1
% of firms	100.0	26.6	9.0	0	9.0	0.6	0.6
8931- Accounting, auditing, bkpg.							
Number of firms	140	6	1	0	0	0	0
% of firms	100.0	4.3	0.7	0	0	0	0
Multiple service							
Number of firms	114	62	38	6	14	1	0
% of firms	100.0	54.4	33.3	5.3	12.3	0.9	0
Total							
Number of firms	607	225	127	20	46	3	2
% of firms	100.0	37.1	20.9	3.3	7.6	0.5	0.3

Source: Federal Reserve Bank of Boston.

services, on the one hand, and New England's fragmented and largely non-hydro energy base (see Chapter 5), on the other hand.

The appendix to Chapter 7 includes a few examples of specific northeastern firms doing cross-boundary work in the business services sector.

Policy Issues

Policy issues surrounding trade across the northeastern boundary necessarily reflect the broader issues of Canada-US trade generally. As indicated in Chapter 1 and the first section of this chapter, trade between the nations has consisted largely of raw materials, energy, and semi-finished goods moving south, and manufactured goods, certain natural products, and services moving north. This north-south pattern is somewhat less obvious in central Canada than in either the eastern or western provinces because of the tendency of Canada's own manufacturing industries to concentrate in Ontario and, to a lesser extent, Quebec. As noted earlier, the Atlantic Provinces fit the traditional pattern of exporter of mostly raw and semi-finished materials, energy, fish, and tourist services (see Table 3.4). Likewise, the Pacific and Mountain provinces sell mostly minerals, lumber, and other crude materials, together with energy and tourist services, to the United States. Ontario's and Quebec's exports, on the other hand, are mixed, with certain kinds of manufactured products competing for top rank with minerals, paper, and a range of other semi-finished goods (Table 3.3). Ontario and Quebec, moreover, depend to a considerable extent on their own manufactures, and on a protected market which raises the price of non-Canadian manufactured goods in the other provinces.

The above pattern suggests divergent interests between central Canada and the other provinces with respect to US trade. This divergence is hardly a recent phenomenon; indeed, it has played an important role in Canadian history and, from time to time, has required offsetting arrangements to maintain the Confederation. The same divergence has been in evidence in recent years with revival of the free trade issue. In that part of the continent that is the focus of this study, the Atlantic Provinces have a good deal to gain from closer trade relations with the United States, including New England. Moves toward free trade would provide Atlantic Canadians with better access to northeastern US markets for their products. It would also lower the cost of some manufactured goods. Both Ontario and Quebec, on the other hand, have more at stake to the extent that their own manufacturing industries would be weakened by lower trade barriers. Quebec in particular continues to support substantial textile, food, and furniture industries whose future would be clouded (at best) by free trade with the United States.

New England occupies a somewhat ambivalent position on the issue. Free trade with Canada would undoubtedly enlarge the markets of a good many regional manufacturers, most of which are located in southern New England. Relaxation of Canadian licensing and regulatory restrictions would probably attract considerable New England interest in the extension of transportation, communication, and financial networks to the north. But the absence of tariffs might also lead to a dramatic restructuring of New England's fishing and fish processing industries, and possibly of northern New England's wood products industry as well. Even now there are periodic and loud complaints about "subsidized" Canadian fish, lumber, and potatoes crossing the boundary into New England.[13] It may be expected, however, that the subsidy issue will be a continuing one. Subsidies in both economies take many forms and come in many sizes, leading to an identification as well as a measurement problem. Indeed, it hardly seems possible that an economy as accustomed to governmental "indicative" and support mechanisms (guaranteed loans, subsidized interest rates, differential taxes, equity participation by both federal and provincial governments) as Canada's will escape criticism from US competitors, even in instances in which the latter enjoy varying degrees of subsidy themselves. Nor is it apt to be clear when US consumer interests in subsidized imports outweigh possible damage to US producers.

Even if this subsidy charge were without merit, it seems likely that economic factors would work in the direction of greater specialization, meaning greater dependence on Canada for at least certain of these primary products, accompanied by expansion of Canadian finished processors in New England itself (see Chapter 7). The benefits of free trade would flow to New England *consumers* and, as indicated, to those New England producers of specialized, finished goods and services ranging from electronic and computer goods to banking, insurance, and consulting services which, without trade restraint, could probably reach the Canadian market at lower cost than is true under present arrangements (see Table 3.5).

As a final point, non-tariff barriers may also be expected to impede trade relations between New England and eastern Canada. It is well known that Canada has not hesitated to utilize such barriers for protective purposes, and that provincial licensing and procurement policies, for example, frequently discriminate against "outside" suppliers.[14] Nor is the United States immune from such criticism. "Buy American" legislation is all too common at the federal if not the state level.[15] It is thus clear that further reductions in tariffs between regions — which are almost certain to materialize — will still leave those regions some distance from achieving a genuine free trade relationship.[16]

Concluding Observations

The foregoing tables and accompanying discussion have tried to summarize the basic dimensions of tri-regional trade among Quebec, the Atlantic Provinces, and New England. It is clear that the volume of trade is substantial and that growth has been rapid over the past decade. There is evidence, moreover, that north-south trade, at least through 1981, has been growing more rapidly than east-west trade within Canada.

While the traditional pattern of Canadian raw materials and semi- finished goods flowing southward in return for US manufactures still prevails, it is also clear that (1) exports from both Quebec and the Atlantic Provinces to the northeastern United States show somewhat greater diversity than in earlier years, and (2) Quebec's manufacturing sector has grown to the point where it now accounts for perhaps one- third of its exports. The northbound flow of goods from New England reflects that region's strength in electronic and various high-technology products as well as the more traditional machinery, equipment, and machine tool categories. There is also a substantial northward flow of raw materials, especially wood-related products. Quebec-New England merchandise trade flows, which were roughly in balance in 1979, had developed a 4:3 ratio by 1983, while Atlantic Provinces-New England flows changed from a 7:1 surplus moving southward in 1979 to an 8:1 ratio in 1983.

A major portion — perhaps over one-half — of trade between eastern Canada and the northeastern United States takes the form of intrafirm shipments. (The 60 per cent figure often cited for Canada as a whole may apply here, although regional proportions could not be identified from available data sources.) Clearly this intrafirm relationship characterizes much of the cross-boundary trade in pulp and pulpwood and fish blocks in the semi-finished category and automobile and aircraft components in the finished category.

Both Canadian and US tariff policies have traditionally favoured raw materials and semi-finished imports over finished manufactures. Given the size and influence of the US market, as well as of US firms, such policies have no doubt intensified the southward movement of raw and semi-finished products, just as they have intensified the "branch plant" characteristic of Canada's manufacturing sector. The intrafirm movement referred to above may be taken as a reflection of the continuing importance of US markets (fish, wood products) *or* as an ongoing rationalization and specialization of manufacturing facilities (autos and aircraft engines) working to offset such tariff preferences. To date, this type of rationalization does not appear to have progressed beyond a few industries.

Scheduled reductions in tariffs during the 1980s may have a substantial effect on some of the observed product flows. If, for example, the final processing of fish, wood, and paper products destined for US markets shifts toward Canada, and if the manufacture of automobiles, appliances, and various kinds of business equipment destined for Canadian users shifts toward the United States, the flow of trade will begin to reflect least-cost production to a much greater extent than at present. Indeed, there has been in recent years a resurgence of free trade commentary on both sides of the boundary. If this trend materializes, and especially if multinational firms continue to expand their market shares, production facilities will tend increasingly to gravitate toward optimum locations (optimum, that is, from the standpoint of the firms themselves) with respect to North American markets, raw materials, and energy. Cross-border trade in business and professional services, which is already quite important in these regions, can be expected to flourish to an even greater extent.

The above, of course, is not the only possibility. Non-tariff barriers in the form of purchase preferences, export subsidies, public sector support, licensing, labelling, and domestic content requirements, are conceivable in infinite variety and are already practised in numerous instances. Indeed, it appears that such banning has already become at least as important as tariffs as impediments to trade. It thus remains to be seen whether future trade negotiations can resolve disputes over what constitutes a "subsidy" and define the allowable limits of non-price competition. But, given the encouraging recent growth of north-south trade, GATT (General Agreement on Tariffs and Trade), and the tendency of east-west ties in Canada to show strains, tri-regional trade can be expected to continue to grow in importance in coming years.

Notes

1. See data sources in Table 3.1. Also see International Trade
    Commission, *Operation of the Trade Agreements Program*,
    35th Report 1983 (Washington, D.C.: ITC, 1984) p. 230. (In
    1982, Canada contained about 13 per cent of North
    American auto assembly capacity, but 23 per cent of larger
    car capacity.)

2. For discussion of the transhipment problem inherent in
    regional export-import data, see p. 65.

3. Information from P.-P. Proulx, Caractéristiques des
    échanges inter-régionaux du Canada et des États-Unis,
    working paper submitted to World Peace Foundation
    (Boston), 1982. See also by Proulx: Quebec-USA Trade and
    Investment Relations, paper prepared for a conference at
    Johns Hopkins University on Quebec- US relations, March
    1980.

4. Data from External Trade Division, Statistics Canada,
    1979 special runoff for the New England states.

5. It has been estimated that over 60 per cent of Canadian
    imports from the United States are intrafirm in nature.
    See P.-P. Proulx, Integration and Mandates, *Policy
    Options*, Vol. 3, No. 2 (March- April 1982). Unfortunately,
    no estimates are available at the regional level.

6. Trade data are also assembled and summarized by the US
    Bureau of the Census, using mainly information from US
    Customs. For present purposes the Canadian data are
    preferable since they do at least confront, if not wholly
    resolve, the transhipment problem.

7. See Proulx, Quebec-USA Trade and Investment Relations.

8. The data in Table 3.13 show a US surplus on current
    account ranging between $4.8 billion and $8.9 billion from
    1977 to 1981. Data for 1982 and 1983 show that the
    surplus disappeared in those years, primarily because of a
    sharp decline in US merchandise exports. There were,
    however, no comparably abrupt changes in the service
    categories under discussion here.

9.   Information from *Statistics Canada Daily*, Ottawa, July 11, 1979 and August 11, 1983.

10.   This apparently is not true for unincorporated affiliates; their *earnings* are included, along with dividends of incorporated affiliates, in the US balance of payments.

11.   David J. Ashton and Branch K. Sternal, *Business Services and New England's Export Base*, Federal Reserve Bank of Boston, 1978.

12.   Ashton and Sternal, *Business Services*, Tables 2 and 4.

13.   In 1983, the US International Trade Commission (ITC) was called upon to investigate the alleged "dumping" of Canadian potatoes and to determine whether subsidies were responsible for injury to New England fishermen. After extensive hearings and debate, the dumping charge was found to be without merit. The final outcome of a case involving fishing subsidies is not known at this time (1984). (See US International Trade Commission, *Fall Harvested Round White Potatoes from Canada*, USITC Pub. 1463, Washington, D.C., December 1983.

14.   Canadian policies concerning investment are also relevant and are discussed in Chapter 7.

15.   The appendix to Chapter 7 considers the experience of Bombardier in attempting to gain access to the US market in mass transit equipment.

16.   For a discussion of the issues surrounding non-tariff barriers, see J. Quinn and P. Slayton (eds.), *Non-Tariff Barriers After the Tokyo Round* (Montreal: Institute for Research on Public Policy, 1980).

4:   A FRAMEWORK FOR ASSESSING THE IMPACT OF FREE TRADE IN NORTH AMERICA

H. McA. Pinchin

Twice in this century, in 1911 and 1948, the United States and Canada came close to embarking on a policy of reciprocal free trade. Now, after more than thirty years – years in which Canada spoke loudly of a third option – the prospect of a bilateral free trade arrangement has come firmly into focus again. Canadians are searching for evidence of the merits of such an arrangement and, while economic evidence is not the only important kind, it will surely have a major impact on the decision.

This chapter is divided into four parts. The first part proposes an abstract framework for viewing the static effects of tariff removal. The second part uses this framework to survey and organize the evidence presented in the recent Canadian literature on the effects of bilateral free trade on North America. The third part is an impact analysis related to the region comprising Ontario, Quebec, and the industrial heartland of the United States. The final part contains a brief excursus from the perspective of the Atlantic Provinces.

A Framework for Analysis
That tariff removal in North America would benefit consumers on both sides of the border through price reductions and a wider range of choices is obvious. It is less obvious, but still true, that the average Canadian consumer has more to gain from tariff removal than his American counterpart. This asymmetry of interest arises because Canadian tariffs are somewhat higher, because a larger proportion of consumer items would be affected, and because so many high-cost Canadian goods are identical to or close substitutes for cheaper items available from the United States.[1]

While tariff removal will clearly benefit all consumers, the effects of a bilateral free trade agreement on production may not benefit all producer interests (income recipients, firms, local and provincial/state governments). To determine whose particular ox is endangered, one must have a clear picture of the production effects of the existing pattern of tariff protection.

Thus, what follows is a brief survey of the static production effects of tariff protection, in the abstract, to focus attention on the real issues and to provide a framework for a subsequent analysis of tariff removal.

Suppose, then, that there are two countries I and II and that country I raises tariffs against manufactured imports from country II. The theory of international trade leads one to anticipate that country I's unilateral action will have "active mode" effects on its own economy and "passive mode" effects on the economy of its neighbour.

As summarized in Table 4.1, in country I the tariff will tend to:

1. Curtail its imports of manufactured goods and improve its balance of payments, while at the same time securing tariff revenues and forcing its neighbour to sell to it at lower prices. These effects, as well as capital flows to be annotated later, would probably cause its currency to appreciate.

2. Reduce its real income while redistributing income shares toward the factors of production used intensively in its protected manufacturing sector at the expense of factors used intensively in the primary, service, and export sectors. The pull exerted on factors toward the protected sectors depends in large part on the relative effective rates of protection implied for specific manufacturing processes by the prescribed set of nominal tariff rates.[2] The effective rate of protection will be negative in the unprotected sectors of production because of the higher cost of intermediate inputs.

3. Change the market areas of its producers of import substitutes in ways that affect their location decisions and their ability to achieve economies of scale in production. Production facilities will tend to move to the centre of the newly protected market area. The reduced competition from imports may allow these producers to achieve some increased economies of scale and lower prices, depending on the size of the protected market and

Table 4.1: Schema of Production Effects of Protection in Neighbouring Countries I and II

I Active Mode	II Passive Mode
• *Trade Effects* - Terms of trade P_x/P_m - Manufactured imports - Duty collected - Balance of trade - ER appreciation (X)	• *Trade Effects* - Terms of trade P_x/P_m - Manufactured imports - Export rents and prices - Balance of trade - ER depreciation (M)
• *Resource Pulls and Income Redistribution* - Real income - Effective protection (t_f) of value added draws factors and resources to protected industries and *away from* primary and tertiary industries. - Redistribution raises average incomes in manufacturing and lowers average incomes of factors elsewhere.	• *Resource Pushes and Income Redistribution* - Real income - (t_f) of I pushes factors and resources *out of* manufacturing into primary and tertiary industries. - Redistribution lowers average incomes in manufacturing and lowers it somewhat elsewhere.
• *Market Area and Scale Effects* - Movement of import-substitution to the centre of the protected area - Scale economies in import substitution industries - Scale economies in export industries (via ER and real income in country II)	• *Market Area and Scale Effects* - Relocation of all industry toward new, reduced market areas - Scale economies in export industries - Scale economies in import-substitution industries (via ER)
• *Intl. Migration and Relocation* - Attraction of II's subsidiaries - Induced immigration of skilled labour and capital specific to protected manufacturing industries	• *Intl. Migration and Relocation* - Outmigration of subsidiaries - Outmigration of skilled labour and capital

Note: P = price, ER = exchange rate, X = exports, and M = imports.

competitive conditions. Economies of scale in the export industries may decline indirectly via negative effective protection and exchange appreciation.

4.   Induce some cross-border relocation into country I. This net immigration may take the form of skilled manpower or capital specific to the protected industries — patents, brand names, and differentiated products. In practice, the latter usually takes the form of wholly owned foreign subsidiaries--tariff factories. Any funds that cross the border into country I will create an upward pressure on the exchange rate.

The passive mode repercussions for country II, if it chooses not to retaliate, are also summarized in Table 4.1. Country II will experience *opposite* changes in trade, exchange rates, resource pulls, and migration. Country I's action will also cause a loss of real income in country II and will generate a tendency for country II's industries (all of them) to relocate away from the border toward the centre of its new market area. The larger the initial trade dependence of country II on country I, the larger will be the passive mode effects to which it is subject.

One could now suppose that country II decides to retaliate by adopting the active mode itself. Country II's tariffs will offset some but not all of its passive mode production effects. By raising tariffs on imported manufactured goods, country II will set in motion each of the active mode effects on its own economy, while imposing the passive mode effects on country I. The net impact of both active and passive mode production effects in each country will depend not only on asymmetries of size and trade dependence, but also on differences in their tariff structures in relation to their endowments and free trade patterns of comparative advantage.

While one cannot be sure what net impact raising tariffs by both countries will have on trade balances, terms of trade, exchange rates, and the domestic resource pulls experienced by each country, one can be certain that each country will be left with a reduced level of real income and reduced levels of imports and exports of manufactured goods, both in absolute amounts and in relation to income, than could have been achieved without the tariffs. The reduced level of real incomes and trade in manufactured goods are associated with

- a relatively inefficient pattern of industrial diversification – the resource pull or *despecialization effect*
- a reduction of effective market size for many producers and the consequent loss of economies of scale – *the scale effect*
- a reallocation of market areas for manufacturers involving the concentration of industry away from the borders – *the relocation effect*
- a large amount of productive capacity located outside the country's borders – *the migration effect*.

The above outline provides a framework for analysing the static production effects of establishing free trade in North America. Free trade offers the potential for increased real incomes and increased trade in manufactured goods to *both* countries by reversing the despecialization, scale, relocation, and migration effects of the two tariff systems. Tariff removal is not a zero sum situation, and losers could be compensated, whether or not this is likely in practice.

While tariff protection creates a burden on a country's real income through these four static production effects, the country might nevertheless resort to protection for the purpose of acquiring dynamic benefits, expecting somehow to induce an increase in the rate of growth of its real income.[3] In practice, this policy might or might not be successful; dynamic (growth) effects can work both ways, and the tariff could become both a static and a dynamic burden. Since disagreements about the production effects of two-tariff systems (i.e., where both countries adopt tariffs) often arise because it is difficult to distinguish between static and dynamic effects, the following points are offered to suggest the distinction.

Ignoring adjustment costs, the two tariffs would represent a *static burden* on a country's aggregate real output to the extent that

1. the real level of productivity of local production factors would be higher in those industries in which, or into which, free trade would direct them
2. any output lost by reversing (via free trade) the migration effects of the tariffs would be more than compensated for by the productivity growth of the factors that remain (point 1 above).

Finessing the problem of the accumulation of static burdens over time, the two tariffs would represent a *dynamic burden* on the rate of growth of a country's aggregate real output to the extent that their continuation

3.   causes a slower rate of growth by discouraging
    a.   savings, investment, initiative, the diffusion of technology, the acquisition of new skills, the development of modes of R&D, or learning by doing
    b.   the speed at which factors flow into fast-growth, high- productivity industries
    c.   the rate of inflow of new factors of production from abroad

4.   causes a slower growth of exports abroad due to retaliatory action on the part of third countries.

Each of these elements (1-4) involves summing up negative and positive effects with respect to a hypothetical, counterfactual situation, a process that is rendered vastly more complicated by reverberations between the elements.

The fundamental methodological question, in discussing the impact of tariff removal, is how to simulate a reasonable free trade counterfactual from existing levels of output and patterns of specialization. This requires exploring in some detail the implications of reversing the four static effects – despecialization, scale, relocation, and migration – of the two tariffs, first at the national level and then at the regional level. Even then, because judgements about the tariffs' effects on elements 1 and 2 are linked to judgements about elements 3 and 4, the inseparability of static and dynamic elements will continue to generate disagreement about what constitutes a reasonable free trade counterfactual. Since the short-run rationalization decisions of firms, and the relocation and migration decisions of individuals and firms, will include *their* judgements about the effects of reversing (removing) the dynamic influence of the tariff, any prediction of the static effects of tariff removal must involve prejudging, by assumption, the dynamic effects of the tariffs encompassed by elements 3 and 4.

The Canadian Literature on the Effects of Bilateral Free Trade

The current literature on the economic consequences of free trade in North America is lopsidedly Canadian in origin and focus.[4] The best evidence now available on changes in manufacturing output and employment that might occur in Canada can be summarized in terms of the predicted outcome of reversing the four static production effects just described. The predictions assume sufficient time for adjustment to and abstract from non-tariff barriers and other forms of governmental interference.

Since the Canadian literature on the economics of bilateral free trade generally favours the pursuit of such an agreement, it is appropriate at the outset to begin with the conclusions of R.J. Wonnacott, the outstanding authority on and certainly the most prolific spokesman for the cause.[5] He has estimated, in a now famous table (reproduced here as Table 4.2), that bilateral free trade might raise the real GNP (gross national product) in Canada by as much as 8.2 per cent.

Wonnacott isolates two primary sources of increased real income, which correspond in the framework presented here to the results of reversing the despecialization and scale effects of the two tariffs, with 28 per cent of the static benefit accorded to the former and 72 per cent to the latter production effect. He does not exclude the migration and relocation effects of the tariffs; his estimating technique simply subsumes these effects, and their related assumptions, under his two primary sources of the static benefits of free trade.

Given the size of the static benefits suggested by this estimation technique ($10.1 billion in 1974 dollars), the significant recognition value associated with the 8.2 per cent figure in the economic literature, and the subsequent thrust of this chapter, it is important to pursue the subtlety of Wonnacott's method of estimation.

Canada's potential gain of 2.3 per cent of GNP from the reversal of the despecialization effects of the two tariff systems is derived from J.R. Williams's conclusion that bilateral free trade would increase real consumption in Canada by 4 per cent (.04 X .575 = .023).[6] Williams used a linear programming, multi-sectoral analysis to estimate the effects of removing the two tariff systems *in 1961*. This analysis not only excluded scale effects by its constant cost assumptions but also excluded migration effects by presuming fixed factor supplies.

Wonnacott ingeniously derives Canada's 5.9 per cent gain in GNP from the reversal of the scale effects of the two tariff systems by using the differential in the productivity of manufacturing in Canada versus the United States as a proxy for the proportion by which productivity could be increased by free trade.[7] Using a figure of 27 per cent for the US productivity advantage in manufacturing, he estimates that free trade would raise real Canadian GNP by (.27) (.22) = .059 (where .22 is the ratio of value added in manufacturing to GNP in 1973).[8] A close

Table 4.2: Estimation of Benefits for Canada of a Free Trade Area with the United States, 1974

Sources of Benefit (real terms)	Per cent of GNP	Realization of these Benefits	Per cent of GNP
A Comparative advantage specialization		I Price reduction	4.0
	2.3	II Increase in equilibrium wage	4.2 (residual estimate)
B Recapture of duty revenue on Canadian exports previously paid to US Treasury		III Increase in equilibrium returns to other factors	
C Increased productivity of labour and other factors of production in Canada because of economies of scale	5.9		
Total benefit, as generated:	8.2	Total benefit, as realized:	8.2

Source: R.J. Wonnacott, *Canada's Trade Options*, Economic Council of Canada (Ottawa: Information Canada, 1975) p. 177.

reading of his text shows that, although Wonnacott attributes these beneficial effects to economies of scale, he intends them to include both the migration and relocation effects.[9]

The right-hand column in Table 4.2 is less important, Wonnacott tells his readers, since it merely shows how the real benefits might be allocated using a particular assumption about exchange parity. With exchange depreciation, fewer benefits would be realized in the form of price decreases and correspondingly more in the form of increased factor rewards. This represents an interesting transition in his estimating technique and one that he discusses at some length.[10] In an earlier effort he chose to estimate the potential benefits in tariff removal by combining the estimated decrease in prices, corrected for exchange rate changes, with an estimate of the potential increase in Canadian income that would occur *if* and when wages in Canadian manufacturing were to rise to the level achieved in the United States.[11]

Wonnacott's estimating procedures involve crucial assumptions about how much productivity (and/or wages) in Canadian manufacturing would increase with free trade and specialization. While these assumptions and the resulting estimates are the best available, they invite objections. The delightful simplicity and cogency of the assumed productivity potential (and/or wage potential) of Canada's manufacturing sector under free trade really begs the question of what the industry-by-industry pattern of Canadian production would be after tariff removal. Before continuing with Wonnacott's estimates this question is pursued in some detail in the following sections using the above framework of production effects. Obviously, the pattern of industrial specialization under free trade relates in part to productivity differences between Canada and the United States. But these productivity differences also depend in important ways on the rationalization, relocation, and migration decisions of firms, investors, and employees, decisions that involve *their* judgements about the dynamic effects of tariff removal.

Despecialization Effects of the Tariffs and Canada's Comparative Advantage

Three techniques have been applied in recent Canadian literature to establish how Canada's trade and pattern of industrial production might change with the removal of the two tariff systems. The first technique involves extrapolating Canada's trading strengths from its current pattern of trade with the United States after correction for the effects of the tariffs.

The second involves industry-by-industry comparisons of differences in Canadian/US productivity corrected for the effects of tariffs, combined with the expectation that Canada would specialize more in producing those goods for which its relative productivity advantage was the greatest or for which its relative productivity disadvantage was the least. The third method builds on the second by inserting factor supply and balance-of-payments constraints into a general equilibrium model of the two economies. Each of these techniques falls short of the goal in that it excludes the influence of scale, relocation, and migration effects on the free trade counterfactual.

The first technique of extrapolating Canada's comparative advantage from the existing pattern of trade in North America figured prominently in staff work undertaken at the Economic Council of Canada for *Looking Outward* (1975) and in Harry Postner's analysis of the factor content of Canada's trade with the United States, which also was ultimately used in *Looking Outward*.[12]

The staff of the Council, following B.W. Wilkinson,[13] used the following formula to convert Canada's 1969 imports and export trade with the United States into the changes in industry shipments that would result from tariff removal. This involved taking the level of Canadian exports to the United States weighted by the elasticity of US demand for imports and US tariff levels and subtracting US exports weighted by the Canadian elasticity and tariff. Using duties on total imports by industry as their measure of the tariff levels, they found that tariff removal would cause exports to increase by 1.85 per cent and imports by 1.84 per cent. Then by assigning export increases by industry as increases in industry shipments, and import increases by industry as decreases in shipments, they concluded that the direct impact of free trade would tip resources out of the Canadian textile, electrical products, machinery, miscellaneous manufactures, and metal- fabricating industries, and would draw resources toward the food and beverage, wood products, primary metals, and even the clothing industries. These changes were then incorporated into the Council's CANDIDE econometric model to simulate the full economic impact reported in *Looking Outward*.[14]

Harry Postner's important conclusions about the factor content of a balanced increase of $1 million in bilateral trade between Canada and the United States are summarized in Table 4.3. Canada exports to the United States the services of natural resources (renewable and non-renewable) and gross fixed capital, and imports from the United States the services of all types of

Table 4.3: **Factor Content of a Balanced Increase in Canadian Bilateral Trade with the United States, 1967**

	\$1 Million Worth of				
	Manufactured Goods Trade			Merchandise Trade	Total Trade
	X	M	$\frac{X-M}{F}$	$\frac{X-M}{F}$	$\frac{X-M}{F}$
Total labour employment (man-years)	103.5	109.2	-1.1	-2.7	n.a.
Elementary	41.6	38.6	1.6	-1.5	-1.2
High school	53.4	61.2	-2.8	-3.8	-3.2
University	8.5	9.4	-1.8	-1.5	-2.6
Total gross fixed capital (thousand \$)	2,756	2,287	4.4	5.2	n.a.
Renewable natural resources (thousand \$)	120	41	16.2	8.2	7.1
Non-renewable natural resources (thousand \$)	128	89	120	37.1	32.0

Note: Each figure in the $\frac{X-M}{F}$ columns has been raised by the power 10^6.

F = factor supply in Canada, X = exports, and M = imports.

Source: Harry H. Postner, *Factor Content of Canadian International Trade: An Input-Output Analysis*, Economic Council of Canada (Ottawa: Information Canada, 1975) pp. 55, 61, and 63.

labour. High school-educated labour is the kind most displaced by Canada's merchandise trade with the United States. Postner concludes from these findings that Canada's comparative advantage is in products that use natural resources intensively and that the source of comparative disadvantage lies in the relative scarcity in Canada of "semi-skilled operatives," "scientific and technical personnel," and the "management and sales distribution" components of the labour force.[15]

Since Postner's conclusions are drawn from the already tariff-laden pattern of trade, one can only draw inferences from them about the free trade comparative advantage characteristics of the two countries. It is apparent that the Canadian tariff has been used to protect industries in which Canada has a comparative disadvantage. Postner's correlation coefficients across ninety-seven industries between nominal tariff level rankings and factor intensity rankings imply that the Canadian tariff serves to pull factors out of non-renewable resource processing and the service sector into more labour-intensive secondary manufacturing industries. This shift away from resource-intensive industry comes about both because of the higher factor rewards generated in secondary manufacturing and because of the higher cost of intermediate inputs in the resource-intensive industries.

If, however, the US tariff system were the same as that in Canada, it would tend to have the opposite effects on the pattern of production in Canada; namely, it would serve to deter secondary manufacturing by discouraging Canadian exports of these goods and to increase the employment of factors in the production of primary resources for the export market (the passive mode). In fact, the cascading of the nominal tariffs of the two countries is not identical. The nominal tariff rates in Canada tend to decline relative to those of the United States as the resource intensity of commodities increases, and they tend to rise relative to US tariffs as the wage costs and labour intensity of commodities increases.[16] Nominal tariffs are very much the same with respect to the capital intensity of commodities. Thus it is reasonable to conclude that these trade-based approximations of Canada's free trade pattern of comparative advantage suggest that it would involve less labour-intensive secondary manufacturing and more resource-intensive production.

The second technique used for estimating Canada's free trade comparative advantage involves arraying the relative productivity difference per worker, by industry, between Canada and the United States, after correcting for the difference in effective protection. This technique builds on the classical theory of trade and forms the basis of a long tradition of empirical tests of comparative advantage.[17] It might be anticipated that under free trade Canada would specialize in those industries in which it has the greatest productivity advantage (or least disadvantage) and cut back production of those goods in which its productivity disadvantage is greatest.

James G. Frank's Canadian Conference Board study (1977) of relative productivity in Canadian and American industry suggests that in 1974 in Canada averaged about 94-98 per cent of US productivity in the area of durable manufactures, and only 68-70 per cent in the area of non-durable manufactures.[18] Table 4.4 shows Frank's findings in detail. To accommodate the difference in wage costs, a second column is added in the table to suggest that under free trade Canada might specialize its pattern of production to emphasize those manufactured goods in which it has the lowest relative for wage costs per unit of output.

Such relative productivity data must be deflated to correct for the effects of protection. This is done by dividing each industry's productivity by $(1 + f)$, where f is the appropriate effective rate of protection, and amounts to multiplying the first column by $(1 + f)^{US}/(1 + f)^{Can}$. This correction serves to blur conclusions about Canada's free trade pattern of industrial specialization because there is independent evidence that "effective protection in Canada varies almost exactly in inverse proportion to relative labour productivity."[19] The most recent application of this technique was made by P.-P. Proulx (1979).[20]

The third and most ambitious technique for estimating Canada's free trade comparative advantage simulates the effects of tariff removal in both economies in 1961 using a multi-sectoral linear programming technique which incorporates general equilibrium considerations by assigning factor and resource supply constraints and balance-of-trade constraints. This trail-blazing piece of research by J.R. Williams (1978) involves fixed consumption coefficients and fixed input-output coefficients and constrains changes in industrial output to no more than 10 per cent. His conclusion that tariff removal would increase output for consumption by 4 per cent has already been discussed. In the present context the more striking conclusion is quoted below:

> The Canadian-United States tariff schedules shifted Canada away from manufacturing and towards earlier stages of processing. The tariff has failed to increase the output of end products in Canada above the level that would be expected in free trade.

Table 4.4: Relative Productivity per Worker and Relative Wage Costs per Unit of Output in Selected Canadian Manufacturing Industries, 1974

	Canada/US Productivity per Worker		Canada/US Unit Wage Costs	
Sawmills, sash and door mills	1.41	(1)	.85	(2)
Veneer and plywood mills	1.24	(2)	.94	(3)
Woollen textile mills	1.16	(3)	.84	(1)
Iron & steel mills, steel, pipe, & tube	1.03	(4)	.95	(5)
Fish products	1.02	(5)	1.01	(6)
Baked products	.97	(6)	.95	(4)
Motor vehicles, parts & accessories	.95	(7)	1.20	(12)
Men's clothing	.93	(8=)	1.11	(9)
Soft drinks	.93	(8=)	1.27	(15)
Hosiery mills	.91	(10)	1.09	(8)
Other knitting mills	.87	(11)	1.03	(7)
Non-ferrous metal smelting, etc.	.86	(12)	1.26	(14)
Pulp and paper mills	.85	(13)	1.31	(16)
Fruit and vegetable processing	.84	(14)	1.13	(10)
Synthetic textile mills	.83	(15)	1.37	(17)
Breweries	.78	(16)	1.17	(11)
Iron foundries	.77	(17)	1.23	(13)
Heating and air conditioning	.72	(18)	1.43	(19)
Fabricated structural metals	.70	(19)	1.79	(27)
Truck and bus bodies	.67	(20=)	1.40	(18)
Other paper converters	.67	(20=)	1.51	(21)
Household furniture	.64	(22)	1.62	(25)
Slaughtering and meat processing	.62	(23)	1.55	(22)
Paper bag and box manufacturing	.61	(24)	1.74	(26)
Biscuit manufacturing	.60	(25)	1.48	(20)
Major appliances	.59	(26)	1.61	(23)
Soap and cleaning products	.57	(27)	1.61	(24)
Petroleum refining	.55	(28)	1.84	(28)
Dairy products	.50	(29)	2.10	(30)
Tobacco products	.47	(30)	2.38	(32)
Confectionary products	.45	(31)	2.09	(29)
Paint and varnish manufacturing	.44	(32)	2.20	(31)
Cotton, yarn and cloth mills	.24	(33)	4.42	(33)

Source: J.G. Frank, *Assessing Trends in Canada's Competitive Position: The Case of Canada and the United States* (Ottawa: Canadian Conference Board, 1977) pp. 26-28 and pp. 62-65.

Industries that were classified with those expanding in free trade were *ceteris paribus*, those which produced the fewest intermediate products and which made relatively the smallest purchases of resources in dollar terms.[21]

This startling conclusion, which at first appears counterintuitive, means that Canadian tariff policy aimed at increasing end product production in Canada failed to provide sufficient effective protection to producers of these goods – that is, the nominal protection they received was insufficient to offset the higher costs of intermediate inputs to which the tariff gave rise.

The detailed industry-by-industry results presented by Williams are important because they constitute the only fully developed free trade counterfactual, and because they can be contrasted with those suggested by the other, more direct techniques. However, since his industries are subdivided into just three components – export (E), domestic (D), and import competing (E), on the basis of their orientation in 1961 – direct comparison by industry is not possible.[22]

In Table 4.5, column (1) ranks the ten industries that, according to Williams, will experience the largest absolute expansion under free trade and the corresponding ten industries with the largest absolute decline in output. While it is not surprising to find that most of the contracting industries are characterized with an M, it is surprising to find that the principal expanding industries are also import-competing industries and not export industries. This is, of course, due to the effect of the tariff in raising the costs of intermediate inputs, which the previously discussed techniques tend to short-change.

For the twenty industries in Table 4.5, column (2) shows the proportion of end product to total production and column (3) their purchases of resources per dollar of output. Although only a subset of Williams's sixty-three industries, these twenty account for most of the changes in end product and resource orientation covered in his conclusion cited above. Under free trade, the expanding group increases production, in 1961 dollars, by $480.7 million and the declining group decreases production by $436.2 million (expansion exceeds contraction by 10.2 per cent). The expanding group increases its use of resources by $3.2 million, while the contracting industries curtail their use of resources by $13.6 million (contraction exceeds expansion by 76.5 per cent). Finally, and here is the surprise, the expansion of end products *in this subset of industries* is $237.1 million, while the contraction of

Table 4.5: **Ten Largest Expansions and Contractions of Canadian Industries in J.R. Williams's Simulation of the Effects of Bilateral Free Trade, 1961**

	Amount of Expansion or Contraction ($ millions) (%) (1)		Per cent End Product (2)	Resources per $ (3)
Expanding industries:				
Autos, trucks and parts NES (M)	120.7	(10.0)	66.0	.002
Electrical products (M)	88.4	(10.0)	57.0	.002
Non-ferrous metal prodts. (M)	68.9	(10.0)	12.5	.002
Printing (M)	58.6	(10.0)	42.7	.000
Liquor and beer (M)	40.9	(10.0)	91.3	.003
Aircraft incl. parts (M)	34.8	(10.0)	79.5	.001
Rubber products (M)	30.7	(10.0)	31.6	.007
Transportation equipment (M)	14.1	(10.0)	93.8	.001
Inorganic chemicals (E)	12.1	(5.5)	4.9	.065
Plastics (M)	11.5	(10.0)	22.1	.018
Total	480.7			
(Weighted average)			(49.3)	(.007)
Contracting industries:				
Other textile products (M)	-150.0	(9.4)	67.3	.017
Machinery and equipment (M)	-87.9	(10.0)	60.6	.011
Processed foods (M)	-52.3	(5.6)	67.1	.155
Pharmaceuticals (M)	-29.5	(10.0)	71.0	.009
End products NES (M)	-28.6	(10.0)	61.6	.009
Cotton textile products (M)	-25.0	(10.0)	12.8	.004
Industrial chemicals (M)	-24.1	(10.0)	13.1	.032
Leather products (M)	-22.5	(10.0)	92.1	.001
Chemicals (M)	-11.2	(2.1)	17.0	.042
Leather (D)	-5.1	(9.0)	0.3	.009
Total	-436.2			
(Weighted average)			(58.9)	(.031)

Note: M = import competing, E = export, and D = domestic.

Source: J.R. Williams, *The Canadian-United States Tariff and Canadian Industry* (Toronto: University of Toronto Press, 1978) from the tables in Part II.

end products is $256.9 million (contraction of end products does, after all, exceed expansion by 7.7 per cent).[23]

The industry-by-industry detail of Williams's simulation of the effects of bilateral free trade in 1961 is important for what it indicates about anticipated changes in the pattern of production. It is presented in Table 4.5 in the context of a discussion of the despecialization effects of North American tariffs. But, in view of Wonnacott's (1975) use of Williams's conclusions as the basis for his estimates of the benefits of free trade, it is worth noting two points. First, if Williams had not constrained his industries to change by no more than 10 per cent, his estimates of the static burden of the tariff would have been higher than 2.3 per cent of GNP. Second, and more important, it must be obvious to all that the burden of those tariffs remaining after the institution of the Auto Pact in 1965 is much lower than that found by Williams for 1961. In Table 4.5, "autos, trucks, and parts NES (M)" and "transportation equipment (M)" constitute 28 per cent of the output growth of the "expanding industries"; both expand to the limit, and both can be classified as end products.

From this survey of trade and relative productivity-based estimates of Canada's comparative advantage under free trade, a compromise conclusion emerges about the despecialization effects of the two tariff systems: the net effect of both sets of tariffs on resource *extraction* is really unimportant. The first two estimating techniques suggest that the tariffs have tipped Canada's pattern of specialization away from resource *fabrication*, which means that the level of production, productivity, and factor rewards in resource fabrication, relative to other Canadian industry, would be increased with the removal of the price and market constriction effects of the US tariff and with the removal of the input cost disadvantages created by the Canadian tariff. If the static despecialization effects of the tariffs serve to tip the pattern of specialization away from resource fabrication, does this mean that they enlarge Canada's secondary and end product manufacturing sectors relative to the levels suggested by a reasonable free trade counterfactual? Williams's negative response to this question is controversial, pre-dates the Auto Pact, and conflicts with perceptions drawn from the other two estimation techniques. But these techniques have problems in treating adequately the impact of effective protection on factor usage and the production of end products. It is difficult to accept Williams's conclusions that the removal of tariffs would serve to increase output and factor productivity in this sector relative to other sectors, drawing factors in from elsewhere, especially without analysing the other three framework effects. It is plausible, on the other hand, that free trade would increase the relative productivity of secondary manufacturing. Therefore, the factor usage and output of this sector, relative to other Canadian sectors under free trade, are too close to call from the evidence studied thus far, and cannot be divined without going beyond Williams's assumptions to incorporate consideration of the scale and migration effects.

None of this compromising about the free trade structure of production, however, affects the conclusion about Canada's overall comparative advantage in trade with the United States. It resides, as Postner says, in products that require intensive use of resources and gross fixed capital. And, while Postner's findings, based on existing trade, overstate Canada's disadvantage in labour-intensive products, these products are still the basis of Canada's relative disadvantage.

Scale Economies and the Despecialization Effects of the Tariffs

In his own analysis, R.J. Wonnacott pays scant attention to comparative advantage. This is not surprising since so much of his case for free trade rests on the benefits of reversing the scale effects of the two tariff systems. Rather, his analysis focuses on the question: "Towards which section of North America would economic activity tend to gravitate in a free trade area with the US?" He posits that:

> If the issue is to be sensibly addressed, it is essential to ask ... how costs (and here he lists labour costs, resource costs, capital costs, transportation costs, and certain non- quantifiable costs) would compare after adjustment to a free trade situation. Specifically, what would be the locational pressures on an industry free to pick the optimum spot from which to supply an integrated North American economy of 220 million people?[24]

It is to his analysis of this question that Wonnacott directs his readers for the justification of the dramatic 27 per cent increase in productivity in Canadian manufacturing that is finally attributed to economies of scale (see Table 4.2).[25]

Wonnacott's question thus pertains to much more than the scale effects of wider markets. It explicitly includes the effects of internal economies of scale in production *and* distribution, as well as economies that are external to the firm. Implicitly, it includes the implications of reversing the impact of tariffs on the pattern of industrial specialization in Canada, as well as both the location and migration effects. Considering just the scale effects for now, Wonnacott's presupposition is that plants in the United States have already achieved available economies of scale, while plants in Canada have much to gain from access to the wider US market.

A large body of Canadian literature attests to the detrimental scale effect on Canada of the two sets of tariffs.[26] The limited size of the Canadian market and the deterrent effect of the US tariff against Canadian exports of manufactured products have led to short production runs and insufficiently specialized plants, with an excessive amount of down-time necessitated by the conversion process needed to produce differentiated product lines. At the same time, the problem of low relative productivity in Canadian manufacturing is enhanced by the fact that the Canadian tariff has drawn subsidiaries of each of the major US producers across the border into Canada, where the "miniature replica effect" results in inadequate competition.

The problem that arises in predicting how the pattern of production in Canada would be affected by reversing the static scale effects of protection is that this pattern depends a great deal on the rationalization, location, and migration decisions of foreign-owned firms. These decisions in turn will be affected by their judgements about the relative productivity of US and Canadian plants in the recent past, as well as judgements about the particular strengths of a Canadian plant in relation to plants in the United States in the future (comparative advantage,[27] distance, and the dynamic effects of tariff removal).

In the presence of increasing returns, history matters. The theoretical literature of international trade does not preclude the possibility that tariff removal will have detrimental effects on a country when there are widespread opportunities for economies of scale.[28] The initial productivity disadvantage of Canadian plants and the extra complications introduced by foreign ownership give rise to legitimate concern in Canada that much of the benefits of free trade will be taken up by new plants located in the United States. While in theory the presence of economies of scale can be shown to give rise to trade between countries even when there are no international differences in factor endowments, tastes, or technology, Canadians could be more sanguine about potential scale economy benefits if these economies tended to accord with Canada's resource strengths.

Using data on a number of quantifiable characteristics of 129 Canadian industries drawn from Postner,[29] Baumann,[30] and

Statistics Canada, and US-based indicators of economies of scale from Hufbauer,[31] this author's analysis suggests that the scale potential characteristic, not surprisingly, correlates positively with the concentrated nature of an industry in Canada, as evidenced by the industry's four firm concentration ratio (SCAF r = .27) and with the existence of an establishment-size differential between US and Canadian industry (SIZE r = .25).[32] The scale characteristic is also positively associated with the height of the industry's tariff, as evidenced by the ratio of duties to dutiable imports (TAR I r = .14) and the degree of foreign ownership (OWN r = .11). But, although positive, the degree of association here was not significant at the 5 per cent level.[33]

While this evidence of the association between the potential for economies of scale and the tariff, foreign ownership, and industrial concentration is consistent with the Canadian literature on the topic, more pertinent to the impact of reversing the scale effects of the tariff is the finding that the scale characteristic correlates negatively with resource utilization (COAL r = -.21); forestry, fishing, and mining (FFM r = 0.12); and energy (EN r = -.11); and with the use of operatives (CRAF r = -.22) and unskilled labour (LAB r = -.20). The industries most prone to economies of scale are those with high expenditures on research and development (R&D r = .21) and with a large proportion of managerial, clerical, and sales personnel (MCS r = .25) and university- educated labour (UN - EMP r = .20).[34] Scale economies, then, appear to be allied most strongly with industrial characteristics rooted in the US comparative advantage and to be negatively correlated with the characteristics of Canada's comparative advantage.

It then follows that any conclusion that Canadian manufacturers would rationalize their pattern of industrial production to obtain dramatic productivity benefits from the scale effects of free trade, without the help of special dispensation for dumping or other non-tariff assistance (such as the safeguards in the Auto Pact), must rest to a high degree on the peculiar *locational* advantages of plants in Canada.

Location in Relation to the New Market Areas

When writing about bilateral free trade from a home base in London, Ontario in 1967 (Wonnacott's location), one would have been understandably struck by the fact that the industrial heartland of North America lay in a large triangle that ran from Chicago to Boston to Baltimore and back, and that, were it not for two sets of tariffs that increase economic distances, southern Ontario would (in terms of a gravity model of market potential) offer one of the best locations. Perhaps it is equally understandable that, writing from the Utica-Syracuse-Binghamton area of central New York — smack in the middle of the triangle — in the 1980s, one is more skeptical about the importance of such a location. The talk in central New York, as in so much of the US Northeast, is of the advantages of a location in the South or West with low heating and energy costs, low taxes, and more rapidly growing incomes and population.[35] Figure 4.1 dramatizes the recent population shifts. The black area on the map represents the regions where between 1970 and 1980 population grew at least twice as fast as the national average of 11.4 per cent. Lighter areas indicate the seven regions where population growth in the 1970s was below average or where it declined.[36]

Traditionally in Canada tariff protection has correlated negatively with the importance of transportation costs to a product's value. Industries that are naturally protected from foreign competitors by distance and transportation costs receive lower tariff protection.[37] Higher tariffs apply to the products of industries where transportation costs are least important in determining the location of production.

Tariff removal, by redefining economic distance and therefore market areas and sources of supply, would set into motion a process of industrial rationalization in which plants on each side of the border would re-evaluate their existing locations, product lines, and markets in the light of transportation costs, border risks, and the assumed locations of their competitors and their subsidiaries. Since more than half the trade that currently crosses the border can be defined as intracorporate trade, much of the rationalization will depend upon actual (and potential) patterns of ownership and control of *existing* production facilities. Leaving the discussion of ownership as it affects location decisions to the next section on migration effects, one can still determine, using location theory, that the process of reversing the effects of protection on relocation consists of three tendencies:[38]

- the tendency for plants to convert from their current east-west orientation toward a north-south orientation for both markets and sources of inputs
- the tendency for plants (other than those in high-weight loss industries) to relocate closer to the centre of their new market areas or at least, in the context of border risks, closer to the border

Figure 4.1

Population shifts in the United States between 1970 and 1980.

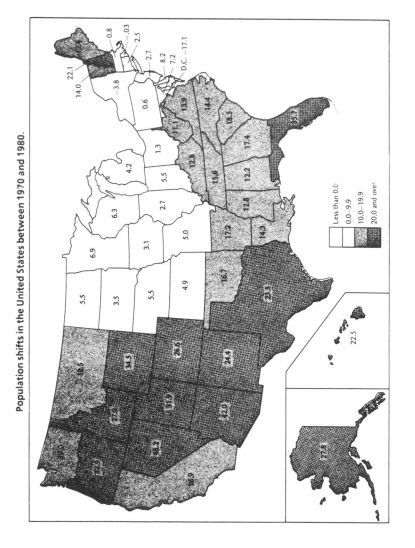

- the tendency for greater intra-industry specialization and, as a consequence, the increased hauling of the differentiated products from the same industry across the international boundary.

The net impact of these relocation tendencies, including the shake-out of industrial duplication, could substantially change the pattern of industrial specialization in border regions of both countries from coast to coast. The peculiar shape of the protected market area currently enjoyed by manufacturers in Canada permits the concentration of three-quarters of their production facilities along the St. Lawrence Valley to Lake Ontario and Lake Erie, servicing a vast market area that represents a thin strip across the continent. While tariff removal would open up opportunities for the existing plants in central Canada to acquire scale economies by competing for a share of the larger and more proximate markets of the US "industrial triangle," it would at the same time open them up to the possibility of losing opportunities for economies of scale from serving more distant eastern and western markets. This reapportionment would tend to occur whether firms in Boston, Minneapolis-St. Paul, and Seattle take advantage of their increased market potential or whether these distant markets go to firms in Vancouver, Calgary, Winnipeg, or Saint John.

The framework developed here suggests that as market areas and sources of inputs are redefined toward a north-south orientation, competing firms would respond to tariff removal by relocating their more footloose production operations toward the centre of their new market areas. In the absence of border risks, the loss of markets in the East and West would probably lead some producers in Ontario and Quebec to locate production facilities inside the US border (regardless of ownership).[39] Reversing the relocation effects of tariffs in the presence of post-free trade agreement border risks (as yet unspecified) might be expected to pull competing production facilities toward the common border. With so much of Canadian manufacturing capacity already close to the border, given the location there of most of Canada's population, this particular relocation effect might be less important on the Canadian side of the border than on the US side.[40]

Finally, although the process of reversing the relocation effects would be dominated by intracorporate control and market sharing decisions, firms would tend to specialize their production facilities to obtain economies of scale in limited product lines, selecting for production in Canada those lines peculiarly suited to

Canadian circumstances (whether this derives from the Canadian resource base, peculiarities of the market, initial advantage in terms of productivity and distance, or sunk costs). This would certainly serve to increase trade, for example, through cross-hauling over the border of more intermediate and end products within industrial classifications.

Migration: Ownership and Control Considerations in the Relocation Process

US firms control a large proportion of the assets, sales, profits, and taxable income of manufacturing operations in Canada. The degree of foreign *ownership* of taxable income in Canada's manufacturing sector varies by industry from around 20 per cent in printing and publishing, leather products, paper and allied products, wood, and furniture, to around 90 per cent in petroleum and coal products, transportation equipment, rubber products, chemicals and chemical products, machinery, electrical products, and tobacco.[41] The trade that currently flows between Canada and the United States reflects such patterns of ownership in complex ways. It is often claimed that intracorporate trade across the border accounts for as much as 60 per cent of the total trade in both directions. With so much of the bilateral trade based on administrative decisions, representing something less than arms-length transactions, it is crucial that one explore the nature and peculiarities of interaffiliate trade relations before judging the effects of a move to free trade.

In 1979, 76 per cent of US imports from Canada entered free of duty, while the remainder was subject to an average tariff duty (duties to dutiable imports) of 5.5 per cent. Items covered by the Auto Pact and entering free of duty accounted for 26 per cent of US imports from Canada. US Department of Commerce data on US imports from "related parties" in Canada for 1979 show that 50 per cent of US imports from Canada fit this classification (Table 4.6).

The Canadian government's study of foreign direct investment in Canada (*Direct Investment in Canada* or the so-called Gray Report, 1972) expresses considerable concern about the size and nature of exports from US subsidiaries in Canada to their affiliates in the United States (which constitute most of the "related parties"). The Report notes that subsidiaries in Canada export less of their output than US subsidiaries in Europe, and that 31 per cent of the 823 US subsidiaries studied were subject to internal corporate export restrictions which prevented them from exporting output back to the United States. Two statements are particularly pertinent to the theme of this chapter:

Table 4.6:   US Imports from Canada and Percentage Share from Affiliated Firms, 1979

	Total US Imports from Canada ($ millions)	Per cent Attributed to Related Parties
Animal and vegetable products	1,841	32.8
Wood, paper, and printed matter	7,359	25.9
Textile fibres, textile products	81	53.0
Chemicals and related products	7,616	54.1
Non-metallic minerals and products	620	34.6
Metals and metal products	17,915	60.9
(Excluding Auto pact items)	(8,115)	(13.6)
Specified and misc. products	561	48.1
Total imports from Canada	37,766	50.0
(Excluding Auto Pact items)	(27,966)	(32.4)

Source: Data cited in US International Trade Commission, *Background Study of the Economies and International Trade Patterns of the Countries of North America and the Caribbean* (1-12-332- 119), Washington, D.C., September 1981.

The evidence on the existence of restrictions and
their potential economic impact suggests that the
contention, that Canadian subsidiaries do not export
more because they are "high cost," needs to be
examined industry by industry and firm by firm to
determine the relative importance of higher costs
and export restrictions (if any). While the Canadian
business environment (the tariff and other economic
policies) within which Canadian subsidiaries
operate has probably had a significant impact on
export performance through the cost structure, it is
difficult for a subsidiary to lower its costs if it cannot
obtain access to export markets because of arbitrary
export limitations. (p. 170)

It should be noted that aside from resource-based
industries only the transportation equipment sector
exports a large proportion of output. In other
industry groups the proportion of sales exported was
in the area of ten per cent. It is significant that the
only secondary manufacturing sector that is highly
export oriented is transportation equipment, where
government intervention in the form of the Auto
Agreement led to North American rationalization
and a rapid increase in exports. The Defense
Production Sharing Agreement — another example
of government intervention — also led to some
rationalization and increased exports. This
indicates that government intervention in the
foreign controlled sector can, in some circumstances,
help to promote the establishment of a sounder
industrial structure (involving both increased
exports and imports) and raises the question as to
what further steps the government could or should
take to gain what advantage it can from the nature
of the MNE (multinational enterprise) by
negotiating for the location of more rational
economic activity in Canada. (p. 176)

In 1979, 69 per cent of US-origin imports entered Canada
free of duty, with Auto Pact imports constituting around 32 per
cent of all imports from the United States. The difference
between the trade-weighted tariff rates on Canadian dutiable
imports (14.1 per cent) and on US dutiable imports (5.5 per cent)
reflects primarily the different stages of fabrication of the two

import bundles, a difference that is readily confirmed in the trade statistics. The Gray Report expresses Canadian concern about the procurement and import practices of US subsidiaries.[42] The Report notes that

> industries in which imports represent a high proportion of purchases have the following common characteristics: (1) a high degree of US ownership; (2) US parent companies that spend significant amounts on research and product innovation; (3) US parent companies that export a large proportion of sales; (4) Canadian exports that are low as a percentage of sales. (p. 188)[43]

A number of reasons were found for the high propensity of subsidiaries to import from parents and affiliates. These range from parental corporate strategy, the incremental costing of supplies produced from the parent's existing capacity and sunk costs, the protection of patents and the assurance of quality specifications, the timing of deliveries, and the benefits of bulk purchase by parents, to "non-economic" considerations such as inertia, union or government jaw-boning, tax concessions and Domestic International Sales Corporations (DISC), and the procurement restrictions of formal licensing agreements. The Report concedes that this behaviour is rational from the parent's point of view since "purchasing from incremental production probably leads to greater profits for the entire operation and reduces investment risks."[44] But it then shows that negative implications for the Canadian economy are involved.[45] Here again the Report sees a role for the intervention of the Canadian government in encouraging MNEs toward a beneficial rationalization of their procurement policy.

The pattern of Canada's trade in manufactured exports and imports, the high cost and low productivity of its secondary manufacturing industries, and the apparent untapped opportunities for scale economies, all must play a role in predicting Canada's comparative advantage under free trade, and yet they all reflect the activities, policies, and interests of US subsidiaries and their parent companies. Those who make assertions about the dramatic benefits to be obtained by Canadian industry from economies of scale resulting from removal of tariffs must come to grips with the interests of the parent companies and, in the framework proposed here, with the implications of reversing the migration effects of the two tariff systems.

It is generally acknowledged that the Canadian tariff is largely responsible for the number and significance of US subsidiaries engaged in secondary manufacturing in Canada for the local market. Without the Canadian tariff many of these subsidiaries – which are now characterized as having high concentration ratios, potential for economies of scale, high expenditures on R&D, and widespread utilization of managerial, clerical, and sales personnel and university-educated labour (with correspondingly high wages) – would not have been drawn into Canada. With removal of the tariff, some would be withdrawn so that the Canadian market could be serviced from production facilities in the United States. The importance of the potential disinvestment and emigration to total output and overall productivity in Canadian manufacturing has not been adequately treated in the recent literature, although it was the principal concern of a previous generation. It would, of course, severely limit the benefits of bilateral free trade if a reverse migration of tariff factories was concentrated in Canada's high-wage, high-technology, rapid-growth industries and was accompanied by an outflow of skilled labour.

Thomas Horst's 1972 analysis, entitled "The Industrial Composition of US Exports and Subsidiary Sales to the Canadian Market," has special relevance to the repatriation of R&D-intensive production.[46] He believes that US companies export and produce abroad on the basis of a technological advantage. His regression analysis suggests that US exports (Xi) and US subsidiary sales (Pi) by industry for the Canadian market are substitutes and that the proportion of exports to total sales (Xi/Xi + Pi) can be explained simply by the height of the Canadian tariff and the size of the Canadian market. If he is correct about the technological (R&D) basis of total US corporate sales in Canada and the crucial role of the tariff in limiting the proportion provided by exports from US-based plants, tariff removal could be associated with the loss to Canada of a large amount of R&D-intensive production.

In its 1978 report entitled *Canada's Trade Relations with the United States*, the Canadian Standing Senate Committee on Foreign Relations unearths a number of interesting responses regarding free trade from industry spokesmen.[47] The report, which incidentally favours a bilateral free trade agreement with the United States, contains a sensitive discussion of "the causes of relocation and disinvestment"[48] and concludes – on the issue of the repatriation of US branch plant production – that it is "the most serious risk of bilateral free trade" (p. 119). The committee records experiencing a defensive attitude toward tariff liberalization on the part of both Canadian companies and US subsidiaries, with the exception of the smallest. Reduced Canadian tariffs were seen as offering firms increased incentives to curtail investment in Canada and to relocate in the States.[49] Exporting firms were found to be already moving south to minimize risks and to protect access for their products to 90 per cent of the North American market.[50] Furthermore, the committee devotes considerable emphasis to the importance of R&D in the relocation decision. R&D expenditures by firms in Canada were shown, by international comparisons, to be very low. The number of patents recorded by Canadian nationals and residents were also shown to be relatively insignificant. Finally, the committee notes that R&D activities tend to cluster in a limited number of nodes, principally in the United States where there is a concentration of creative talent.[51]

Faced with tariff removal, most subsidiaries of US corporations would, in the short run, be expected to stay in Canada, rationalizing their product lines to secure a return on their existing Canadian investments by intracorporate specialization. They would, nevertheless, have a choice as to where to locate the plants producing manufactures most prone to economies of scale. These economies tend to be tied in with R&D and the labour skills that constitute Canada's comparative disadvantage, and tend to be less rooted in resource utilization.

There are other causes for concern. The Standing Senate Committee's report contains an intriguing map that shows the historical drift of the geographic centre of the US population in relation to a line drawn at a 500-mile distance from the Canadian border.[52] In 1970, the centre was already to the south of this line. Were one to throw in the population of Canada and compute the path traced by the centre of the North American population between 1950 and 1980, one could could see clearly that locational desirability *with respect to markets* of production facilities in Quebec and Ontario is a wasting asset.[53] The process of adjustment is slow due to sunk costs, but can one doubt that the shock effect of a free trade agreement would spur on the adjustment of more firms to the growth markets of the South and the West?

In contemplating new locations in Canada, firms will not only have to make judgements about how tariff removal will affect local market growth, they will also have to evaluate the post-free trade agreement border risks. With 90 per cent of the potential market lying to the south of the border, there is an obvious asymmetry in vulnerability to any subsequent reversal in the trade agreement or to certain types of non-tariff barriers that the US government might erect at some later date. Parent companies that locate plants along the US border to serve the Canadian market may increase the proportion of their production subject to reduced control because of government interference with business decisions, taxes, union-management relations, language requirements, etc. Such benefits of a US border location could, at least for some types of firms, outweigh the advantages that they might anticipate with a Canadian border location and the downward flexibility of the Canadian dollar.

Finally, it is worth remembering that long before the Canadian tariff induced the duplication of production facilities north of the boundary, the tariff served to maintain, in certain inefficient Canadian- owned enterprises, the use of capital and labour that would have otherwise moved to the United States. Simple economic models of free trade assume that production factors will be released to find employment in industries having higher productivity within the same country. The Canadian situation is unique not only because of the magnitude of the US subsidiary phenomenon, but also because the loss of protection that raised the returns and job opportunities for certain highly mobile labour skills may lead them to migrate.[54] This could apply particularly to the young and more recent graduates, but it would also apply to those of any age who would rather switch countries than jobs. On the other hand, removal of the US tariff might well cause some inefficient US producers to move to Canada for lower wage costs and some Canadian subsidiaries now in the United States to return home. Here again there is an asymmetry. Canadian subsidiaries in the United States have an established record of competitiveness in the large market, which those that moved north have not established. Furthermore, US producers have more options in the Third World open to them.[55] The direction of any net migration is clear; the amount and significance of the outmigration from Canada must be a prime cause for concern.

This review of the literature on the effects of bilateral free trade between Canada and the United States has emphasized the reversal of four effects – despecialization, scale, relocation, and migration – of the two tariff systems. And it casts some doubt on the size of the static benefits promised by R.J. Wonnacott's findings.

The use of "productivity parity" assumptions to estimate Canada's potential is thoroughly suspect, since this sort of parity is not achieved even between regions of the same country under conditions of high factor mobility. As an assumption, its usefulness depends heavily upon the industry mix, and even the process mix, of production being the same in the two countries. In the context of the rationalization of production patterns to conditions of free trade, it is apparent that these mix effects *must* differ. Just how they will differ cannot be derived from industry-by-industry comparisons of productivity, as was done in the preceding discussion of comparative advantage, because such comparisons do not simply reflect potential for economies of scale. Many producers in Canada could indeed achieve increases in productivity and economies of scale from the creation of a free trade area, but the realization of these economies would be confined to specific manufacturing processes that were consistent with the migration decisions of corporate decision makers and with Canada's relative factor and resource endowments. Any loss of output due to the departure of factors from Canada would reduce the static benefits of higher productivity that arose from the despecialization and scale effects.

To conclude that the case for bilateral free trade, based on substantial static benefits, has too optimistic a ring to it is not necessarily to defend the status quo. In Britain's decision to enter the European Economic Community, dynamic elements appeared to outweigh the rather small static benefits. One could make the case that the static costs of exclusion (although larger for Canada than for Britain) are small indeed compared to the dynamic costs of continued exclusion from its neighbours' large market at a time when the latter is undergoing a dramatic process of industrial reorientation.

The Impact of Free Trade on the Industrial Heartland

Production in Canada's industrial heartland area[56] is concentrated on durable manufactured goods, especially transportation equipment, rubber and plastics, metals, electrical and other machinery, and chemicals.[57] It does not produce much in the way of wood, food, tobacco, textile, and petroleum products.

Table 4.7 shows, for 1970, the importance of each two-digit manufacturing industry to Quebec and Ontario trade with the United States and to each province's manufacturing employment. A comparison of the three columns gives a quick impression of interprovincial differences in specialization and trading strengths. The bulk of provincial exports to the United States was provided by three industries: transportation equipment, primary metals, and paper products. In the US tariff-laden situation, with extensive intra-corporate trade, 67 per cent of

Ontario's exports and 59 per cent of Quebec's exports were accounted for by these three industries.

The differences between the employment structures of Ontario and Quebec reveal fundamental differences in provincial specialization that will have an important bearing on the impact of free trade. Ontario is more specialized in transportation equipment, primary metals, electrical products, machinery, and miscellaneous manufacturing, while Quebec is more specialized in clothing, textiles, and knitting, and paper and wood products.

As a first approximation, a province might be described as having an established trading strength with the United States in those industries (see the asterisks in Table 4.7) in which the share of exports to the United States exceeds the share of imports as well as the share of employment in manufacturing. On this basis, the wood products industry joins the three main export industries, and Ontario appears to have an additional trading strength in machinery. Quebec's apparent export strength in machinery, as in food and beverages and non-metallic minerals, is offset by the size of its import shares. While the number of Quebec industries meeting the export criteria may have grown during the 1970s, possibly to include electrical and telecommunications products, the relative trading strengths would not appear to be fundamentally different today.

Industry-by-industry ratios of provincial exports (X^{US}) to shipments and of imports (M^{US}) to provincial disappearance support these conclusions about provincial trading strengths and underscore the dependence of both provinces on US-origin imports from the machinery, textiles, miscellaneous, rubber, chemicals, and electrical products industries (Table 4.8). The implications of such interprovincial differences in industrial structure and trading strengths (especially once the data are more appropriately disaggregated) are that each province will be affected somewhat differently by reversing the despecialization and scale effects of the two tariff systems.[58]

With bilateral free trade certain Canadian industries will expand, others will contract. The provincial incidence of these impacts will certainly differ because the pattern of industrial specialization – the industry mix – differs between provinces. But at the same time free trade would bring about changes in provincial shares of particular industries – the provincial/competitive effect. Different growth rates of the same industry in different provinces is bound to accompany the reorientation of markets and the relocation and migration effects of removing the tariffs.

Table 4.7: Employment, Export, (X), and Import (M) Shares by Industry (Per cent), Ontario and Quebec, 1970

Industry		Quebec			Ontario		
		Emp. Shares	X Shares	M Shares	Emp. Shares	X Shares	M Shares
1.	Food and beverages	4.18	5.31	18.49	5.46	3.34	14.04
2.	Tobacco products	1.53	0.04	1.86	0.63	0.36	1.00
3.	Rubber products	1.27	0.46	1.40	2.13	0.52	2.14
4.	Leather	3.31	0.81	1.81	2.14	0.58	0.87
5.	Textiles	6.39	2.35	8.49	3.59	1.02	3.53
6.	Knitting mills	2.68	0.55	2.74	1.14	0.06	0.53
7.	Clothing	23.22 *	3.74	7.23	5.59	0.50	1.33
8.	Wood products	3.52 *	6.03	2.25	1.49 *	1.75	1.23
9.	Furniture and fixtures	2.56	0.99	2.15	2.08	0.62	1.50
10.	Paper and allied products	10.63 *	22.31	5.86	6.07 *	8.68	3.92
11.	Printing and publishing	1.13	0.60	3.76	1.86	0.32	3.92
12.	Primary metals	8.46 *	22.52	1.95	10.63 *	19.25	6.50
13.	Metal fabricating	5.00	2.76	6.65	6.95	2.71	9.10
14.	Machinery	2.38	3.13	4.52	7.58 *	9.05	8.33
15.	Transportation equipment	7.42 *	14.32	7.28	21.34 *	39.28	15.35
16.	Electrical products	6.39	5.86	5.93	10.16	5.16	8.13
17.	Non-metallic minerals	1.25	1.31	2.59	1.62	1.13	3.03
18.	Petro and coal products	0.15	0.06	4.57	0.08	0.08	2.56
19.	Chemical products	3.92	3.46	6.32	3.52	1.75	7.32
20.	Miscellaneous mfg.	4.60	3.38	4.14	5.96	3.87	5.66
	Total shares	100.00	100.00	100.00	100.00	100.00	100.00

Note: Shares of provincial exports to the United States, shares of direct provincial imports from the United States.

Source: Statistics Canada.

Table 4.8: Provincial Exports (Xi) to United States as a Percentage Share of Total Shipments (Si), and Imports from United States (Mi) as a Percentage Share of Total Provincial Disappearance (Di), by Industry, 1970

Industry		Quebec		Ontario	
		Xi/Si	Mi/Di	Xi/Si	Mi/Di
1.	Food and beverages	5.53	2.42	6.09	4.22
2.	Tobacco products	0.37	1.13	0.49	0.90
3.	Rubber products	4.01	9.60	4.85	15.00
4.	Leather	4.55	5.38	5.40	4.13
5.	Textile	1.77	10.37	3.24	14.15
6.	Knitting mills	2.29	3.48	0.80	3.73
7.	Clothing	2.80	1.04	2.58	3.30
8.	Wood products	21.13	5.81	14.78	10.57
9.	Furniture and fixtures	4.50	2.83	4.51	4.95
10.	Paper and allied products	37.00	4.80	31.89	8.95
11.	Printing and publishing	2.91	5.96	1.34	16.10
12.	Primary metals	34.02	10.32	23.67	14.48
13.	Metal fabricating	4.91	9.49	4.32	11.65
14.	Machinery	17.21	53.77	27.73	52.50
15.	Transportation equipment	36.29	34.99	73.24	69.84
16.	Electrical products	12.40	13.13	9.27	19.89
17.	Non-metallic minerals	7.55	7.30	6.66	13.03
18.	Petro and coal products	2.40	1.15	4.67	3.76
19.	Chemical products	9.94	16.00	6.59	18.30
20.	Miscellaneous Mfg.	9.53	34.09	10.45	30.86
	Total manufacturing	13.82	11.18	22.76	25.14

Note: "Provincial disappearance" consists of shipments less all exports plus all imports.

Source: From various special tabulations.

Correcting for industry mix effects involves extrapolations from the current pattern of industrial specialization in each province, using any evidence of the specialization effects of tariff removal for each Canadian industry *on the assumption that current provincial shares, by industry, are maintained*. Abstracting from the scale effects of tariff removal in this manner produces the following conclusions:

- Resource-intensive industries would *expand* somewhat under the impetus of new markets in the United States for the further processing of current resource exports. This would result in proportionately greater increases in the manufacturing output of Quebec.
- Significant *contractions* would be expected in the textile, leather, processed food, chemical, machinery, and miscellaneous products industries. Such contractions would have a proportionately larger impact on the manufacturing sector of Quebec.
- Certain import-competing industries would *expand* as their intermediate input costs fell with the removal of the Canadian tariff. In the post-Auto Pact situation, this growth might roughly approximate the current shares held by Ontario and Quebec in total manufacturing in Canada.

When one incorporates a correction for the scale effects of tariff removal, a dramatic relative increase appears in the static benefit for Ontario, accompanied by a less than equivalent decline (if any) for Quebec (because of the other provinces). This correction arises because of Ontario's relative trading strength in industries subject to economies of scale, as well as from the small size of Canadian establishments, compared to those of the United States, in such industries. One should remember that in Wonnacott's estimates 72 per cent of the national benefit was attributed to "scale effects." Of course, to the extent that Canada has to *share* the benefits of scale economies with the United States, due to the repatriation of subsidiaries in the most concentrated, oligopolistic industries, then Ontario's large advantage over Quebec related to the industry mix effect would be reduced.

Sizing up the relocation and migration effects of bilateral tariff removal involves reasoning less from provincial trading strengths and relative factor scarcities, and more from distances, market areas, patterns of ownership, and location strategies for various corporate functions. It appears likely that the static benefits of both provinces should be corrected downward to take account of the outmigration of managerial and research functions resulting from the shake-out that would accompany free trade in the "Great Lakes Megalopolis." But here again, provincial differences are to be expected.

The relocation and migration effects of tariff removal appropriately call into play provincial/competitive effects, which involve *removing the previous assumption of constant provincial share, by industry.* The first expectation, on removing this assumption, must be that Ontario, with its locational advantage, its apparent potential for economies of scale, and its initial dominance of trade with the United States,[59] would see its share of various industries grow. In this sense, the provincial/competitive effects would clearly favour Ontario relative to Quebec.

On the other hand, the fact that Ontario has been the favoured location for US subsidiaries,[60] and so much of its current trade flows are administered, means that Ontario's clear provincial/competitive advantage is peculiarly sensitive to decisions by head offices about the form of the rationalization of their various plants. The concentration of relatively inefficient US subsidiaries in Ontario, with widespread opportunities for scale economies, leaves in doubt which industrial processes will expand. Repatriation of only a few lines of production by a principal user of some intermediate products would have effects on the supplier of those products and on all other domestic users. There can be no certainty how much might unravel with the migration effects of free trade and with what effects on productivity in Ontario.

The undoubted locational advantages of southern Ontario in terms of distance and market potential both for Canadian firms and for US subsidiaries that produce in Canada should not be overstated, for they would be compromised under free trade by the loss of markets in eastern and western Canada, by the drift of the US market toward the South and West, by initial cost disparities in comparison with plants in the United States, by the amount of unused capacity south of the border, and by border risks that arise when 90 per cent of the market lies south of the border.

Dodging once again the question of the absolute size of the static benefits of free trade, this discussion of the different provincial implications of removing the despecialization, scale, relocation, and migration effects of the tariffs within the industrial heartland points to the following conclusions. The static benefits for Ontario would be substantially larger than these for Quebec due primarily to the scale and locational advantages of the former. Ontario would, however, be vulnerable to the loss of significant operations to the United States. The smaller static benefits that would emerge in Quebec might be further reduced by loss of operations to Ontario, to the extent that widespread productivity increases reduced the costs of production in that province. In sum, free trade appears to imply a further concentration of Canada's manufacturing sector in Ontario.

The expectation from the first principles of economics is that relative factor scarcities would then cause factor prices to change in the two provinces, directing firms to relocate more of their production in Quebec, or inducing yet more migration of labour from the latter. In the past the market response has proven relatively weak, whether because of the overriding importance of external economies, head office policy, Quebec's language policies, the drift of the North American market, or because of the maintenance of traditional wage parities in the face of changing interprovincial relative productivities. Here, of course, are the roots of a political problem for the Canadian government which seems inevitably to require a regional policy solution.

If the absolute size of the static, real-income benefits of bilateral free trade to each of these two provinces was large enough, the regional balance issue could be dismissed as not politically significant. But, if the static benefits appear to be low — and the analysis in this section supports this possibility — then the regional policy issue assumes some considerable importance. Furthermore, the discussion of static benefits overlooks what effects "tariff cash cost transfers" from the remaining provinces will have on the current *real* income (pre-free trade agreement) of these two provinces. The concept of cash cost transfers is developed in the next section. Once can say here, however, that income recipients in Ontario and Quebec are receiving indirectly, as producers and taxpayers, amounts in excess of the cash cost mark-ups they actually pay as a result of the Canadian tariff.[61]

In the light of these admittedly tentative conclusions, there appear to be sound reasons for Canadians to prefer specific sectoral arrangements as a means of pursuing free trade with the United States. These would permit their government not only to monitor the rationalization decisions of foreign subsidiaries, but also to achieve flexibility with respect to varying regional impacts. Since, in the absence of intervention, free trade in the industrial heartland seems to imply a greater concentration of Canada's manufacturing sector in Ontario, the Canadian government might be expected to pursue a sectoral approach that permits the promotion of an industrial strategy for Quebec. One might also hazard a guess that the core of such a strategy (a "third option" for Quebec) might involve the exploration of ways to enhance the long-run viability of that province's durables industry via sectoral trade arrangements between firms in Quebec and New England, making use of the province's advantages in hydropower.

The Perspective of the Atlantic Provinces[62]

Since the early days of Confederation, Maritimers (and since 1949, Newfoundlanders) have insisted that free trade is in their best interests. They protest that the Canadian tariff forces them to pay higher prices for the benefit of the residents of central Canada. Bilateral free trade with the United States, it is believed, would give the Atlantic Provinces an opportunity to buy their imported manufactured goods more cheaply, as well as a chance to market more of the products of their resource base to the eastern United States, thus increasing income and employment opportunities.

In considering first the consumption effects of the Canadian tariff on the Atlantic Provinces the concept of the *cash cost* of the Canadian tariff—the amount paid by the populace because the tariff prevents them from buying from the cheapest source—is a simple one to grasp, and Atlantic Canadians still rely on it. For the year 1970, the gross cash cost to final users was estimated at 4-5 per cent of personal income. With the recent reductions in tariffs and increases in incomes, the current figure would be substantially lower.[63] This cash cost was derived from Canadian tariffs against imports from all foreign sources, and it does not take into account the fact that tariff removal would raise the price of foreign goods through an associated devaluation of the Canadian dollar. Since the cash cost of the Canadian tariff represents roughly the same proportion of personal incomes in each region of the country, Atlantic Provinces frustration with the tariff is less with the size of the cash cost and much more with the distribution of the benefits of this implicit tax.

The beneficiaries of the extra costs paid by final users in Canada as a result of the tariff are the federal government if the goods are imported from abroad, and domestic producers (stockholders and employees) if the goods are produced in Canada. It can be safely assumed that government tariff revenues are returned to the provinces in some—perhaps varying – proportion to personal incomes in the form of government services and transfers. What then becomes of the provincial distribution of the cash cost component encompassed by the higher cost of domestically produced goods? These monies are received by producers, and their allocation among the provinces depends upon the provincial distribution of protected production in manufacturing.

Estimates for 1970 show that 32.2 per cent of manufactured goods used in the Atlantic Provinces were produced locally (L), 52.9 per cent came from interregional imports from the rest of Canada (M_R), and 14.9 per cent came from abroad (M_F).[64] Furthermore, 17.1 per cent of Atlantic Provinces manufacturing workers were employed by industries subject to tariff rates (duties to dutiable imports) of 17.5 per cent or higher. The figures for Quebec and Ontario were 40.0 per cent and 18.5 per cent, respectively. Clearly, little of the cash cost paid by Atlantic Provinces residents in the form of higher prices for Canadian-produced goods was received by Atlantic Provinces producers in their own much smaller manufacturing sector. When account was taken of the interregional transfers from Atlantic Provinces consumers to other Canadian producers, the Atlantic Provinces experienced an unrequited loss of 2 per cent of personal income, while Ontario and Quebec experienced a net benefit of, respectively, 1.1 per cent and 0.9 per cent of personal income.[65]

The introduction of bilateral free trade would indeed permit Atlantic Provinces consumers to buy many goods more cheaply from the United States and would force down the prices of Canadian producers, thereby reducing much of the cash cost of the tariff. However, since tariffs against third countries would remain in place, some cash cost and some unrequited transfers within North America would continue. The net gain probably would not exceed 3 per cent of personal income in the region.[66] While this is a sizeable gain (especially when translated into the present value of a stream of income increments into the future), it appears small beside the apparent 18 per cent per capita income disparity between this region and the neighbouring state of Maine (Table 1.4).

What then would be the production effects of removing the two tariff systems? Would this involve higher prices for products of the Atlantic Provinces, more job opportunities, higher productivity, and therefore higher incomes? Once again, the answer depends upon how one reads the repercussions of reversing the despecialization, scale, relocation, and migration effects of the tariffs.

The current pattern of production and employment reveals that the Atlantic Region is an open economy which specializes heavily in the production of primary products and depends upon imports for its use of secondary manufactured goods. In 1970-1973, a mere 12 per cent of employment was in manufacturing — 6 per cent in fishing-related manufactures, 3 per cent in food and fibre processing, 2 per cent in mining, and 1 per cent in forestry.[67] Of the 12 per cent in manufacturing, only 52 per cent were employed in secondary manufacturing compared to 83 and 88 per cent, respectively, in Ontario and Quebec. Figures for 1979, derived from Table 3.11, show that goods for local use (L*) represented approximately 45.2 per cent of the total production of manufactured goods.[68] The remainder of production was exported to other regions (X_R) or to other countries (X_F).

The concentration of the region's manufacturing employment in 1970 is apparent from the list of two-digit industries with more than 2,000 employees shown in Table 4.9. These six industries accounted for 80 per cent of employment in manufacturing. Five industries contributed almost 90 per cent of manufactured exports to foreign markets and 49 per cent of exports to the rest of Canada. Two industries — transportation equipment and primary metals — were more obviously oriented toward production for interregional distribution in Canada (X_R). As shown in Chapter 3, Atlantic Provinces exports to the United States in 1979 accounted for 60 per cent of the region's commodity exports, with fully 60 per cent of this taking the form of pulp and paper and fish products.[69]

Atlantic Provinces imports of manufactured goods are dominated by secondary manufactures from central Canada. As noted in the earlier discussion of consumption effects, only 32.2 per cent of manufactured goods used by the Atlantic Provinces themselves was produced locally in 1970, while 52.9 per cent was imported from other regions and 14.9 per cent was imported from abroad. How might this pattern of specialization be changed by the removal of the tariffs? Regionalization of the impacts of bilateral free trade set forth by the Economic Council of Canada offers a first impression of the implications of reversing the despecialization effects of the tariffs.[70] (The impression is, however, misleading in that it makes no pretense at covering the effects of scale economies, relocation, or migration.) This shows that Canada's export growth, or *expanding industries*, appears to lie in food and beverages, clothing, wood, and primary metals. Import growth, or *contracting industries*, appears to be electrical products, machinery, metal fabricating, textiles, and miscellaneous. The regionalization procedure suggested a net

Table 4.9: Percentage Shares of Employment and Exports (X) in Atlantic Provinces Manufacturing, 1970

	Share of Emp.	Horizontal Shares[a]		Vertical Shares[b]	
		X_R	X_F	X_R	X_F
Food and beverages	36.75	26.0	31.2	21.0	29.5
Paper and allied products	14.91	9.7	82.3	6.6	49.9
Transportation equip.	9.66	80.1	9.4	8.9	1.8
Wood products	9.10	15.6	20.0	1.9	3.4
Primary metals	6.10	49.4	28.2	10.5	5.1
Metal fabricating	4.16	31.5	5.2	1.0	0.5
Shown	80.86			49.9	90.2
Total	100.00	31.5	31.1	100.0	100.0

a   Horizontal shares: $L* + X_R + X_F = 100\%$, where $L*$ = local production, X_R = interregional exports, and X_F = foreign exports.

b   Vertical shares: Summations across all industries equal 100 per cent.

Source: Various special tabulations.
       See H. McA. Pinchin, *The Regional Impact of the Canadian Tariff* (Ottawa: Economic Council of Canada, 1979).

increase in the Atlantic Provinces of a mere 233 manufacturing jobs, with gross employment increments only in the food and beverage industry.

As previously noted, this trade-based exercise is severely flawed, both as an indicator of regional comparative advantage in trade with the United States and as a guide to the implications of removing the despecialization effects of the tariffs. The actual pattern of pre-free trade agreement trade, while it reveals something about industry-by- industry trading strengths, also reflects both ownership patterns and trade subject to the exclusion of products where tariffs have had their prohibitive effects. Even the tariff rates used are trade-weighted averages, which reflect the non-effect of the tariffs. Having looked at Atlantic Provinces exports to the United States and the pattern of employment and specialization in the region's manufacturing sector, it is readily apparent that products could be upgraded or further processed in Canada where low US tariffs (or quotas) have represented very high levels of effective protection for the US processing industry. Further processing could bring significant increases in the value of exports not encompassed in the Economic Council's study but clearly in line with the region's comparative advantage. Increased employment and productivity would be expected, for instance, in upgrading current exports of fish blocks, wood pulp, wood, and primary metals. The installation of production facilities to advance such a step would enhance the region's capacity to corner more of the Canadian market for finished, resource-intensive products. Any conclusions about the expansion of Atlantic Provinces production of resource-intensive products under bilateral free trade, however, must be predicated upon optimistic assumptions concerning the supply elasticities of these industries and on a favourable interpretation of the costs involved in processing so far from the principal markets. In the British Columbia study previously cited (1971),[71] J.H. Young's conclusion in this regard about the B.C. case is guarded:

> The extent to which removal of foreign tariffs would encourage the processing of primary products within the Province is hard to determine. All that can be said at present is that we have encountered less concrete evidence than we expected at the outset. What can be said is that guaranteed free entry would be a major source of encouragement for firms to search for opportunities of this kind, and no doubt

some unsuspected possibilities would be brought to
light. (p. 86)

Shearer's conclusion in the same study is more direct: "We have
not been able to estimate possible gains from the expansion of
export-oriented manufacturing and from the establishment of
new export industries. We suspect these would be minor" (p.
201). Haviland, *et al.*, studied the prospects for different tariff-
protected grades of paper under free trade.[72] They suggest that
producers in eastern Canada with the ideal technology and scale
could compete in the Northeast, but that they would experience
marketing problems since distribution channels are controlled by
US companies.

Extrapolations from existing Canadian imports to indicate
the prospects for US exports to the Atlantic Provinces involve the
same kind of underestimation. In Canada certain sectors
considered highly vulnerable are highly protected (for example,
poultry processors, breweries, dairies, and bakeries), and these
industries are of considerable interest to the Atlantic Provinces.
Thus, the increases in both imports and exports resulting from
bilateral free trade should far surpass those reflected in the
Economic Council's study.

Free trade with the United States would be expected to
bring with it a major reorientation of Atlantic Provinces exports
and imports away from the rest of Canada and toward the
proximate northeast region of the United States. Although
subject to the weakness of actual trade as an indicator of
potential changes, a brief survey of the pattern of Atlantic
imports (1970) follows. Table 4.10 ranks eight two-digit
manufacturing industries according to the value of Atlantic
Provinces imports from the United States (M_{US}).[73] In addition,
the importance of these products in relation to total imports to
the Atlantic Provinces from the rest of Canada (M_R) is shown.
The dollar value of M_{US} is, of course, small compared to that of
M_R. The table also shows for these selected industries the
horizontal shares of local use of local production (L) and local use
of imports from the rest of Canada (M_R).

These eight industries accounted for 90 per cent of the
Atlantic Region's imports from the United States which entered
around or over the Canadian tariff, and they accounted for 68 per
cent of the region's imports from the rest of Canada. Under free
trade, US producers in the Northeast might supplant the
producers of central Canada in servicing Atlantic markets,
especially where Canadian tariffs are higher than US tariffs and
where the horizontal M_R share is high in the Atlantic Provinces,

Table 4.10: Percentage Shares of Atlantic Provinces Imports and Local Use, by Industry, 1970

Industry	Vertical Shares [a]		Horizontal Shares [b]	
	M_{US}	M_R	L	M_R
Machinery	43.6	4.5	3.6	36.8
Transportation equipment	15.7	7.3	35.7	38.3
Metal fabricating	7.8	10.5	25.3	64.5
Miscellaneous	6.3	3.6	12.6	67.6
Food and beverages	5.6	20.2	55.7	37.4
Electrical products	5.1	10.3	8.8	82.9
Chemicals & allied products	3.5	9.1	17.7	74.8
Textiles	2.9	3.2	8.7	68.7
Total shown	90.5	68.7		
Grand total	100.0	100.0	32.2	52.9

[a]   Vertical shares of imports from the United States and interregional imports, by industry.

[b]   Horizontal shares of Altantic Provinces disappearance (production for local use plus all imports): $L + M_R + M_F = 100\%$, where L = local production, M_R = imports from rest of Canada, and M_F = foreign imports; M_{US} = imports from the United States.

Sources: Various special tabulations.
See H. McA. Pinchin, *The Regional Impact of the Canadian Tariff* (Ottawa: Economic Council of Canada, 1979).

as in electric products, chemicals, textiles, miscellaneous, and metal fabricating. But, from the perspective of Atlantic Provinces producers, what is important is that import substitution for local production might threaten employment in these industries as well as in such small and vulnerable industries as leather, knitting mills, and furniture.

These vulnerable industries account for a small proportion of domestic employment, however. Thus, removing the despecialization effects *per se* of the tariffs on vulnerable Atlantic Provinces industries might turn out to be of less importance to local per capita income than the reversal of the relocation and migration effects of the tariffs. Faced with the challenge of free trade, secondary manufacturers in vulnerable sectors might see the advantage of locating production facilities inside the US border through mergers, acquisitions, and investments to command larger market areas. R&D-oriented producers might be attracted to the Boston area. Moving south of the border might be particularly attractive to those foreign subsidiaries, US and other, for whom the Canadian tariff provided the principal reason for their current location. Corporate rationalization of multi-plant firms under free trade might be expected to reduce the attractiveness of Atlantic Provinces locations, except for resource-intensive industries, due to distance, market potential, and the need to acquire economies of scale.

The traditional Atlantic Provinces perception that free trade would permit the region to buy in a cheaper market and sell its resources in a manner that increases real incomes is, therefore, as true as it ever was. The gains from bilateral free trade resulting from *consumption* effects might amount to as much as 3 per cent of personal incomes. But would the restructuring of the region's manufacturing sector for bilateral free trade bring further increases in incomes from increased factor productivity?

Any rise in incomes from increased resource extraction would be miniscule because of the inelasticity of supply curves and the dominance of world prices, before and after any trade agreement. Incomes would increase only where there has been negative effective protection. The extent to which the growth of *further processing* for the US market would serve to increase incomes in the Atlantic Provinces is unknown. The combination of advantages such as access to electricity, pulp, fish, iron ore, offshore gas, coal, and port facilities suggests that the region has a potential that requires only the removal of US tariffs to be realized. On the other hand, the market power of the established US producers of brand name products, built upon their vast advertising and distribution systems, would probably result in the acquisition of some Canadian resource companies, leaving the processing decisions to be allocated according to existing incremental productivities arising out of sunk costs both in the present companies and in their auxiliary suppliers.

Free trade, therefore, offers no panacea for increased incomes and employment in the Atlantic Provinces. While incomes would increase for those involved, directly and indirectly, in the further processing of resources, such increases would have to be spectacular to raise the average productivity of all income recipients. The regional multiplier effects are, after all, bound to be small in such an open regional economy, and there are then the offsetting influences of the relocation and migration effects on incomes. It seems unlikely that tariff removal would attract many firms in market-oriented industries into the region, and the reverse flow out of the region would serve to reduce employment opportunities, creating an inducement for labour to migrate or a drag on the wage and salary scales of employees at all levels, but particularly professional, technical, managerial, and sales personnel. The net effect on incomes (and employment) from greater resource specialization, at least in the absence of a coordinated regional and industrial strategy, might at best be negligible.

This conclusion is at odds with traditional perceptions in the Atlantic Provinces about the unmitigated benefits of free trade, but it is consistent with Shearer's conclusions about the effects of free trade on British Columbia. In both peripheral regions, free trade is popular and appears politically viable. The reasons for this popular appeal derive from the obvious benefits of "trade reversion" – the substitution of US for extraregional Canadian markets as sources of supply. These benefits appear to require only modest reorganization of the pattern of productive activity, while in Quebec and Ontario, where the potential benefits of free trade based on location and economies of scale in secondary manufacturing are that much greater, the general public appears cowed into skepticism by the extensive industrial reorganization that might be necessary.[74] The static benefits of unrestricted bilateral free trade could be large, but they would tend to be highly concentrated within the industrial heartland.

Notes

1. In 1979, only 5 per cent of total Canadian imports from the United States came from New England. Exports from Quebec and the Atlantic Provinces to New England amounted to only 4.3 per cent of Canada's total exports to the United States.

2. Effective protection relates the tariff on an industry's inputs to the tariff on its output. The effective rate of protection shows the percentage mark-up on domestic value added per unit of shipments that is facilitated by a given nominal tariff.

3. The static burden might, of course, be considered an acceptable cost in terms of a long list of other benefits such as defence, independence, diversification against instability, regional balance, or other such socio-political ends.

4. The US Trade Act of 1974 stated that "it is the sense of the Congress that the United States should enter into a trade agreement with Canada" and that "the President may initiate negotiations" for an agreement. The Trade Agreements Act of 1979 reaffirms the 1974 resolution but then calls on the president to "study the desireability of entering into such an agreement" and to report on his "findings and conclusions" by July 1981. A broad review of current trade relations is contained in US International Trade Commission, *Background Study of the Economies and International Trade Patterns of the Countries of North America and the Caribbean* (1-12-332-119), Washington D.C., September 1981.

5. R.J. Wonnacott and P. Wonnacott, *Free Trade Between the United States and Canada, the Potential Economic Effects* (Cambridge: Harvard University Press, 1967); R.J. Wonnacott, *Canada's Trade Options*, Economic Council of Canada (Ottawa: Information Canada, 1975); R.J. Wonnacott, Controlling Trade and Foreign Investment in the Canadian Economy: Some Proposals, *Canadian Journal of Economics* (November 1982); and P. Wonnacott and R.J. Wonnacott, Free Trade Between the United States and Canada: Fifteen Years Later, *Canadian Public Policy*, Supplement VIII (October 1982).

6.   J.R. Williams, *The Canadian-United States Tariff and Canadian Industry* (Toronto: University of Toronto Press, 1978).

7.   Economies of scale are elsewhere referred to as economies of market size, which include both economies in production and distribution as well as economies external to the firm. Wonnacott, *Canada's Trade Options*, pp. 14-15.

8.   Wonnacott, *Canada's Trade Options*, pp. 177-181.

9.   Wonnacott directs the reader to an appendix "for reasons why productivity in Canada could rise with free trade to the United States level." It contains an abridged version of Wonnacott and Wonnacott, *Free Trade Between the United States and Canada*. In this appendix, he studies "the various locational forces that cause a firm to choose a particular location" in North America — in other words, the very forces that account for the size of any migration and relocation effects.

10.   Wonnacott, *Canada's Trade Options*, pp. 177-181.

11.   In *Free Trade* (Wonnacott and Wonnacott, pp. 297-304), of the 10.5 per cent of GNP obtainable from tariff removal, they attributed 4.0-4.5 per cent to the burden of the Canadian tariff and the remainder to the impact of the US tariff on Canadian incomes.

12.   Economic Council of Canada, *Looking Outward, a New Trade Strategy for Canada* (Ottawa: Information Canada, 1975) (hereafter cited as *Looking Outward*); Harry H. Postner, *Factor Content of Canadian International Trade: An Input-Output Analysis*, Economic Council of Canada (Ottawa: Information Canada, 1975).

13.   Bruce W. Wilkinson, A First Approximation to Free Trade Alternatives for Canada, in *Canada in a Wider Economic Community*, edited by H.E. English, Bruce W. Wilkinson, and H.C. Eastman (Toronto: University of Toronto Press, 1972) Ch. 4.

14.   *Looking Outward*, p. 168. The loss in manufacturing RDP came out as 1.69 per cent and the loss of overall employment was 0.32 per cent. My objections to this

procedure can be found in H. McA. Pinchin, *The Regional Impact of the Canadian Tariff*, Economic Council of Canada, (Ottawa: Information Canada, 1979) pp. 78-81.

15.   Postner, *Factor Content*, pp. 40 and 68. A very convenient list of ninety-seven of Canada's industries ranked by tariff level, resource intensity, and labour intensity is included as Appendix B in *Looking Outward* (pp. 200-203).

16.   These conclusions are derived from J.R. Williams, *Resources, Tariffs and Trade: Ontario's Stake* (Toronto: Ontario Economic Council, 1976) Table II, p. 60. Williams found a correlation coefficient of -.315 across eighty commodities for the weighted average tariff in Canada less that of the United States as against the commodity's resource content. He found a coefficient of .274 for the same tariff difference against wage costs per commodity. At the 10 per cent level of significance, the critical r value is .186.

17.   G.D.A. MacDougall, British and American Exports: A Study Suggested by the Theory of Comparative Costs, *Economic Journal* (December 1951). The technique is applied to Canada-US data in M.E. Kreinin, The Theory of Comparative Cost — Further Empirical Evidence, *Economia Internationale* (1969) pp. 662-673.

18.   James G. Frank, *Assessing Trends in Canada's Competitive Position: The Case of Canada and the United States* (Ottawa: Canadian Conference Board, 1977) p. 66.

19.   R.S. Saunders, The Political Economy of Effective Tariff Protection in Canada's Manufacturing Sector, *Canadian Journal of Economics* (May 1980) p. 346.

20.   P.-P. Proulx, L. Dulude, and Y. Rabeau, Etude des relations commerciales Quebec-USA, Quebec-Canada, options et impacts, constraintes et potentiels," Ministère des affaires intergouvernementales, Gouvernement du Québec 1979.

21.   Williams, *The Canadian-United States Tariff*, p. 33. Notice that the data for this study pre-date the Auto Pact and that Williams adds (on p. 34) the apparent qualification that "with the exception of textiles,

chemicals, food and agriculture there would be a general shift toward end product production in free trade."

22. Unfortunately, Williams reports neither the effective tariff rates (two sets) nor the counterfactual pattern of trade for his industries. Moreover, the difference in dates renders fruitless any direct comparison by industry.

23. Williams actually bases his conclusions on a "discriminant analysis" involving sixteen expanding and sixteen contracting industries (pp. 24-27).

24. Wonnacott, *Canada's Trade Options*, p. 196.

25. Wonnacott, *Canada's Trade Options*, p. 178.

26. This literature, which springs from J.H. Young, Some Aspects of Canadian Economic Development, unpublished Ph.D. dissertation, Cambridge University (1955) and from the work of H.C. Eastman and S. Stykolt (*The Tariff and Competition in Canada* (New York: St. Martins Press, 1967) is well summarized in Wonnacott, *Canada's Trade Options*, p. 19.

27. Since free trade in North America would not be accompanied by monetary unification, and considerable immobility of land and labour between the two economies would remain, Wonnacott's question does not bypass the need for reviewing the basic pattern of Canada's comparative advantage.

28. Paul R. Krugman, Increasing Returns, Monopolistic Competition and International Trade, and J. Eaton and A. Panariya, Gains From Trade under Variable Returns to Scale, Commodity Taxation and Factor Market Distortions, *Journal of International Economics* (November 1979) pp. 469-501.

29. This author is grateful to Harry Postner for permission to use his unpublished data.

30. H.G. Baumann, The Pattern of Interregional Trade in Canada, mimeographed, October 1975.

31. G.C. Hufbauer, The Impact of National Characteristics and Technology on the Commodity Composition of Trade in Manufactured Goods, *The Technology Factor in International Trade*, edited by R. Vernon (New York: National Bureau of Economic Research, 1970).

32. Pinchin, *The Regional Impact*, pp. 118-129.

33. The critical value for these simple correlations, at the 5 per cent level, is r = .16.

34. Pinchin, *The Regional Impact*, pp. 122-123.

35. *Newsweek* (March 24, 1980) predicted that the 1980 census will result in a loss of as many as nine congressional seats in a decade for the "Industrial Triangle" of the United States.

36. See *Wall Street Journal*, October 18, 1983, p. 35. The map is taken from the work of Calvin Beale, head of population studies at the US Department of Agriculture.

37. See Saunders, The Political Economy of Effective Tariff Protection, p. 346.

38. A theoretical framework using Hoover-Isard margin lines for delivered prices is developed for this purpose by Gordon Monro. See R.A. Shearer, J.H. Young, and G.R. Monro, *Trade Liberalization and a Regional Economy: Studies of the Impact of Free Trade in British Columbia*, (Toronto: University of Toronto Press, 1971) pp. 102-115.

39. Short-term relocation decisions will involve long-term market projections that take account of the continental drift of economic activity to the South and West.

40. This conclusion is supported by the findings of Prem P. Ghandi, The Effect of Free Trade on Northern New York, *1973-74 Papers and Proceedings*, Vol. VI, New York State Economics Association, pp. 47-63.

41. Government of Canada, *Foreign Direct Investment in Canada* (The Gray Report) (Ottawa: Information Canada, 1972) p. 21. (Hereafter cited as *Foreign Direct Investment in Canada*.) The proportions are somewhat lower today

(1983), partly as a result of the Canadian government's own policy responses to the Gray Report. Current data and foreign investment policy issues are discussed in Chapter 7.

42.   The Report found that from 1964 to 1969 US subsidiaries in Canada, aside from the auto companies, imported 23 per cent of their merchandise purchases and a larger proportion of their services purchases. Seventy per cent of these merchandise imports came from parents and affiliates. The percentage of merchandise purchases imported was higher than for US subsidiaries elsewhere. Specifically, the percentage was high in the areas (again, aside from automobiles) of machinery, electrical products, chemicals, and miscellaneous manufacturing and low in resource-based industries.

43.   All of this tended to confirm the Report's conclusion that the development of a "distinctive capacity" — perhaps through research and development — gives a company the ability to penetrate a foreign market *either* through exports or through foreign direct investment, but where the latter approach permits entry into the foreign market in minimal form with a number of strategic activities retained by the parent.

44.   *Foreign Direct Investment in Canada*, p. 201.

45.   See *Foreign Direct Investment in Canada*. Sourcing decisions made on the basis of incremental cost considerations are short-run decisions which make the fullest possible use of productive capacity already in place. In the longer run it is generally to the parent's advantage to expand production where it is most economic, or to buy at arms length if this is cheaper. This might not occur, however, in industries where competitive pressures are not great because of oligopoly, or where non-economic biases induce parents to produce or purchase from suppliers in their home market (p. 207). The procurement practices of parents and subsidiaries within vertically integrated structures represent a barrier to entry for any potentially efficient Canadian supplier, thus tending to prevent lower costs and maintain a truncation in the Canadian supply industry (p. 202). The savings realized by the parent from internal sources of supply, as a result of low incremental

costs, need not then be reflected in the prices paid by either the Canadian subsidiary or by the Canadian purchasers of the finished goods involved.

46. Thomas Horst, The Industrial Composition of US Exports and Subsidiary Sales to the Canadian Market, *American Economic Review* (March 1972) pp. 37-45.

47. Canada, Standing Senate Committee on Foreign Relations, *Canada's Trade Relations with the United States*, Vol. II in *Canada-United States Relations* (Ottawa: Queen's Printer, 1978). (Hereafter cited as *Canada's Trade Relations*.)

48. *Canada's Trade Relations*, pp. 26-31.

49. *Canada's Trade Relations*, pp. 29, 117, 119.

50. *Canada's Trade Relations*, p. 30.

51. *Canada's Trade Relations*, pp. 20, 26, 54-60. In 1974, Canadian nationals and residents filed only 5.7 per cent of the patents filed in Canada. The corresponding figure for US patents filed in the United States was 69.5 per cent (p. 54).

52. The Committee's observation on this is: "As purchasing power and industry moves towards the South-West, selling to the US market and serving it from Canada will become increasingly difficult and costly. It is little wonder that many Canadian companies anxious to profit from this large and fast growing market throughout the south and west of the United States have established or expanded production and service facilities across the border" (pp. 30-31).

53. J.H.N. Britton, Locational Perspectives on Free Trade for Canada, *Canadian Public Policy* (Winter 1978) pp. 4-18. Also see the relative growth picture evidenced in Figure 4.1.

54. R.E. Caves and R.H. Holton argue that "the threat of heavy labour migration to the United States, taken in connection with the low labour intensity of Canada's major export industries, gives the Canadian tariff a clearer

justification than that of almost any other nation." *The Canadian Economy* (Cambridge: Harvard University Press, 1959) p. 67.

55.   It is well known that bilateral free trade would cause at least some trade diversion by allocating some low-productivity activities to Canada that belong more appropriately to the Third World.

56.   The industrial heartland referred to here includes the Canadian industrial centres along the Windsor-Quebec City "axis" and the US industrial centres of Illinois, Indiana, and Wisconsin (the West Lake Region); the centres of Michigan and Ohio (the East Lake Region); and the northern part of the Mid-Atlantic Region, that is, only the northern and central parts of New York and Pennsylvania, excluding both the southern portion of these states as well as the whole of New Jersey and Connecticut. This area encompasses more than a third of the North American population (roughly 80 million people), but its share of manufacturing output is much higher.

57.   In 1978, 60 per cent of US manufacturing employment was in durable goods production, but in Michigan, for instance, the figure was 80 per cent, and in Indiana it was 77 per cent.

58.   The reversal of the other two effects is addressed later in this section.

59.   Ontario exports to the United States 80 per cent of its total exports whereas the same figure for Quebec is only 56 per cent.

60.   The percentage of taxable income of foreign-owned corporations in manufacturing in 1965-1968 attributable to Ontario was 58.2 per cent; to Quebec, 23.7 per cent, and to the Atlantic Provinces, 2.7 per cent. *Foreign Direct Investment in Canada*, p. 24.

61.   Estimates of the size of these interprovincial cash cost transfers depend on the assumptions used. This author's findings for 1970 suggest net receipts for residents of Ontario of 1.1 per cent of personal income and 0.97 per cent for residents of Quebec (Pinchin, *The Regional Impact*, pp.

31-49). See also Ontario, Ministry of Treasury and Economics, Interprovincial Trade Flows, Employment, and the Tariff in Canada, Supplementary material to the 1977 Ontario budget, April 1977.

62.   Some 2.2 million people live in this part of Canada, or about the same number of people who live in the neighbouring states of Maine and New Hampshire. Wages, productivity, and per capita income in the region are low. In 1981, personal income per capita was 73 per cent of the Canadian average, 67 per cent of the US average, and 76 per cent of that of Maine and New Hampshire (see Table 1.4).

63.   Pinchin, *The Regional Impact*, pp. 31-49. This approach was first used by N. McL. Rogers in *A Submission on Dominion Provincial Relations and the Fiscal Disabilities of Nova Scotia within the Canadian Federation*, Halifax, 1934.

64.   Pinchin, *The Regional Impact*, Ch. 2 and p. 150.

65.   Pinchin, *The Regional Impact*, p. 48. All figures are uncorrected for changes in the value of the Canadian dollar.

66.   In their study of British Columbia under free trade, Shearer, *et. al.* estimate the cash cost rebate at 5.2 per cent of personal income (*Trade Regionalization*, p. 201). Their figures for 1963 (which pre-date the publication of official interregional trade data, the Auto Pact, and the Kennedy Round) are substantially higher than this author's estimates for 1970 (Pinchin, *The Regional Impact*, Ch. 3).

67.   Auer, L., *Regional Disparities of Productivity and Growth*, Economic Council of Canada (Ottawa: Information Canada, 1979) p. 178. (See also Table 1.10.)

68.   From Table 3.11, in 1979 manufacturing production of the Atlantic Provinces was distributed (per cent) as follows:

	L*	X_R	X_F	
1979 Manufacturing	45.23	23.89	30.88	100.00

Similar estimates for 1970 in the areas of manufacturing, mining, and forestry were:

Manufacturing	37.37	31.50	31.13	100.00
Mining	20.30	15.00	64.70	100.00
Forestry	76.80	7.70	15.50	100.00

The 1970 estimates are from Pinchin, *The Regional Impact*, p. 156.

69.   Tables 3.7 and 3.8 show the details of Atlantic Provinces exports to New England. They include food and beverages, mostly fish products, 4.4 per cent; wood chips and ores, 3 per cent; fabricated materials, including wood pulp, electricity, petroleum and coal products, lumber, and newsprint, 50 per cent; and end products, only 3 per cent.

70.   Pinchin, *The Regional Impact*.

71.   Shearer, *et al.*, *Trade Regionalization*.

72.   W.E. Haviland, N.S. Takacsy, and E.M. Cape, *Trade Liberalization and the Canadian Pulp and Paper Industry* (Toronto: University of Toronto Press, 1969).

73.   This exercise is subject to all the limitations of the first-destination recording of imports.

74.   Shearer, *et al.*, *Trade Regionalization*, pp. 202-203.

5: ENERGY FLOWS: PAST PRESENT, AND FUTURE

W.D. Shipman

Energy Trade Patterns from World War II to 1982

The northeastern states have long had close ties with the eastern Canadian provinces in matters of energy. Power development at Niagara Falls and on the St. Lawrence River has for many years been coordinated to obtain maximum benefits. This has been accomplished through formal treaties and, in some cases, joint construction and operation. The earliest of the major US-Canadian power ties at Niagara Falls permitted the exchange of surplus energy and provided back-up capacity, thus strengthening both the New York and Ontario systems. Even today this tie is the major entry point into the United States for Ontario electric energy. To the east, the St. Lawrence Project has been providing electric energy to both Ontario and New York since 1958, as well as a minor amount to Vermont through the lines of the Power Authority of the State of New York (PASNY).[1]

Quebec has been exporting electricity to the northeastern United States for many years, but only relatively small quantities were involved before the 1970s. During the 1970s, imports increased substantially, from less than 200 million kilowatt-hours (kWh) annually to more than 800 million.[2] Completion of the direct, high-voltage line linking Hydro-Quebec and PASNY in 1978 resulted in a further jump, and by 1980 the export total was in excess of 8 billion kWh.[3] Moreover, the export total now included seasonally firm (from April to October) as well as surplus energy.[4] All but a small fraction (less than 5 per cent) of this energy went to New York; the balance was distributed among several New England states. (The post-1980 expansion of Canadian exports to New England is detailed shortly.) Quebec also relays minor amounts of Canadian natural gas and petroleum products to New England, as will be discussed later.

On the New England side, large flows of foreign crude oil have been transmitted from Portland, Maine to Montreal refineries via the Portland Pipeline. Smaller quantities of oil products, especially gasoline and residual oil, have come into

141

New England coastal ports from refineries located in the Atlantic Provinces. Even prior to planning for the St. Lawrence Project, feasibility studies were undertaken for tidal power development in Passamaquoddy Bay, lying between Maine and New Brunswick. These studies did not produce positive results, but New England did begin to import electric energy on a significant scale from New Brunswick in the early 1970s, and by 1980 the total southward flow approximated 4 billion kWh.[5] Since New Brunswick has imported perhaps 30 per cent of its electric energy supply from Quebec in recent years,[6] it is reasonable to assume that, in a physical sense, some of that Quebec energy also found its way into New England.

Table 5.1 shows a breakdown of energy imports to New England from eastern Canada in 1978.[7] (New England energy *exports* to Canada are insignificant save for the above-mentioned Portland-Montreal pipeline which conveys overseas crude oil northward.) It shows that liquid fuels, especially gasoline, and electricity were the dominant forms. All but a very small fraction (3 per cent) of the electric energy imported came from New Brunswick. While the high-voltage Maine- New Brunswick line originally carried surplus power from the Mactaquac project on the Saint John River, since 1976 most of the energy has originated (in a legal or contractual, if not physical, sense) from generating units using imported oil at the Coleson Cove station near Saint John. Since 1982, the line has also been used to convey nuclear-generated power from the Point Lepreau plant.

Table 5.2 shows year-to-year variations in quantities for each of the major product components between 1971 and 1981. Within the oil products category, gasoline moving into Boston from refineries in the Atlantic Provinces and fuel oil (both distillate and residual) entering New England more broadly appear to be of greatest importance.[8] It is clear that there is considerable variability in these flows, however, and some reason to believe that such variation is attributable primarily to fluctuations in residual oil purchases by New England utilities and industry. Over the period in question, output from Canadian refineries first increased in importance, and then was displaced, probably by a combination of alternative sources of residual oil and the expanding use of nuclear power. (Nuclear generation grew from 14 per cent of total New England electric output in 1972 to 34 per cent in 1981; the proportion has since been fairly stable.[9]) During the years under consideration, there also was a substantial volume of propane coming across the Canadian boundary into New England, much of it destined for gas distribution systems in the northern tier states.

Table 5.1: Energy Imports from Eastern Canada to New England, 1978

	Quantity	Value (thousand $ US)	
Oil products, by type (thousand bbl)			
Fuel oils	832	11,594	
Gasoline	2,538	41,508	
Propane and butane	811	9,454	
Jet fuel and kerosene	436	6,513	
Miscellaneous products		18	
Total	4,617	69,084	$69,084
Oil products, by customs district (thousand bbl)			
Portland	999	14,697	
St. Albans	844	10,153	
Boston	2,167	34,450	
Providence	60	1,016	
Bridgeport	547	8,768	
Total	4,617	69,084	
Natural gas (thousand mcf)			
Quebec	4,224	8,200	8,200
Electricity (million kWh)			
New Brunswick	2,552	76,317	
Quebec	109	2,099	
Total	2,661	78,416	78,416
			$155,700

Note: bbl = barrels, mcf = thousand cubic feet.

Sources: US Bureau of the Census (Foreign Trade Division).
Vermont Public Service Board.
New Brunswick Electric Power Commission.
Canadian National Energy Board.

Table 5.2: Energy Shipments to New England from Eastern Canada, 1971-1981

	1971	1972	1973	1974	1975	1976	1977	1978	1979	1980	1981
Oil products (thousand bbl)											
Fuel oils[a]	3,000	14,208	15,082	9,262	3,539	1,999	1,138	832	8512	106	4,481
Gasoline		455	1,872	71	952	188	1,102	2,538	2,655	1,326	1,585
Propane and butane	1,319	1,207	1,206	887	1,131	1,063	1,457	811	967	1,291	1,475
Jet fuel and kerosene	17	79	405	1		124	837	436	7	7	143
Miscellaneous					2		1			6	4
Total	4,336	15,949	18,565	10,221	5,624	3,374	4,535	4,617	4,474	2,736	7,688
Natural gas (thousand mcf)	2,810.	3,745	3,912	4,891	4,124	4,066	4,263	4,224	4,543	4,224	4,589
Electricity (million kWh)				2,573	1,705	2,470	4,087	2,661	4,066	4,210	3,596

a   Includes minor amounts of crude oil (Rhode Island) prior to 1973.

Sources: Canadian National Energy Board.
US Bureau of the Census.

Natural gas imports arrive in Vermont by a branch line from Quebec connecting with the main Trans-Canada pipeline near Montreal. This connection, which has been in existence since 1966, carries small but significant amounts of natural gas to communities in northwestern Vermont served by Vermont Gas Systems, Inc.[10] Table 5.3 shows annual volumes and the price paid at the Canadian border for natural gas imported by this system. The significant feature of this table is the column showing the export price charged by Canada; that price increased from less than $1.00 per thousand cubic feet (mcf) in the early 1970s to $4.94 (US) in 1981. It has since declined moderately.

Table 5.3: **Canadian Natural Gas Exports to Vermont, 1971-1983**

	Export Volume (thousand mcf)	Price Paid at Boundary ($ US/mcf)
1971	2,820	
1972	3,745	
1973	3,912	
1974	4,891	1.00
1975	4,125	1.00-1.60
1976	4,066	1.60-2.10
1977	4,263	2.10-2.16
1978	4,224	2.16
1979	4,543	2.16-3.45
1980	4,224	3.45-4.47
1981	4,589	4.47-4.94
1982	4,518	4.94
1983	4,610	3.40-4.40 [a]

a   Since July 1983, the incentive price for quantities in excess of the "base" amount (equals 50 per cent of licence authorization) has been $3.40.

Source: Canadian National Energy Board.

Such increases reflect an export pricing policy rather than the inherent cost of the gas itself. The Canadian government until recently used a formula that had the effect of keying the export price of gas and oil to that of imported oil.[11] Both federal and provincial government revenues from this source grew rapidly, reflecting primarily the large export flows to the western and central United States. Revenues accruing to the federal treasury were, in effect, used in part to subsidize the price of foreign oil imported into eastern Canada. Interestingly, the price of electricity imported into New England from New Brunswick in recent years—until 1981—reflected that underlying oil price subsidy. A 1981 decision by the Canadian government removing the subsidy element in the export price was followed by curtailment of New England imports.[12]

During several years in the early 1970s, liquefied natural gas (LNG) was trucked from Quebec into southern New England to help meet seasonal peak requirements of gas distribution systems. That flow, however, was not significant after 1972, by which time it had been replaced by gas from Algeria and other sources.

The northward flow of crude oil through the Portland-Montreal pipeline peaked in 1973 at about 170 million barrels (bbl) and declined thereafter due to a number of circumstances, the most important of which was completion of the Sarnia-Montreal pipeline (see Table 5.4). The Portland Pipeline (which is actually three lines, with diameters ranging from 12 to 24 inches) has thus been operating at less than a third of its capacity in most recent years. While the flow increased temporarily in 1981 due to curtailment in cross-continental shipments by Alberta (reflecting that province's reactions to Ottawa's energy policy), a relatively low level of Portland-to-Montreal shipments is likely in the 1980s. This pipeline is owned by five (formerly six) of the major international companies and dates back to World War II.[13] As will be discussed shortly, marketing areas served by the Montreal refineries are Quebec, parts of eastern Ontario, and the Maritime Provinces, as well as the northeastern United States.

While the flow of petroleum is pretty clear-cut in north-south trade—products moving southward from Canada into New England and crude oil northward through the pipeline—trade between Quebec and the Atlantic Provinces presents a more complex pattern. (Natural gas will not figure in such trade unless a once-proposed Quebec-Maritimes pipeline is built—a subject to be discussed later.) In general, it appears that there is substantial cross-shipment of petroleum products from refineries in either region to markets in the other. Table 5.5 provides a cross-sectional view of such shipments in 1980, considering Atlantic Canada as a unit.

| Table 5.4: | Portland-Montreal Pipeline, Annual Throughput, 1973-1981 |

Year	Flow (thousand bbl)
1973	169,225
1974	163,062
1975	161,686
1976	140,225
1977	85,359
1978	62,786
1979	47,688
1980	51,613
1981	64,521
1982	41,247
1983	28,157

Source: Portland Pipeline Corporation.

Crude oil input to the Montreal refineries, as already indicated, now comes mostly from western Canada, but with a substantial inflow also from Venezuela, Mexico, and the Middle East, as well as minor amounts from the United States and other parts of the world. The Atlantic Provinces refineries, on the other hand, depend almost entirely on overseas sources. With respect to intra-Canada product shipments, it may be assumed that Quebec's "exports" flow both eastward and westward (as well as southward), but that the Atlantic Region's sales— 1.5 million cubic metres in 1980—are mainly to Quebec, given the higher costs of reaching Ontario or western markets. In viewing these interprovincial data, one should, of course, keep in mind that Quebec had eight refineries in 1980 as opposed to the five in the Atlantic Region;[14] 1980 and 1981 operating levels were not close to capacity in either region.

The pattern of domestic sales in each region (Table 5.5) is for the most part what one might expect given the basic differences in population and industrial base. The one major exception is sales of heavy fuel oil, which are almost as high in

Table 5.5: Petroleum Imports, Interregional Shipments, and Sales in Quebec and the Atlantic Provinces, 1980

| | Quebec | | Atlantic Provinces | |
	Quantity (thousand m³)	%	Quantity (thousand m³)	%
Crude oil input to refineries from:				
Western Canada	16,560.9	56.4	61.2	0.4
United States	1,895.7	6.5		
Central and South America	5,577.8	19.0	4,052.9	25.1
Other areas	5,331.6	18.1	12,034.1	74.5
Total	29,366.0	100.0	16,148.2	100.0

	In	Out	Ina	Outa
Interprovincial shipments of oil products (thousand m³):				
Propane, butane, petro-feedstocks	221.4	82.1	9.0	77.1
Aviation fuel, all types	34.7	286.7	113.2	31.6
Motor gasoline	922.8	1,234.0	340.9	464.4
Stove oil kerosene	114.2	146.7	71.1	83.8
Diesel fuel	281.5	363.9	149.8	99.1
Light fuel oil (Nos. 2, 3)	747.4	778.0	311.7	410.3
Heavy fuel oil (Nos. 4, 5, 6)	665.7	450.2	265.8	315.6
Lubric. oils and grease	121.9	177.2	58.9	3.4
Other	113.6	437.3	56.6	26.9
Total interprovincial	3,223.3	3,956.1	1,377.0	1,512.3

	Quantity (thousand m³)	%	Quantity (thousand m³)	%
Domestic (provincial) sales:				
Propane, butane, petro-feedstocks	1,857.9	6.9	189.2	1.4
Aviation fuel, all types	953.6	3.5	432.0	3.3
Motor gasoline	8,687.1	32.2	3,261.8	24.6
Stove oil kerosene	411.4	1.5	331.2	2.5
Diesel fuel	2,668.4	9.9	1,453.5	11.0
Light fuel oil (Nos. 2, 3)	5,241.5	19.4	2,299.4	17.4
Heavy fuel oil (Nos. 4, 5, 6)	5,854.3	21.7	4,897.1	37.0
Lubric. oils and grease	178.6	0.6	74.4	0.6
Other	1,163.9	4.3	291.3	2.2
Total domestic sales	27,016.7	100.0	13,229.9	100.0

[a] Atlantic Provinces as a whole; shipments *within* the Atlantic Region are excluded. For conversion purposes, 1 cubic metre equals approximately 6.3 barrels.

Source: Statistics Canada, Cat. No. 45-004, various issues.

Atlantic Canada as in Quebec. Without question, this is attributable to the Atlantic Region's heavy dependence on oil for paper production and for electricity generation (see Table 5.9). The Atlantic Provinces' dependence on fuel oil for electricity generation was 65-70 per cent in 1980, if Labrador is excluded.

New England imports of electricity from eastern Canada are shown for selected years in Table 5.6, together with estimated prices and revenues. While Quebec has recently become a dominant supplier to New York, its exports to New England have remained modest. This is due partly to an early, well-organized effort on the part of the Consolidated Edison Company (serving New York City) and PASNY to obtain the needed energy. Up to the present time, Hydro-Quebec has limited its exports to New England to (1) those flowing through low- voltage ties to small, adjacent systems in Vermont, New Hampshire, and northwestern Maine, and (2) a contractual 52 megawatts (mW) to Vermont beginning in late 1980, transported via PASNY lines. New Brunswick, on the other hand, had increased its annual exports to 4 billion kWh by 1979, most of which was delivered to Maine Electric Power Company, a transmission entity jointly owned by several New England utilities. The capacity of this tie is presently 500 mW, roughly comparable to a mid-sized nuclear unit or a full-sized coal unit. Figure 5.1 shows in diagrammatic form the principal electric interconnections and their capacity between eastern Canada and the northeastern United States.

An interesting aspect of Table 5.6 is the rapid price escalation that took place during the 1970s. Since data on revenue per kilowatt-hour reflect a combination of firm and interruptible energy sales (but with their proportions — outside of the New York-Quebec tie — not changing greatly during the 1970s), they must be interpreted with caution. Nevertheless, the effective export price has increased on the order of six to eight times since 1970. The rising average price to 1979 shown for New Brunswick exports reflects primarily (1) a shift from hydro- to oil-based generation in the mid-1970s, and (2) escalation in the cost of fuel oil thereafter — even subsidized fuel oil, as indicated earlier. Quebec's average export price remained lower, probably reflecting the predominance of hydro generation in that province. It is significant, however, that none of the average revenue figures prior to 1981 (Table 5.6) fully reflect the Canadian federal policy of the time which set energy export prices at a level close to the least-cost alternative available to the US purchaser.[15]

Table 5.7 sheds additional light on the strategic position of New Brunswick in relation to electric energy flows. As indicated earlier, the province has recently been purchasing about 30 per

Table 5.6: New England Imports of Electricity from Canada, Selected Years, 1970-1981

		New Brunswick	Quebec	Total
1970	kWh (millions)	756	51	807
	Revenue ($ thousands)	5,010	372	5,382
	Revenue/kWh (¢)	0.66	0.73	0.67
1973	kWh	2,847	66	2,913
	Revenue	20,463	422	20,885
	Revenue/kWh	0.72	0.64	0.72
1976	kWh	2,402	69	2,470
	Revenue	42,714	1,093	43,807
	Revenue/kWh	1.78	1.58	1.77
1979	kWh	3,920	146	4,066
	Revenue	128,343	3,289	131,632
	Revenue/kWh	3.27	2.25	3.24
1981	kWh (000,000)	3,247	349	3,596
	Revenue ($000)	180,586	12,005	192,591
	Revenue/kWh (¢)	5.46	3.44	5.36

Source: Canadian National Energy Board.

Table 5.7: Cross-Boundary Purchases and Sales of Electric Energy by New Brunswick Electric Power Commission, 1970-1982

Year	Purchases from Hydro Quebec			Sales to Maine Electric Power Corporation[a]		
	kWh (millions)	$ Can. (thousands)	¢/kWh	kWh (millions)	$ Can. (thousands)	¢/kWh
1970				136.1	734.4	0.54
1971	126.5	748.5	0.59	781.8	5,763.1	0.74
1972	1,013.9	4,305.7	0.42	1,276.6	9,155.5	0.72
1973	2,447.0	9,248.7	0.38	2,092.4	14,303.3	0.68
1974	3,427.3	16,360.7	0.48	1,709.0	20,612.0	1.21
1975	3,717.3	20,369.9	0.55	900.7	11,371.2	1.26
1976	3,654.1	21,843.1	0.60	1,693.0	31,112.0	1,84
1977	3,648.5	34,349.5	0.94	3,026.6	75,067.8	2.48
1978	3,543.1	42,296.3	1.19	2,059.5	65,504.5	3.18
1979	3,587.8	57,582.4	1.60	3,353.7	111,458.5	3.32
1980	3,674.0	65,762.6	1.79	3,300.3	127,517.1	3.86
1981	4,005.4	94,154.8	2.35	2,683.3	162,823.8	6.07
1982	3,769.0	101,909.9	2.70	2,429.8	137,493.7	5.66

a   Excludes small amounts sold directly to Maine distributing utilities.

Sources: New Brunswick Electric Power Commission.
Canadian National Energy Board.

Figure 5.1

Electric interconnections between the northeastern United States and the eastern Canadian Provinces, 1980.

(Sources: Hydro-Quebec and Northeast Power Coordinating Council)

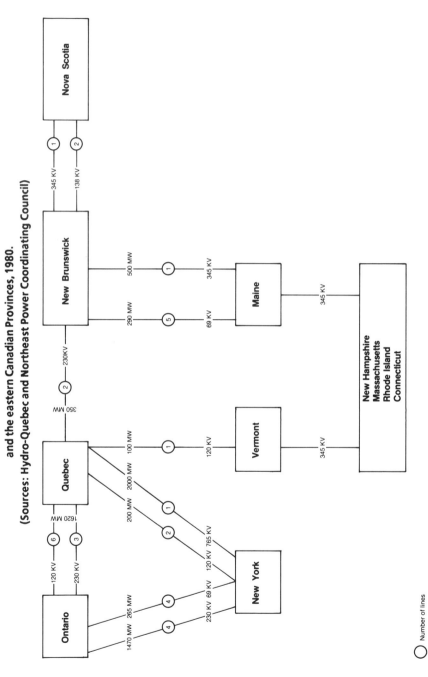

○ Number of lines

cent of its total supply from Quebec (much of this supply originates in Labrador). The price paid is, by 1980 standards, extremely low, despite several increases put into effect by Quebec since 1976. But New Brunswick *exports* at least as much electric power as it imports. As shown in Table 5.7, the effective price of export sales to the largest single New England purchaser, Maine Electric Power Company, in 1981-1982 was close to 6 cents per kWh, reflecting both the high cost of generating fuel and the aforementioned federal policy. The province is thus in the advantageous position of exporting much (perhaps two-thirds) of its thermally generated electricity and using imported hydroelectricity to displace all or most of the amount exported.[16]

Tables 5.8 and 5.9 present data summarizing electric energy supplies originating within each of the three regions. In all areas, utilities have long since taken over the major supply function (Table 5.8), with on-site industrial generation (1981-1983) providing only a minor proportion of total energy except in Quebec (18 per cent) and Maine (26 per cent). Certain mineral industries in Quebec—for example, aluminum—and the paper industry in both Maine and Quebec have traditionally provided most of their own electric energy. The major producers of electric energy are Quebec and Newfoundland (Labrador) in the north, and Massachusetts and Connecticut in the south.

Table 5.9 shows that the "northern" supply is almost entirely hydro, while that in southern New England is primarily a combination of oil- and nuclear-based generation. The table also shows in some detail the relationships between load and capacity, and the breakdown of utility-owned supply by each of the principal consumption categories. Comparisons of capacity and peak load require that Quebec and the Atlantic Provinces be viewed together, since in 1981 Labrador provided a major proportion (21 per cent of capacity, 30 per cent of output) of Quebec's supply. This proportion recently declined somewhat with the completion of additional units at James Bay. Before the James Bay project, the capacity of the Canadian provinces was more closely matched to their peak load than was and is true in New England where very high reserve margins have been maintained in recent years. These are the result of long construction lead time a slackening growth in demand, and a private ownership-public regulation structure that was conducive to overexpansion.

The rationale underlying most of the electric energy flows between Canada and the United States is, of course, differential costs. While enhanced reliability and scale advantages can result from tying systems together across the international—or state

Table 5.8: **Production of Electric Energy (Thousand Gigawatt-Hours) in Quebec, Atlantic Provinces, and New England, 1981**

	Total Production	Utility Production	Utility/ Total (per cent)[a]
Quebec	103.2 [b]	85.0	82
Atlantic Provinces			
Newfoundland	44.8 [b]	44.2	99
Prince Edward Island	[c]		
Nova Scotia	6.6	6.1	93
New Brunswick	9.0	8.3	92
Total	60.4	58.6	97
New England			
Maine		9.3	74 [d]
New Hampshire		5.6	94
Vermont		4.6	97
Massachusetts		32.9	98
Rhode Island		0.8	94
Connecticut		23.8	99
Total	80.9	76.9	95 [d]

a   Utility percentage calculated from finer data than shown.
b   Churchill Falls (Labrador) output is attributed here to Newfoundland; approximately 37,000 gWh were exported to Quebec in 1981.
c   Less than 50 gWh.
d   New England utility/total generation estimated from 1978 data.

Sources: Statistics Canada, Cat. No. 57-202.
Canada Department of Energy, Mines and Resources.
US Bureau of the Census.
Electric Council of New England.

Table 5.9: Electric Utility Capacity, Peak Load, and Sales in the Three Regions, 1981

	Quebec		Atlantic Provinces		New England	
	1981	Per cent	1981	Per cent	1981	Per cent
Utility capacity on Dec. 31 (mW)[a]	19,245		11,558		20,967	
System peak demand (mW)	19,696		4,328		15,702	
Utility generation (gWh)[a]	84,954	100.0	58,639	100.0	76,912	100.0
Hydro	84,852	99.9	48,600	82.9	4,640	6.0
Fossil steam			9,932	16.9	46,226	60.1
Coal (estimated)			3,972	(6.8)	4,467	(5.8)
Oil (estimated)			5,960	(10.1)	41,759	(54.3)
Nuclear					25,785	33.5
Other[b]	101	0.1	106	0.2	261	0.4
Purchases from neighbouring regions (gWh)[c]	35,881		3,829		2,920	
Price/kWh purchased (¢)	0.27		2.44		5.79	
Sales to ultimate consumers (gWh)	84,113 [d]	100.0	17,652	100.0	77,886	100.0
Residential (incl. farm)		37.8		36.1		37.4
Commercial and general		22.7		26.1		32.8
Industrial		39.5		37.8		29.8
Sales to neighbouring regions (gWh)	18,525 [e]					
Revenue/kWh sold (¢)	2.02					
Revenues from ultimate consumers ($ millions)[f]	2,262		764		5,927	
Revenue/kWh sold (¢)	2.69		4.33		7.61	

a   Churchill Falls (Labrador) capacity (4,225 mW) and output is attributed here to the Atlantic
   Provinces, although it is largely transmitted to Quebec.
b   Other includes gas turbine and internal combustion units.
c   Quebec purchases from Labrador; New Brunswick purchases from Quebec; New England
   purchases from New Brunswick, excluding industrial.
d   Hydro-Quebec only.
e   Sales to New Brunswick and Ontario (1.75¢), New York and Vermont (2.36¢).
f   Revenues shown in respective currencies; the average exchange ratio during 1981 was $119.88
   Can. = $1.00 US.

Sources: Statistics Canada, Cat. Nos. 57-202 and 57-204.
        Hydro-Quebec.
        Electric Council of New England.

and provincial — boundary, ultimately the explanation for virtually all of the observed electric power exports is the lower cost of electricity production in Canada. Electric rate and bill comparisons are not an ideal measure of such differentials; however, they do suggest the extent of the difference at the consumer level. Table 5.9 shows differences in 1981 average revenues per kilowatt-hour sold, while Table 5.10 presents a comparison of electric bills for typical amounts and kinds of usage in five Canadian and six New England cities as of January 1, 1982.

In general, Quebec's electric rates are well below those in both New England and the Atlantic Provinces. Indeed, Montreal bills appear to be only about half the New England average. Electric bills in the Atlantic Provinces (except for Prince Edward Island) are also substantially below those of most New England cities, after allowing for differences in currency values, with the exception of Portland, Maine and Burlington, Vermont. Maine's relatively low rates (relative, that is, to New England and the Atlantic Provinces) are attributable largely to a generating mix that emphasizes nuclear and, to a lesser extent, hydroelectric power. (Maine has a large, vintage nuclear plant whose construction preceded the dramatic rise in nuclear costs experienced during the late 1970s.) Burlington, Vermont has a publicly owned electric utility and, in addition, enjoys the cost advantage stemming from importation of some power from the St. Lawrence project.

Along with generating mix, differences in ownership structure are probably a major reason for observed differences in electric rates between most of New England and the Atlantic Provinces. All of the eastern Canadian provinces have publicly owned, province-wide electric systems. Such systems benefit from lower tax and financing costs than are incurred by privately owned utilities, and are less likely to be organized on a less-than-optimum scale. Some (such as the Nova Scotia system) also enjoy explicit government subsidies. While the New England companies have created a regional power pool (NEPOOL) to overcome the scale (and isolation) handicap, there are still an unusually large number of operating companies in the region, with their associated administrative and other overhead costs. Both financing costs and (especially) taxes are very high per unit of plant or output basis and account for a major portion of total expenses.[17]

Without question Hydro-Quebec enjoys the greatest cost advantage of any of these systems as it is publicly owned, has access to extraordinary hydro resources, and is organized on a

Table 5.10: Typical Monthly Electric Bills in Atlantic Canada, Quebec, and New England, 1982

	Residential (750 kWh/mo.)	Commercial (40 kW; 10,000 kWh/mo.)	Industrial (500 kW; 200,000 kWh/mo.)
St. John's, Newfoundland	$44.83	$ 635.70	$ 9,204.18
Charlottetown, P.E.I.	86.90	1,329.36	21,444.78
Halifax, Nova Scotia	44.93	713.93	9,292.70
Saint John, New Brunswick	39.56	639.36	9,139.50
Montreal, Quebec	29.10	510.28	7,954.50
Portland, Maine	50.01	670.30	10,167.00
Manchester, New Hampshire	57.51	755.27	12,804.00
Burlington, Vermont	37.10	460.20	8,663.00
Boston, Massachusetts	67.03	1,031.30	15,585.00
Providence, Rhode Island	51.91	727.40	12,275.00
Hartford, Connecticut	61.93	957.78	13,824.00
New England, weighted avg.	58.69	895.91	n.a.

Note: Bills are as of January 1, 1982, and they are in each country's respective currency. Where more than one rate schedule is applicable (e.g., for seasonal or temporary use), the lower bill is shown. Bills include fuel adjustments but exclude sales taxes. The exchange rate January 1, 1982 was approximately $1.19 Can. = $1.00 US.

Source: Statistics Canada.
US Energy Information Administration.

vast scale. On the basis of capacity, it was, as of 1983, the largest electric utility in North America, and it can sell an average kilowatt-hour of electricity for about one-third the price in New England or one-half that in New Brunswick. These differentials have been intensified by the oil crisis of the 1970s. Between 1973 and 1980, for example, residential electric bills in Montreal increased about 80 per cent; the corresponding increases in the Atlantic Provinces ranged from 140 per cent in Saint John (New Brunswick) to 210 per cent in Charlottetown (P.E.I.), and in New England from 82 per cent in Burlington to 146 per cent in Providence.[18]

Given the cost advantage, it is not surprising that both Quebec and New Brunswick have been viewed as attractive sources of energy for the New England states. The major New Brunswick interconnection, which was completed in 1972, has provided New England with between 1 and 4 billion kWh annually since that time (Table 5.2), and the 4.2 billion kWh imported in 1980 accounted for approximately 5 per cent of total New England requirements.[19] Until recently, New England had not formally approached Quebec for this purpose, nor had Quebec sought this particular type of export market. Several factors seem to have been at work, including (1) Hydro-Quebec's non-synchronous (with New England) mode of operating its electric grid and non-participation in the Northeast Power Coordinating Council, (2) the difficulty of approaching a region comprised of many small utilities, (3) Quebec's own very rapid load growth, and (4) the more limited advantages of export (import) where both systems have winter peaks and thus excess generating capacity mainly during the other seasons. In any event, it was New York State, faced with great obstacles to creation of additional summer peaking capacity, which broke the stalemate. New York built the necessary transmission line, and by 1983 it was importing about 8 billion kWh from Quebec each year.[20]

Developments from 1982 to 1984

Events taking place over the past few years have reduced and in some cases overcome the above obstacles to Quebec-New England energy trade. Chief among these has been a notable decline in Quebec's load growth just as the province was completing Phase I at James Bay. The consequent rapid increase in excess capacity has resulted in a willingness to enter into longer-term export contracts. NEPOOL signed a contract with Hydro-Quebec in 1982 (the so-called Phase I contract) calling for the import of 33 billion non-firm kilowatt-hours over an eleven-year period beginning in 1986, by which time a new 600-mW transmission line linking Sherbrooke, Quebec and west-central New Hampshire (via northeastern Vermont) will have been completed. Negotiations between Hydro-Quebec and NEPOOL in 1983 and 1984 have resulted in plans for augmenting this energy flow through contracts for semi-firm capacity and energy (Phase II) starting in 1990. The transmission tie will be planned so that its ultimate capacity will be 2,000 mW. Vermont has now negotiated a separate contract for 150 mW or firm capacity, which will require a new but shorter transmission line in the northwest corner of that state. Thus, a real possibility exists that Quebec hydroelectric energy will come to account for a substantial fraction, quite possibly more than 10 per cent, of New England's electricity requirements by 1990.

In 1983, New Brunswick signed up several New England buyers for about half of the 600-mW capacity of the first unit of its Point Lepreau nuclear power station. Preliminary talks have been held concerning the temporary export of virtually all the output of a proposed second unit. Indeed, the second unit, if it is built, would in effect be committed to the export market for perhaps the first ten years. If this export materializes, by 1990 New England might be deriving perhaps 6-7 per cent of its electricity from New Brunswick, or 15-18 per cent from eastern Canadian sources generally. Development of the Bay of Fundy tidal power might substantially increase this figure, but the economics of that project remain tenuous.

Finally, the prospect of major natural gas shipments from offshore Nova Scotia to the northeastern United States, a subject to be discussed shortly, raises the possibility that within this coming decade, New England may be importing from the Maritimes as much as 15 per cent of its natural gas supply. (A limited amount of southern New England's gas will in any event be coming from Canada by 1990 by way of a new link across New York State, connecting at Niagara.) Current negotiations over available offshore volumes, cost sharing, levels of taxation, and hence the boundary price, make it hazardous at this point (1984) to predict the outcome.

Prospects for the 1990s and Beyond
Electric Power from Quebec
For north-to-south energy flows in the remainder of this century, the principal sources of new energy exports are likely to be the very large, undeveloped hydro capacity of northern Quebec and Labrador and the offshore oil and gas fields adjacent to Newfoundland and Nova Scotia. Additionally, it is possible that natural gas from either or both western Canada and the Arctic

will be available in sufficient quantities to permit substantial exports. Nuclear energy from New Brunswick will also probably play some role. Finally, there is the less certain possibility of tidal energy being harnessed in the Bay of Fundy on a scale that would permit — and perhaps require — export to the United States.

New England is a relatively energy-poor region, as it has been throughout most of the twentieth century.[21] At one time it was thought that nuclear power would usher in a new era of low-cost energy that would lessen, if not eliminate, New England's disadvantage. That was actually beginning to happen up to about the mid-1970s, but the deteriorating prospects for nuclear power attributable to long lead times and high litigation and political costs, as well as to inherent construction and safety requirements, is once again placing the region in a distinctly have-not position. It is not surprising, therefore, that New England, unable to pursue the nuclear option as aggressively as before, hesitant about the trade-off between its own offshore oil and gas versus fishing and recreational uses, and unable to achieve a consensus concerning development of its remaining hydroelectric resources (e.g., the Saint John and Penobscot Rivers), should be looking to Canada for at least part of its future energy requirements.

Quebec is, of course, the logical place to look. Its hydroelectric resources alone are sufficient to give the province a commanding energy position in eastern North America. As indicated earlier, Hydro- Quebec, relying on hydro resources for 99 per cent of its output (Table 5.9), supplies electric power to provincial users at rates averaging about half those in New England.[22] Because of the winter peak load and an ability to maintain substantial year-round water flows, a large amount of excess energy can be (and is being) exported on a seasonal basis. The immediate questions are to what extent exports will be increased in the future, and what types of energy might be made available to New England.

The potential for hydroelectricity exports from Quebec is truly impressive. Hydro-Quebec's developed electric capacity as of 1983 was about 21,000 mW, including several of the new units at James Bay. Churchill Falls contributes an additional 5,200 mW, most of which is committed to the Quebec market. Combining these, total capacity is roughly 20 per cent greater than that of all six New England states. Thus, on a per capita basis Quebec has well over twice the electric capacity of New England. By 1986, Quebec-Labrador capacity will have reached 30,000 mW with completion of the so-called Phase I construction at James Bay. Incremental capacity which could be added to the then-existing plant is in excess of 5,000 mW. *Potential* hydro capacity in northern parts of the province is such that an additional 25-30 mW might be developed by the end of the century. (This does not include undeveloped capacity in Labrador.) But much of the additional capacity is located in remote regions, is subject to social and environmental constraints, and ultimately may be unable to compete with other sources, e.g., nuclear.[23]

Hydro-Quebec's load growth during the 1970s averaged approximately 7 per cent annually, but tended to decrease during the latter half of the decade. In 1980, the utility was still estimating that its firm power requirements would increase about 6 per cent annually, from 19,000 mW to 48,000 mW by 1996.[24] But recent forecasts have been revised downward substantially. A forecast made at the end of 1983 assumed only about a 3 per cent annual load growth during the 1980s, arising mainly from a combination of rising electric rates, conservation, and increased penetration of the Quebec market by natural gas.[25] Given this forecast for a lower load, there is clearly a substantial amount of capacity already scheduled, and an even larger amount that could be developed on an accelerated schedule, available for export to other regions, possibly on a long-term basis and certainly in a time frame encompassing the next 20-30 years.

It is important to recognize that New England is only one of several regions interested in obtaining energy from Quebec. While New England will seriously need, and probably will be willing to pay for, the extra energy, it is also true that Ontario and the Atlantic Provinces may be interested, and that the Middle Atlantic region almost certainly will be. Much will depend on the future course of Ontario's own load growth and nuclear program (the province currently has a substantial surplus — mainly coal-fired), and on efforts by the Atlantic Provinces to develop their own new electricity resources, including additional Labrador hydro, nuclear, Nova Scotia coal, and possibly Bay of Fundy tidal power.

In any event, completion of the Phase I expansion of Hydro-Quebec's generating capacity at James Bay is yielding substantial surplus energy from May through October, and could well permit exports of firm capacity during the time between completion of the remaining Phase I units and full absorption of their output by Quebec's own load growth. Construction of James Bay Phase II, originally scheduled to commence in 1988 but now deferred, would allow export of longer-term, firm capacity to the extent that load growth in Quebec continued at currently forecast levels. An essential element concerning this possibility is, of course, the province's own desire or willingness to schedule the Phase II development program in order to export energy.[26]

In looking first at the certainty of substantial amounts of seasonal surplus energy from Phase I units being available for export, one could argue that because much of New England continues to experience a winter peak such energy may find its principal outlets farther south, probably in the Middle Atlantic states. Indeed, this would appear to explain the large exports recently negotiated with New York.

Nevertheless, New England does have an interest in such energy, as evidenced by its high-capacity tie with Quebec currently under construction, for New England also has a secondary summer peak, with load valleys in the fall and spring months. There appear to be possibilities for using seasonal Canadian energy to add flexibility to the scheduling of maintenance, repair, and refueling of generating units in New England. The tie will permit transfer of energy on a daily basis to take advantage of Quebec's considerable "storage" capacity to replace high-cost fuel generation at peak hours. As indicated above, these possibilities recently led NEPOOL and Hydro-Quebec to sign contracts calling for the construction of the above-mentioned 600-mW interconnection to be completed by 1986, energy "banking" on a daily basis, and the sale of 33 billion kWh over the period 1986-1997.[27]

It remains true that the demand for seasonal, surplus energy is even greater in the Middle Atlantic region. Since the market is considerably larger there, it is reasonable to expect that the bulk of Quebec's seasonal exports will flow in that direction. Current plans are to increase Quebec's interchange capacity with PASNY from 1,300 to 2,400 mW. And, as indicated above, a new contract calling for exports of up to 111 billion kWh over a thirteen-year period starting in 1984 was announced in March 1982.[28]

The possibility of Quebec exporting *firm* or *semi-firm* capacity to New England from Phase I plants over an intermediate period has also been recognized as a real one, and negotiations have continued with this end in view. Deferring additions to the region's own power supply, on the other hand, is seen from various viewpoints by the New England utilities. While such a program would grant a breathing spell in their own efforts to built new plants, it would ultimately mean higher dollar (if not real) construction costs due to postponement,[29] assuming that New England's load growth eventually requires the new capacity. Whether the augmented transmission line required to bring intermediate-term, firm power into New England can be made to pay for itself will presumably depend on the line's load factor and the ultimate price paid by the New England companies.

Both the new PASNY and NEPOOL agreements stipulate an effective export price (for at least two-thirds of the energy) that is set at 80 per cent of the buyers' weighted average cost of fossil fuel generation. Earlier contracts generally used the utilities' "decremental" cost as a benchmark. Since decremental (or incremental) energy would normally be generated by the highest-cost fuel in the system, the new contractual arrangements are marginally more beneficial to New England and New York than the old ones. Moreover, since New England depends more heavily on oil-fired generation than New York, and has a less ambitious oil-to-coal conversion program under way, the effective import price in New England is apt to remain significantly above that paid by PASNY.

It can be argued that what New England really needs is a major infusion of firm, long-term electric energy that will be available year-round and can be used to displace oil as a base load source or provide for future growth in the base load. This substitute is needed at a price that is sufficiently low to make the risk of importation (as well as the transmission line) worthwhile. New England's own load growth has fallen to only about 2 per cent per year (from 7 per cent plus in the early 1970s); nevertheless, the region needs to find new sources of capacity to meet that growth requirement, to alleviate its dependence on oil, and to meet capacity shortfalls in the event of nuclear outages, cancellations, or shutdowns. On the Quebec side, while firm exports could be justified for perhaps 10-15 years given the excess capacity yielded by Phase I at James Bay, longer-term, firm contracts would require either (1) the creation of substantial incremental capacity at existing plants, (2) an accelerated construction schedule for Phase I of James Bay, or (3) possibly the planning of more remote power developments at an earlier date than is presently envisioned.

Long-term export of electric power on the scale indicated might well prove attractive to Quebec for several reasons. First, some economies would accrue from a sustained, large-scale construction program undertaken in advance of load growth and stretched over several decades. While these might appear at first glance to be purely financial rather than "real" savings, they need not be exclusively so; there should be significant economies related to scale and continuity factors as well. Even purely financial economies, moreover, would benefit owners and ultimate Quebec users to the extent that the latter are able to obtain electricity at prices reflecting historical costs.

Second, the cost of financing construction needed to supply exports might be lower than otherwise if the exports were backed up by firm US purchase agreements. The bonds should have a receptive market in the United States.

Third, and most important, the cost of the energy so developed and delivered to the international boundary probably would be well below its value to New England purchasers. (This is a tentative conclusion since much depends on the trend of hydro construction costs in Quebec versus the trend of fossil fuel and nuclear construction and generating costs in New England.) Not only is there a logical basis for trade, but the terms should also be distinctly favourable to Quebec given the alternative cost of energy to New England and the region's relative inelasticity of demand for electric energy.[30] The resulting profits could be used to keep Quebec's own electric rates low, thus enhancing further its present energy cost advantage.[31] It seems likely, therefore, that long-term (10-25 years) exports of firm electric capacity might prove to be one of Quebec's strongest suits in further economic negotiations with the United States.

Having said this, it is necessary to add that it may be premature to conclude that *firm* Quebec hydro energy will in fact become a major export to New England. First, it is not possible to say at this point whether, or to what extent, Quebec will want to plan its future hydro capacity with so much emphasis on exports. The fact that hydroelectric energy is a renewable resource should make the province less apprehensive than, say, members of OPEC (Organization of Petroleum Exporting Countries) who must deal with a depleting resource. But there still is fairly strong sentiment in Quebec in favour of "keeping the energy at home."[32] It is perhaps because of such a sentiment that Quebec is setting aside a minimum of 2,000 mW as a means of attracting new industry to the province.[33]

Second, Quebec's present contract for power originating in Labrador is not totally immune to revision. Table 5.9 shows that over 35,000 gWh flow from the Churchill Falls plant each year at a cost to Hydro-Quebec of less than 3 mills per kWh. But the contract in fact only conveys 80 per cent of firm capacity to Quebec. Newfoundland, not surprisingly, has pursued a number of strategies for recovering part of the energy and/or moving the price toward market levels, all thus far to no avail. But there will unquestionably be further attempts to negotiate a higher price, if not terminate the contract, and Quebec always faces the possibility, however remote, of curtailment. With at least

1,000 mW — and conceivably up to 5,000 mW — at stake, Quebec has had to follow a conservative policy in committing itself to firm exports. While it is quite probable that any large amount of power recovered by Newfoundland would be made available to New England or New York (either directly or via a federal corridor through Quebec), such a contingency can hardly be contracted for between Quebec and New England.

Third, political considerations in Canada may play a role. Quebec might well trade off voluntarily more of her surplus energy to Ontario and the Maritimes in return for their support in other matters, including negotiations with the federal government.[34] While Ontario and New Brunswick seem committed at present to the nuclear option, it is unlikely that this option can be developed at a lower cost than Quebec's incremental hydro capacity.

The fourth consideration which may dampen the potential for Quebec hydroelectric exports arises from circumstances on the US side of the boundary. It is well known that New England's privately owned electric utilities have not been particularly enthusiastic about importing energy from Canada. Some of the reasons are entirely justified from a reliability standpoint. Canadian exports of energy have been curtailed before in the context of changing political circumstances and world events.[35] Thus it is doubtful whether contractual obligations across the international boundary would be made without some form of escape clause.[36] Hydro-Quebec's system is somewhat vulnerable to outages arising from the great length and exposure of transmission lines, not to mention the potential insecurity of Churchill Falls power. The political environment in Quebec itself is not wholly reassuring to those seeking long-term guarantees, particularly in an area (electric power) known to be politically sensitive, without good substitutes, and requiring heavy fixed investments in transmission facilities. There is no reason, in other words, to think that New England utilities, would be willing or able to solve their supply problem simply by substituting dependence on Quebec for the present 40 per cent dependence on imported oil.

In addition to this justifiable hesitancy to become energy-dependent in another direction — even assuming that sufficient Quebec electricity were available on a firm basis — there has been an equally strong influence at work with New England utilities, making them reluctant to pursue any such goal. This influence stems from the fact that they are privately owned companies only partially integrated in this region, with high-capacity reserve margins and operating under (1) a system of regulation that until recently gave them an incentive to expand their own capacity rather than buy from outside the company (and region), and (2) a system of taxation that provides generous credits and deductions for internal construction programs but not for purchased power, except for the transmission investment involved.[37]

The only partial integration of New England electric utilities makes it difficult for them to speak with one voice in negotiations with Canada. Their co-ordinating body, NEPOOL, functions more as a committee than as an authority. Experience with the 1970s import contract with New Brunswick suggests less than unanimous agreement on terms or shares on the New England side,[38] and the same kinds of disagreement will no doubt be at work in negotiations with Quebec. This fragmentation of ownership in New England (which, at times, has appeared odd, to say the least, to managers of systems the size of Ontario Hydro and Hydro-Quebec) probably discouraged initiatives on the part of Canada when earlier, large-scale projects with export potential were being discussed.[39] Moreover, the *political* fact that Hydro-Quebec has sought and been able to bargain directly and enter into formal contracts with a public agency — New York's Power Authority — has without question enhanced the *physical* fact of seasonal load diversity between the two systems as a basis for power exchange. New England has no such agency, largely because of the utilities' own opposition to its creation.

Finally, the New England utilities have made very large investments in nuclear generating plants, a number of which are not yet completed. In fact, their completion has become a controversial issue. To the extent that buying firm power from Quebec weakens the case for completion, the utilities might well refrain from seeking firm imports on a large scale.

New England political leaders and regulatory officials have helped to some degree to offset the utilities' reluctance, however. In the past few years several governors have journeyed northward to sound out Quebec officials on the possibility of greater exports, and Governor Richard Snelling's 1980 proposal that Quebec embark on a major pre-build effort with capital funds supplied by US utilities represented a true "bull by the horns" initiative. While Hydro-Quebec has not taken up the financing suggestion, the provincial government is clearly more favourably disposed toward New England exports than was true as recently as 1980. Thus, it may turn out that, even if New England utilities themselves remain lukewarm, the advantage to New England of an augmented supply of firm power and to Quebec of an ample export price, yielding profits that could help keep Quebec's own rates low and provide extra revenue to the provincial government, will lead to a major flow of firm electric energy into New England by the 1990s.

It should be noted that the 2,000-mW tie negotiated with NEPOOL in 1982 and 1983 calls for the export of what might be termed semi-firm capacity — that is, energy would be available for most of the year but not necessarily at 100 per cent during the winter peak, unless Quebec's own reserve margins are sufficiently high to permit such export. This implies that without a "Phase III" contract stipulating truly firm capacity a substantial fraction of New England's winter peak load might continue to be met by oil-fired generation (which mostly accounts for the region's high reserve margins) and that such plants could thereby legitimately remain in the rate bases of the importing utilities. To the extent that this is true, New England consumers will not be benefiting from Canadian imports nearly as much as if the capacity and energy were firm on a year-round basis, thus permitting retirement of older oil-burning stations and possibly the cancellation of one or more unfinished nuclear plants.[40]

Electric Power from the Atlantic Provinces

Prospects for electric energy flowing from the Atlantic Provinces to New England are less dramatic but nevertheless favourable. Even before the contract between the New Brunswick Electric Power Commission and the Maine Electric Power Company (based on oil generation at Coleson Cove) expires in 1985, the Commission is signing up New England buyers for part of the output of its Point Lepreau nuclear station, which was completed late in 1982. Indeed, there has been ample transmission capacity in the Maine-New Brunswick line since 1980 when the export price of Coleson Cove energy ceased to benefit from the Canadian fuel oil subsidy. Just how much of the Point Lepreau energy will flow to New England apparently will depend in part on the willingness of New England utilities and regulators to commit themselves for a share of the plant's fixed charges.[41] Even if additional commitments fail to materialize, it is likely that within a few years exports will account for close to half of New Brunswick's total electric revenues.[42]

Looking farther ahead, both Nova Scotia and Newfoundland have an eye on the New England-New York market in hopes that future power plant construction at, respectively, a Bay of Fundy tidal site and Labrador's Lower Churchill River will be rendered feasible by at least temporary exports. Both projects face major obstacles — primarily economic in the case of Fundy tidal power and political in the case of the Lower Churchill River. Newfoundland's request for a corridor through Quebec to market its energy has not been granted by that province.[43] Quebec, not surprisingly, prefers the role of middleman in any transaction between Newfoundland and the United States, and New Brunswick is equally opposed to the corridor idea for fear that the device might be used to move Fundy or other Nova Scotia energy southward. The competitiveness of Fundy tidal power will not be known for several years; the economic feasibility of such a project is highly sensitive to interest rates and the price of fuel.[44] In the meantime, a smaller tidal project (without export potential) has been built in the Annapolis Basin.

Natural Gas

As indicated earlier, the only significant trade in natural gas between eastern Canada and New England at present is the relatively small volume of imports across the northern Vermont boundary. New England's weak energy position, however, together with large surpluses of gas in western Canada and the prospect of new supplies from offshore Nova Scotia, have recently generated proposals calling for substantial new imports. One proposal is to build a new pipeline – the so-called boundary project – across New York State, paralleling existing lines. This pipeline would transmit Canadian (Albertan) natural gas from Niagara to markets in southern New England and the Middle Atlantic states. Another proposal calls for building a new line that would traverse Maine, southern New Hampshire, and eastern Massachusetts. This line would deliver offshore Canadian gas from the Maritimes to similar markets in New England and the Middle Atlantic states (see Figure 5.2). While the Maritimes project was originally conceived as a US spur of the projected Quebec-Halifax line (which would have permitted Albertan gas to flow to Canada's eastern seaboard), rising costs, arguments over an optimum route, and improved offshore prospects resulted in an indefinite deferral of this Trans- Quebec and Maritimes (TQM) project.

Following the Canadian National Energy Board's 1982 decision concerning the amounts of gas that could be demonstrated to be clearly surplus to projected Canadian requirements, authorization was granted in early 1983 for the export of approximately half the applied-for quantities at Niagara.[45] The context involved several additional applications for new gas exports to companies in the western and midwestern states and also sizeable quantities to Japan in the form of LNG shipments from British Columbia. The Board's decision favoured the latter but acknowledged the strategic importance of north-

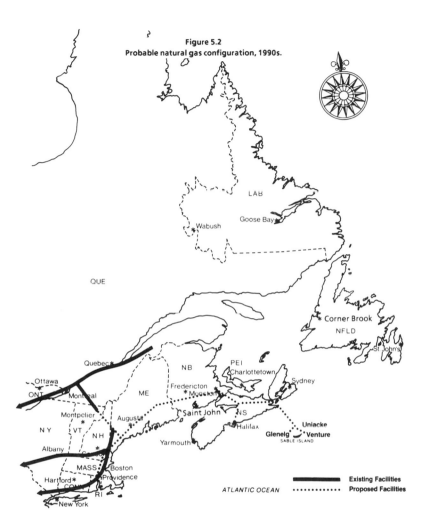

Figure 5.2
Probable natural gas configuration, 1990s.

LAB

Goose Bay

Wabush

QUE

Corner Brook

NFLD

St. John's

Quebec

Ottawa
ONT

Montreal

NB

PEI
Charlottetown

Sydney

Fredericton
Moncton

ME

Montpelier

Augusta

Saint John

NS

N Y

VT

N H

Uniacke
Glenelg   Venture
SABLE ISLAND

Albany

Yarmouth

Halifax

MASS

Boston
Providence

Hartford
CONN

RI

New York

ATLANTIC OCEAN

━━━━ **Existing Facilities**
•••••••• **Proposed Facilities**

eastern US markets to Canadian suppliers.[46]

To the east, it seems probable that the proposal to export Nova Scotian gas will receive the necessary approvals and that, as a consequence, New England's natural gas supply might be increased on the order of 15 per cent. Either of the two competing firms on the US side would deliver initially some 100 million cubic feet per day to New England (about 14 per cent of 1982 regional sales) and perhaps twice that amount to the Middle Atlantic states. The line will cost in excess of $700 million (in 1982 dollars) on the US side, and possibly $4 billion overall if the underwater portion is included.[47]

Canadian policy during the 1970s called for a uniform export price for natural gas at the boundary – a price that rose rapidly after 1974 (Table 5.3). By 1983, that price was well above the average US domestic price at comparable distances from the major "city gates." (The current US policy of phased deregulation is gradually raising the price of natural gas to consumers, but, in most areas, not to a level equivalent to the cost of imported oil to which the Canadian export price has been keyed.) Despite the fact that the price of Canadian gas is generally "rolled in" to the regulated price of gas from older US fields, deliveries of Canadian gas to western and midwestern US markets had fallen well below contractual maximums by 1983. A combination of recession, conservation, and falling oil prices has intensified this result.

Changes in Canadian energy policy may restore or even enlarge Albertan gas exports to midwestern markets.[48] It is possible, moreover, that if supplies in the West become redundant, efforts will be made to export additional gas to eastern (including New England) markets. Without adequate resources in the West, however, New England's chances of obtaining Canadian gas will be far more closely tied to prospects for new offshore resources.

While market forces are tending to lower gas prices – or at least temper their rate of increase with deregulation – the high cost of offshore production, together with Nova Scotia's desire to achieve an adequate profit margin, are working to keep the export price up. There is some question, therefore, of whether offshore Canadian natural gas, even allowing for high alternative costs in the eastern United States, will find a ready market in New England. The situation bears some resemblance to that in Alaska, where abundant gas supplies cannot at present be transmitted to the lower forty-eight without transmission costs pricing the gas out of the US market. Not surprisingly, producers and distributors of competitive fuels in the northeast are skeptical and, indeed, can be expected to oppose the

Maritimes-New England pipeline before various US licensing authorities.

Presumably, if Canada wishes to export gas to the northeastern United States, it clearly has the ability to set a price or prices that would accomplish that objective. For one thing, natural gas produced on federal (i.e., non-provincial) lands, including offshore areas, is subject to a variable export tax. Provincial royalty payments are likewise flexible. The provinces (and states) through which the pipeline will run will clearly gain by the employment impact. But the return to the Canadian pipeline company and to sponsoring provincial governments — apparently the line will be a joint public-private venture--may have to be very low indeed. Moreover, the offshore producer will have exploration, extraction, and platform-to-shore transmission costs that must be covered. In the end, therefore, federal subsidies may play a significant role.

On the New England side, there is little doubt that a strong market exists for Canadian natural gas at prices at or near those of competitive fuels. As already indicated, the region's remote location from US natural gas-producing areas has meant high prices and low market saturation. Quite apart from New England's vulnerability to overseas oil curtailments, a "premium" fuel such as natural gas could, given a near-comparable price, readily displace oil in areas where distribution systems are in place (mainly southern New England) and could probably make inroads even where such systems have to be built from scratch. Depending on the prices eventually established, moreover, it is entirely possible that Canadian gas could replace some gas from US sources over a period of years. But this may not be the primary function. With US transmission lines now operating at below-normal capacity, Canadian gas may be needed in southern New England just to keep the lines full and to meet the needs of existing customers.

Petroleum

Trade in crude oil and petroleum products among the three regions was summarized earlier. The principal flow is northward from Portland to Montreal via the Portland Pipeline. As indicated, that line has been operating at a fraction of capacity ever since the eastern extension of the Interprovincial Lakehead Pipeline from Sarnia to Montreal was completed. Given the fact that Montreal refineries have also been operating at less than capacity and some have closed, it does not seem likely that increased trade in crude oil is a realistic prospect.

Petroleum products may be a different matter. Canada unquestionably would like to increase product exports to New England. As indicated in earlier chapters, this happened on a moderate scale during the 1970s. Moreover, US import duties were suspended for a time following the 1979 oil crisis. But the broader effect of rising oil prices in New England markets has been to dampen the demand for such imports; indeed, oil consumption in the New England states has been essentially flat for several years now.[49] While it is possible to imagine situations in which Canadian product exports to New England would rise substantially in the 1980s – for example, if US demand resumes its growth and US refineries are unable to meet that demand, or if a price differential in favour of Canadian refinery output emerges, perhaps due to a conjunction of large oil discoveries in the North Atlantic and a pricing policy aimed at undercutting American oil (not a likely circumstance given the structure of this industry) – it is much more likely that trade in oil products will remain at a relatively low level. From the standpoint of New England, of course, it is nevertheless desirable to minimize import duties on Canadian oil. It is possible that, *should* the New England product market improve, Canadian output at Montreal might find its way to Portland and points south via a reversed flow in the Portland Pipeline.[50]

Coal

Currently, trade in coal across boundaries of the three regions is negligible. Nova Scotia has significant coal reserves in the tri-region area (there are minor deposits in New Brunswick and Massachusetts), but the rate of extraction there had fallen off until very recently. That province is currently undertaking a number of new developments based on these resources, however, and there is reason to believe that coal will increasingly displace oil as a primary energy source in Nova Scotia itself. Indeed, coal is already the principal source of electricity generation in the province, having grown from less than 20 per cent in the early 1970s to 51 per cent in 1982.[51]

Whether or not Nova Scotian coal will become an important commodity in northeast interregional trade cannot be determined as yet. While it appears that coal reserves are sufficient to permit substantial exports, the price of the coal will be of critical importance. New England has access to different grades Appalachian coal from different sources. Thus, at the moment it is doubtful whether Nova Scotian coal will be competitive in the region. Nova Scotia has found some attractive markets in Europe and elsewhere, and seems more likely to pursue exports in that direction.

Policy Issues

Policy questions inevitably centre on the possibility and advantages of enlarged energy flows from north to south. Barring some entirely new, unforeseen development, New England will continue to be an energy-deficit area. Quebec will most likely move toward an equilibrium position, with surplus hydroelectric resources roughly offsetting its fuel deficit. The Atlantic Provinces as a whole would be in a heavy deficit position were it not for the hydro energy produced in — but exported from — Labrador. The Maritimes should be able to reduce their deficit, but they will probably not achieve anything like a balance unless (1) offshore oil and gas reserves prove to be substantial, or (2) tidal power can be developed at costs below those of imported energy. (Particular provinces such as Newfoundland may, of course, become important oil and gas exporters.) Canada as a whole will probably continue to be an exporter of energy to the United States, primarily in the form of natural gas, uranium, and electricity.

Looking at the three regions together, it appears that most policy questions will relate to the quantities and particular forms of energy that may be available for export, and to the prices that make such exports mutually advantageous. While there has been much discussion of appropriate energy import policy in the northeastern United States, the fact is that Canada will be the key player in future negotiations. As former Canadian Minister of Energy, Mines and Resources Marc Lalonde said in 1980 to a gathering of US business and public leaders who were emphasizing the advantages of a free trade, continental energy policy, it is all very well to talk about policy but, after all, "We have the energy, you have the policy."[52]

It was indicated earlier that Canada — both the nation and provinces — must consider the advisability of energy exports in the light of its own prospective needs and resources. It is quite important for interested parties in the United States to understand that, at least in a political sense, the presumed abundance of energy resources in Canada has a bearing on exports only when account is taken of appropriate time horizons and the Canadian provinces' own rates of growth. Generally export licences have been granted only when it has been shown that reserves are reasonably in excess of prospective domestic requirements. This also explains the severe cut-backs in oil exports to the United States during the 1970s and the decision made at that time to phase out all such exports by the mid-1980s. The past decade has witnessed a serious debate in Canada concerning long-term supplies of energy, particularly gas and oil, and the results are by no means conducive to a US assumption of indefinite imports.[53] Nevertheless, recent gas discoveries and enhanced hydro potential, as well as changes in government, may influence the Canadian position.

Assuming that energy resources do and will exceed prospective Canadian domestic demands, the other, and almost as important, question concerns the export price, hence the net benefits to Canada and net cost to the United States. Net benefits are germane to the United States as well, since imports from Canada are beneficial largely in the sense that they displace higher-cost alternatives. Thus, the second basic policy consideration is necessarily the export/import price. Other policy issues do arise from time to time: for example, the possibility of curtailment within contract periods, the desirability of US importers sharing investment costs and risks, or even the broader questions of national security. But such questions usually partake of, or are a manifestation of, the crucial issues of export quantities and price.

It might be thought that the two central issues — availability and price — are essentially separate. Thus, Canada, or a particular province, would first determine prospective or proven reserves and domestic demands (while the United States considered whether a given level of imports would be acceptable in the light of security and related requirements), and would then, only after this issue is resolved, turn to the question of terms of trade. Indeed, the political and legal apparatus governing such export/imports on either side of the boundary would lead one to believe the issues were largely separate.

But, perhaps unfortunately, the economic realities of international trade, even in such a vital commodity as energy, suggest that the two issues are not only closely connected but in many instances inseparable. The primary reason is uncertainty: uncertainty concerning the extent of energy reserves and their cost of development; uncertainty about forecasts of domestic demand growth; uncertainty about what constitutes adequate security; uncertainty surrounding the prospects for alternative forms of energy; and uncertainty about a number of other non-price aspects of trade. A consequence of this uncertainty is that the prospective price may indeed influence what values or standards are applied on the availability side.

To take an example — electricity exports — that is important to Quebec and New England, it is quite unlikely that the availability issue can be settled without due consideration of export price. Quebec's as yet undeveloped hydro resources will not all cost the same. Rather, they reflect an array of ascending real costs depending on their remoteness, scale of development, and a host of other factors. Indeed, they are quite similar to western Canada's gas and oil reserves in the sense that future quantities will require deeper wells, longer distances, and more complex technologies, all of which translate into higher real costs. Quebec would like to be assured that its lowest-cost sources of electric energy will be available if and when the province's own consumption (including consumption by the new industries it wishes to attract) grows to the point where such resources are required. Since there are inevitably large questions surrounding the actual development of such new demands, Quebec has faced a question of whether to enter into contracts for long-term, firm electricity exports. It would seem obvious that the price it receives will have an important bearing on whether or not it is deemed worthwhile to assume some risk of exporting more now than might prove advisable over the longer term.

In this instance, the question is further complicated by the relationship of the export price to Hydro-Quebec's profits, and hence its ability to keep domestic rates low (and thus attract new industry) and to contribute to the provincial government's own revenues. Until 1981, the position of Hydro-Quebec was that, given the province's future requirements, there could be no long-term export of firm or even semi- firm power.[54] But some Quebec government officials apparently thought that this position underestimated the advantages of substantial export profits now.[55] There is reason to believe that the recent Quebec government decision to promote at least limited, firm hydro exports to the United States (including New England) was closely related to its decision to reform the financial structure of Hydro-Quebec so as to receive a larger portion of its profits.[56]

Looking at this same example from the US side, to what extent does the price factor impinge on the willingness to import electric energy from Canada? Again, the answer is fairly obvious. If new England utilities can obtain even non-firm energy at a price significantly below the alternative cost of thermal generation using imported oil, they will probably do so. But the closer the export price is to the alternative cost, the stronger is the argument to use existing generating capacity in New England itself. The matter is further complicated by growing legal and environmental pressures on New England utilities to buy energy from independent producers (sometimes customers) in their own service territories.

With respect to firm-capacity imports, the utilities are again confronting alternatives, but in this case they are uneasy about importing power that might have the effect of making domestic capacity (existing or under construction) redundant. It is probably not overstating the case to say that, without a fairly substantial price differential in favour of Canadian power, the inherent preference of New England utilities' for developing their own capacity (as discussed earlier) will prevail. Beyond the decision preferences of the utilities, moreover, is the national security argument which, for some reason, seems much stronger when the Canadian export price is high than when it is low.

It is important to recognize that Quebec is not the only Canadian province in which there are strong sentiments working against electricity exports. While Ontario is not an important exporter of energy to New England, and thus is not an appropriate focus for this particular study, it is clear that political opposition to the export of both coal-generated and nuclear-generated electricity to the United States is growing in that province. The general arguments are in part those one hears in Quebec about keeping the lower-cost energy at home, and in part the arguments surrounding the creation of domestic nuclear and thermal pollution at home to produce clean electricity for export. In the Maritime Provinces, there is some serious argument developing as to the advisability of exporting nuclear energy from New Brunswick to New England if that energy indeed is the lowest-cost source over the coming few years in those provinces.[57] A sufficiently high export price will, of course, help to overcome the latter type of argument. Whether a high export price will do much to belay fears of domestic nuclear and acid rain pollution remains to be seen.

Another example of this interrelation between price and availability, and one of particular interest to New England, is the question of future natural gas exports from Canada. In a report dated June 1981, the Canadian National Energy Board took the position that Canada did not have a surplus of reserves sufficient to support additional gas exports.[58] It turned out, however, that even as the report was being prepared, gas deliveries to the US West Coast and north-central region were falling below existing contract volumes, in part because of escalation in the Canadian export price above the cost of alternative US sources. Thus, this Canadian gas could have been available to markets such as New England in which the Canadian export price was still competitive with that of gas from other sources. The ability to consummate long-term contracts at the higher prices, moreover, would unquestionably have an impact on the development of new, higher-cost reserves in western Canada. Once again, there is no real possibility of answering the availability question without considering the export price; for that matter, reserves of gas and oil, like those of any other commodity, are at least partly a function of price.

Having said this, it nevertheless seems useful, for purposes of the present discussion, to consider the availability question resolved in favour of additional gas and electricity exports and to concentrate on the terms of trade, since most of the difficult policy questions are to be found here. It is clear that New England's own energy costs are high enough to make this region a (perhaps *the*) preferred export market for both Quebec and the Atlantic Provinces. It is also clear that, if basic resource costs were the only determinant of price and if there was no international boundary, New England would almost certainly derive its future electricity supply largely from the north. An additional factor working to enhance New England's receptivity to, and willingness to pay for, Canadian energy is the high level of environmental sensitivity in the region. The situation has elements of irony; the US region having the highest energy costs by reason of its meagre resource base, distance from oil and gas reserves, and preference for private ownership of its utilities incurs still higher energy costs because of opposition to further hydro development and any but the "cleanest" technologies for using coal. On the other hand, the conservation ethic has taken hold in New England at least as strongly as it has elsewhere in the United States so that incremental demands for energy would be modest were it not for the need to displace oil for heating purposes and electricity generated in oil-fired stations. The region's continued heavy dependence on oil means that the price of that fuel, at least in the short run, will determine the selling price of Canadian gas and electricity.

Is it possible for New England and Canada to negotiate a lower export price – e.g., one more nearly approximating actual cost? The answer may depend on whether New England, and perhaps the northeastern United States generally, would be willing to broaden the area of trade negotiations so that existing impediments to Canadian fish and finished goods exports were lowered.[59] This is, of course, a national issue as well as a regional one, and the political obstacles to further reduction in tariffs on, say, Quebec shoes, textiles, and furniture or Atlantic Provinces wood products and processed fish are somewhat awesome. But, if that kind of concession cannot be granted by the United States, there is no apparent reason for Canada to sell its energy at anything less than the highest possible price, which means a price just enough below New England's alternative cost to overcome the national security argument and the built-in incentives for US utilities to construct their own plant.

The remaining impediments to energy imports can be grouped under the heading "getting New England's own house in order." It is abundantly clear that negotiations between the region's utilities and the Canadian provinces would have proceeded much more slowly had it not been for intervention by the New England governors. The stand-off relationship between the privately owned utilities and most political leaders in New England has in no way furthered the public interest in taking advantage of lower-cost Canadian energy. Indeed, threats were needed before the utilities would allow representatives of the public sector to sit in on negotiations.[60] A recent response to the situation has taken the form of legislation passed by several New England states which enables their energy directors or public utility commissions to negotiate directly with Canada and, if necessary, build the transmission lines. Unfortunately, not all of the states have done this; thus the utilities can, if they wish, still shape or even stall negotiations in the presumed interest of their stockholders rather than that of the public at large.

A related housekeeping item is the impasse that develops when an import agreement with Canada for either electricity or natural gas has a "take or pay" clause requiring the US buyer to share in the risks of delayed construction or poor operating performance, or some other type of situation requiring shut-down of the generating plant or transmission line. Most New England utilities argue that there is no incentive for their stockholders to assume the risks of such a purchase agreement unless they are assured in advance of being able to recoup the loss (stemming from paying without taking) from rate payers. Some state utility regulatory commissions, on the other hand, are reluctant to give this guarantee since it appears to lift entirely the risk element from stockholders who nevertheless insist on being granted a competitive rate of return on whatever investment is necessary to obtain the imported energy.

The impasse stems in large part from private ownership of the region's utilities. A large-scale public entity such as PASNY might well agree to such a contract, or at least one in which some capacity risks were shared, and, if something went wrong, it would have to cover the losses from consumers. But those consumers would also be benefiting (as they do benefit) from the lower financing and tax costs of the public corporation or authority in the first place. As things stand, New England's multiple private utilities and their multiple regulators all appear to be wound up in a strait-jacket of risk avoidance.

If the region is serious in its search for firm electricity and gas supplies from Canada — firm in the sense of involving long-term capacity commitments on the Canadian side — it would seem important that this issue be resolved soon, on a regional basis. This will require the cooperation of New England's six governors, their public utility commissions, and the major gas and electric utilities. Its resolution will, of course, require some sort of compromise as the interests of both consumers and security holders are at stake. Since the expiration of the NEEPS organization (New England Energy Policy Staff) in 1973, there has been no built-in public mechanism to lay the groundwork for such a resolution. Thus, it may require the efforts of several state-level groups acting together to resolve the issue. Certainly, New England cannot afford to let itself get into the position of refusing imports of lower-cost Canadian energy simply because its utilities balk at anything less than a risk-free agreement, or because they face losses from nuclear plant cancellations.

Once again, it is essential to keep energy trade benefits in perspective. This chapter has demonstrated the advantages of such trade and has discussed in some detail progress to date. If New England can obtain access to new energy supplies from eastern Canada — either temporary or long-run — at significant savings, then the trade option should be pursued vigorously, regardless of the distribution of benefits. If the Canadian provinces can channel a major portion of export revenues toward diversification of their own economies, this will obviously be of some benefit to them, and even New England will, in all likelihood, benefit once again through enhanced demand for its own products. Interregional trade flows that may seem one-sided at first glance frequently turn out to diffuse "first-round" benefits very widely.

Notes

1. John T. Miller, Jr., *Foreign Trade in Gas and Electricity in North America* (New York: Praeger, 1970). An up-to-date reference is US Energy Information Administration, *US-Canadian Electricity Trade*, Pub.   DOE/EIA 0365 (Washington, D.C.: US Department of Energy, 1982).

2. The unit of electrical *output* or *sales* used most commonly in this chapter is the kilowatt-hour (kWh), equivalent to 1,000 watt- hours. The corresponding unit of *capacity* is the kilowatt (kW); however, most capacity data herein are expressed in terms of megawatts (mW), equivalent to 1,000 kW.

3. Canadian National Energy Board, *Annual Report*, Ottawa, various dates from 1972 to 1980. The Hydro-Quebec system is not synchronized with that in New York. Consequently, exports originate in generating units that have been isolated from the Quebec network.

4. Bulk sales of electric energy can be classified according to degrees of "firmness" or dependability. Truly dependable capacity implies year-round availability of a given number of kilowatts. Purely surplus energy, at the other extreme, can be interrupted or varied at the seller's discretion.

5. Canadian National Energy Board, *Annual Report*, 1979, 1980.

6. New Brunswick Electric Power Commission, *Annual Report*, Fredericton, 1977-1982. Much of the energy exported from Quebec to New Brunswick actually originates in Labrador (Newfoundland). See Table 5.9.

7. The years 1978 and 1979 are used extensively for comparison purposes in this chapter. They appear to have been typical "full employment" years for the late 1970s.

8. This information is based in part on import data details not shown in table. Data covering liquid fuels are derived from census tabulations applicable to New England's five customs regions.

9.   New England Electric Council, *Electric Utility Industry in New England, Statistical Tables, 1983,* Boston, 1984.

10.   Vermont Public Service Board, *Biennial Reports.* Montpelier, Vermont, various dates.

11.   Canadian National Energy Board, *Annual Report 1980,* Ottawa, 1981, p. 26. In 1981 and 1982, the export price remained somewhat below the level that would be dictated by strict adherence to the formula, largely because of slack demand on the US side. Future export prices, moreover, are apt to reflect specific market conditions to a much greater degree.

12.   Canadian National Energy Board, *Annual Report,* 1981, p. 44 and Appendix E-V. Curtailment of firm power imports was partially offset by expansion of "interruptible" (lower-cost) imports, however.

13.   This information is from the Portland Pipeline Corporation. The recent closure of two Montreal refineries — both part owners in the pipeline — increases the likelihood of diminished throughput.

14.   See Statistics Canada, Cat. No. 45-205 (*Petroleum Refineries 1979*), p. 24. The conversion ratio for liquid petroleum is 1 cubic metre = 6.3 barrels.

15.   This policy in effect ties the price of exports to the cost of imported oil, or to coal, or to a combination of these. See Canadian National Energy Board, *Annual Report,* 1980, pp. 25-26.

16.   See New Brunswick Electric Power Commission, *Annual Report,* 1981.

17.   Hydro-Quebec's taxes in 1980 were about one-tenth those levied on New England's electric utilities, despite kilowatt-hour outputs being roughly the same; 1981 taxes rose sharply, however. Taxes on electric utilities in the Atlantic Provinces are similarly low or non-existent.

18.   See Statistics Canada, Cat. No. 57-203, various dates; and US Energy Information Administration, *Typical Electric Bills,* Washington, D.C., 1973-1980.

19.   Electric Council of New England, *Statistical Bulletin 1980,* Boston, 1981.

20.   A new energy contract was signed in late 1982, moreover, calling for an additional 4 billion kWh per year starting in 1984 or 1985.

21.   W.D. Shipman, An Inquiry into the High Cost of Electricity in New England, Middletown, Conn., 1962.

22.   See Table 5.10. As indicated earlier, the difference in average revenue per kilowatt-hour sold (reflecting differences in both rates and usage) was even more striking — something on the order of 2.5:1 in favour of Quebec. See also Table 5.9 and, for more recent data: Hydro-Quebec, *Annual Report,* Montreal, 1983; and Electric Council of New England, *Statistical Bulletin 1983.*

23.   Hydro-Quebec, *A Strategy for the '80s,* Montreal, 1980, pp. 44-51 and Figure 3.2.

24.   Hydro-Quebec, *A Strategy for the '80s,* pp. 15-17. Load growth was approximately 10 per cent in 1980 and 3 per cent in 1981. See Hydro-Quebec annual reports for the respective years.

25.   Hydro-Quebec, *Annual Report,* 1983; the recent load growth estimate was obtained directly from the company.

26.   See, in this connection, Energie Québec, *Electricity: Exchanges Between Quebec and the United States,* Quebec City, 1979. Also, Hydro-Quebec, *A Strategy for the '80s.* The decision to defer Phase II was announced in October 1982. Prior to this announcement Quebec's Energy and Resources Minister Duhaime had indicated on more than one occasion his willingness to consider such a program. See Quebec Govt. Delegation in New England, *Quebec Update,* February 16, 1982. Also, revised estimates of Quebec's own growth prompted the minister to pledge additional exports to New England. See *New York Times,* June 12, 1982, p. A17.

27.   Hydro-Quebec and NEPOOL press releases dated March 21, 1983. The eventual capacity of this tie will probably be

2,000 mW. Most of the energy is to be "prescheduled" on an annual and weekly basis.

28. *New York Times*, March 20, 1982, p. 1. Also, Hydro-Quebec news releases, various dates.

29. The real costs of deferred construction may also rise if later plants require additional pollution control or other types of equipment.

30. John Stuart Mill first demonstrated that the lion's share of the gains in such circumstances would accrue to the seller. See J.S. Mill, *Principles of Political Economy*, edited by W.J. Ashley (London: Longmans, Green, 1921) pp. 587-588.

31. In a separate study of the distribution of benefits under existing contracts, this author estimated that Hydro-Quebec receives "profits" that are on the order of three times the "savings" realized by New York buyers. Hydro-Quebec's own electric rates will probably be lower by up to 15 per cent, depending on the Quebec government's "take" of such profits. Paper presented at a conference of the Association for Canadian Studies in the United States, Rockland, Maine, September 1983.

32. See Government of Quebec, *Challenges for Quebec, A Statement of Economic Policy*, Quebec City, 1979, pp. 127-128.

33. Talk given by Honourable Yves L. Duhaime, Quebec Minister for Energy and Resources, before the Council on State Government Eastern Regional Conference, August 18, 1981. Hydro-Quebec is also encouraging the province's paper mills to substitute purchased for self-generated electricity, some of which uses oil.

34. The trade-off may not be entirely voluntary since, as noted above, Quebec's claim to Churchill Falls power continues to be challenged in the courts.

35. Contracted oil deliveries to New England were sharply reduced at the time of the Arab oil embargo.

36.   The US government's position on large-scale imports is not clear at this point, but the Department of Energy may well be brought under pressure by Midwest utility interests (and perhaps others) wishing to sell surplus capacity to limit such imports.

37.   This inference is drawn from discussions by the author and others within the Northeast International Committee on Energy. See also Stephen Quick, Canadian Power and the New England Energy Crisis, *New England Journal of Business and Economics* (Spring 1980). The New England utilities are especially reluctant to sign "take or pay" contracts for Canadian capacity without prior endorsement by their respective regulatory commissions, their argument being that stockholders have no incentive to assume any such risks.

38.   In the early 1970s, Maine's share of the New Brunswick energy was scaled down to 10 per cent despite its proximity to that province and the considerable length of transmission line traversing the state.

39.   The author recalls an earlier discussion with the original promoters of Churchill Falls who were trying, unsuccessfully, to sound out New England utilities' interest in the purchase of some of that 3-mill power.

40.   Under the Phase II contract Hydro-Quebec and NEPOOL reached broad agreement on an almost firm sale of electric power, the only "soft" part of which is Quebec's right to restrict deliveries by a yearly total of 400 gWh — or about 5 per cent of the time. See the interview with Phillip C. Otness, executive director of NEPOOL, which appeared in *Power Lines,* July 15, 1984.

41.   At least one-third of the capacity will be exported in the early years, according to a favourable decision of the Canadian National Energy Board dated April 1982. New Brunswick had asked for permission to export *half* the total capacity, but, as of mid-1983, it had not been successful in obtaining firm commitments from New England for the difference. It has, however, negotiated a new contract with the Central Maine Power Company calling for the sale of 150 mW of *system* energy under less stringent conditions than is true of the Point LePreau

contracts. See Point LePreau Unit Participation Agreement between New Brunswick Electric Power Commission and Massachusetts Municipal Wholesale Electric Company, dated October 24, 1980; also, Power Purchase Agreement between the New Brunswick Electric Power Commission and Central Maine Power Company, dated January 21, 1983.

42. See New Brunswick Electric Power Commission, *Annual Report*, 1983/84, p. 13.

43. See articles in the Halifax *Chronicle-Herald*, June 26, 1981, p. 1, and Montreal *Gazette*, June 25, 1981, p. 1. Only if the federal government itself creates the corridor and builds the line – an unlikely prospect without some major compensating concession to Quebec – is the corridor likely to materialize.

44. See *Reassessment of Fundy Tidal Power*, a report by the Bay of Fundy Tidal Power Review Board, 1977, and *Fundy Tidal Power Update '82*, a report to the Tidal Power Corporation, Halifax, 1982.

45. Canadian National Energy Board, *Reasons for Decisions in the Matters of Phase II – The Licence Phase, and Phase III – The Surplus Phase of the Gas Export Omnibus Hearing, 1982*, Ottawa, January 1983.

46. Canadian National Energy Board, *Reasons for Decisions*, pp. 42-44.

47. This information is from New England States Pipeline news releases, various dates. See also *Prospects for Natural Gas Exchange Between New England and Eastern Canada*, a report prepared by E.J. Curtis Associates for the New England Regional Commission, 1980; and *New England Energy Forum*, Fall 1981, pp. 11-13.

48. See *The Financial Post*, March 19, 1983, p. 1.

49. US Energy Information Administration, *State Energy Data Report*, 1979. Volumes have actually fallen since 1980.

50.   A reversed flow would require some new or possibly relocated pumping stations, together with revamped terminal facilities. Using the line to transmit natural gas is also a possibility, but, again, it would require substantial new investment.

51.   Nova Scotia Power Corp., *Annual Report*, Halifax, 1982-1983.

52.   *New York Times*, November 19, 1980, p. D1.

53.   See J.E. Gander and R.W. Belaire, *Energy Futures for Canadians*, Department of Energy, Mines and Resources, Long Term Energy Assessment Program (LEAP), Ottawa, 1978, Ch. 5. Also see B.F. Willson, *The Energy Squeeze — Canadian Policies for Survival*, (Toronto: Lorimer, 1980) Ch. 3.

54.   Letter from Robert Boyd, president of Hydro-Quebec, to New England Power Pool, dated September 18, 1979.

55.   See speech by the Honourable Yves L. Duhaime cited in note 33. More recently, it appears that long-term exports from Phase II units at James Bay may become a political issue separating the two leading parties in Quebec itself.

56.   Montreal *Gazette*, June 16, 1981, p. 7.

57.   Fight against power exports stepped up, *The Financial Post*, December 5, 1981, p. 20.

58.   Canadian National Energy Board, *Canadian Energy Supply and Demand, 1980-2000*, Ottawa, 1981. On the surplus gas problem, see *New York Times*, March 6, 1980, p. D4.

59.   This position has been developed particularly by Professor John E. Carroll, former New Hampshire representative to the Northeast International Committee on Energy. See *Halifax Herald*, July 31, 1981, p. 1.

60.   The NEPOOL committee established to carry on discussions with Hydro-Quebec originally had no member from outside the industry. After protests were made by the governors, the utilities agreed to permit the chief engineer

of the Vermont Public Service Board to sit in on their meetings.

6:   FISHERIES: THE IMPACT OF POLITICS AND ECONOMICS ON TRADE

H. Mills and M. LeBlanc

Introduction

The fishing industries of Quebec, the Atlantic Provinces, and New England have close historic ties and remain firmly interlinked. For example, Canada and the United States share one of the world's greatest fishery resources, Georges Bank, and Canada is heavily reliant upon the United States as a market for its fish products. There are also important links between the harvesting and processing sectors of each country. Canada and the United States are presently entering a new era in fisheries relations as a result of the delimitation of the boundary line in the Gulf of Maine by the International Court of Justice (ICJ).

This chapter examines the impact of politics and economics on the fisheries trade among Quebec, the Atlantic Provinces, and New England. It includes an examination of the structure of the fishing industry on each side of the border and the complications that arise because the structures are significantly different and are increasing in their divergence. It also examines differences between management systems and philosophies. Trade in the fisheries is examined in detail before concluding with a summary of current bilateral fisheries issues.

The New England Fishing Industry

The fishing industry has been important to New England for over 300 years. For much of the period, the industry thrived to a greater extent than is true today. In past years the fleet ventured into more distant waters, while today its efforts are kept close to home on Georges Bank, Nantucket Shoals, and the Gulf of Maine. Even through the 1950s, the American fleet dominated the resource-rich Georges Bank. It subsequently went into decline,

The authors wish to acknowledge the research assistance of Andre d'Entremont in the preparation of this chapter.

however, in the face of competition from foreign fleets (including Canadian) over the next two decades.

Both the New England fleet and the resource stocks were in serious decline when the 200 nautical-mile (NM) fishing zone was enacted by the US Fishery Conservation and Management Act of 1976 (Magnuson Act). Prior to this, fish beyond the 3-NM limit were a common property resource and, despite the best intentions of the International Commission for Northwest Atlantic Fisheries (ICNAF) to manage and conserve stocks, political realities were such that serious overfishing by foreign fishing fleets occurred. The 1976 Magnuson Act gave the US government jurisdiction over fishery resources between 3 and 200 NM offshore, and established a management network of eight regional councils, including the New England Fishery Management Council. The Act also greatly reduced foreign fleet operations within the 200-NM fishery conservation zone (FCZ), except for a disputed area on Georges Bank where the claims of Canada and the United States overlapped. This dispute was resolved in October 1984 when the ICJ handed down its boundary decision. Today both the industry and the resource stocks are still in a period of recovery and adjustment.

Although of significance, New England is not the dominant fisheries region in the United States. Table 6.1 gives the 1982 commercial landings for each region by weight and by value. The Pacific and Alaska region is the most important, landing 29.8 per cent of the weight and 40.3 per cent of the value of all US commercial landings, followed by the Gulf region with 36.1 per cent and 25.7 per cent, respectively. The New England region ranks third, landing 687.3 million pounds of fish valued at $373.9 million, with 10.8 per cent of the weight and 15.6 per cent of the value of all US landings.

Regional Aspects of New England Fisheries

In New England, the leading state for commercial landings is Massachusetts with 344 million pounds, representing 54.6 per cent of the value of all fish landed at New England ports (see Table 6.2). Maine follows at 30.9 per cent, with Rhode Island accounting for 14.8 per cent. New Hampshire and Connecticut combined account for only 3.6 per cent of the total landed value.

The species composition of the New England fishery is quite diverse, and varies considerably from state to state. The top five species for each state (by value, 1978) yields no less than twelve significant species: scallops, lobster, oysters, clams, cod, haddock, pollock, yellowtail flounder, blackback flounder, butterfish, redfish, and herring.

Table 6.1:   US Commercial Landings, 1982

Region	Weight (million lbs)	Value ($ millions)
Pacific and Alaska	1,872.1	964.3
Gulf	2,300.4	613.9
New England	687.3	373.9
South Atlantic	426.6	164.1
Chesapeake	791.2	120.2
Middle Atlantic	129.5	92.6
Great Lakes	36.5	12.9
Hawaii	14.2	14.4
Other	109.5	33.7
Total	6,367.3	2,390.0

Source: US Department of Commerce, *Fisheries of the United States, 1983*, Current Fishery Statistics No. 8320, April 1984.

Table 6.2:   New England Commercial Landings, 1982

State	Weight (million lbs)	Value ($ millions)
Massachusetts	344.0	204.2
Maine	217.4	100.9
Rhode Island	112.9	55.4
New Hampshire	7.6	3.8
Connecticut	5.5	9.6
Total	687.4	373.9

Source: US Department of Commerce, *Fisheries of the United States, 1983*, Current Fishery Statistics No. 8320, April 1984.

In Massachusetts, scallops are the most important (27 per cent), while lobster dominates in Maine (49 per cent), New Hampshire (47 per cent), and Rhode Island (20 per cent). Oysters (46 per cent) dominate the Connecticut fisheries.[1]

Table 6.3 summarizes commercial landings at major ports in New England from 1978 to 1982, by the ex-vessel value of landings. New Bedford and Gloucester are clearly the dominant fishing ports, with New Bedford's sizeable lead primarily the result of the high price of scallops, the specialty of the New Bedford fleet in recent years. Gloucester is the leading port for groundfish landings.

Table 6.3: **Commercial Landings at Major New England Ports ($ Millions): 1978, 1980, 1982**

Port	1978	1980	1982
New Bedford, Mass.	54.6	71.3	84.6
Gloucester, Mass.	28.9	34.7	44.5
Newport, R.I.	10.7	19.5	?
Portland, Maine	7.5	13.6	13.7
Boston, Mass.	8.1	12.3	11.8
Pt. Judith, R.I.	9.5	11.5	19.9
Provincetown, Mass.	9.1	10.4	?
Rockland, Maine	?	8.4	11.1
Sandwich, Mass.	?	7.4	?

Source: US Department of Commerce, *Fisheries of the United States, 1983,* Current Fishery Statistics No. 8320, April 1984.

Structure of the New England Industry

The structure of the New England fishing industry is highly decentralized. The fishing fleet itself is characterized by small, owner-operated vessels. While recent years have seen a significant addition of new scallop draggers to the New Bedford fleet, as well as new and larger mid-water trawlers to the groundfish fleet, there is little indication of a shift toward significant concentration of ownership. In the finest Yankee tradition, fishermen in New England are proud of their profession and of their independence as entrepreneurs, and they strongly resist all attempts to alter the structure of their industry. Many of the vessel owners are young and well educated. Ethnic groups such as Portuguese and Italians form important segments of the fishing communities and carry on a tradition of fishing within their families. Although the fishermen have not organized into unions, numerous associations and some cooperatives have been formed throughout the region, giving fishermen a more effective voice in fisheries issues.

There is very little vertical integration in the New England fishing industry, with an almost complete separation existing between the fish catching and fish processing sectors. Even at the processing level, the industry is not highly concentrated. In 1974, for the entire United States, the sales of the top fifty companies represented less than 3 per cent of the total.[2]

In 1978, there were 158 processing plants operating in New England producing $403.9 million in fish products. By 1982, the number of plants had increased to 221, employing 6,923 yearly employees and 9,427 on a seasonal basis.[3] But even the larger of these plants do not command a major share of the processing market. Table 6.4 shows the five important fish processing regions within New England, each of which focuses on a major port but with some processing plants located in the surrounding country. In 1978, the Gloucester region led the way with thirty-eight processing plants employing a seasonal average of 1,885 employees and producing $151.6 million in fish products. The other important processing regions include those of New Bedford, Boston, Rockland, and Portland. The small size of the processing plants made several of them particularly vulnerable to the recession of the early 1980s.[4]

New England processors specialize in products from groundfish, including fish sticks, fish portions, fillets, and steaks, using a combination of domestic landings and imported blocks and slabs. Cod is the leading species, with 57.8 per cent of the imported blocks and slabs, but haddock, pollock and whiting are also used. For cod, domestic landings account for 22.4 per cent, and 77.6 per cent is imported. In 1982, the United States imported a total of $273.9 million in frozen blocks and slabs, including more than $10 million from each of seven countries: Canada, Iceland, South Korea, Norway, Denmark, Greenland, and Poland. Although Canada was the leading supplier of blocks and slabs to the United States nation-wide, her percentage share was only 36.9 per cent.[5] A large proportion of the imported blocks and slabs from Canada, however, is processed in New England.

Table 6.4:New England Fish Processing, 1978

Region	No. of Plants	Average No. Seasonal Employees	$ Millions Processed
Gloucester	38	1,885	151.6
New Bedford	20	761	87.1
Boston	41	765	70.9
Rockland	12	848	51.4
Portland	26	496	36.8
Provincetown	8	69	2.9
Point Judith	5	169	2.2
Newport	4	34	0.5
Connecticut	4	35	0.5 (est.)
Total	158	5,062	403.9

Source: US Department of State, Draft Environmental Impact Statement on the Agreement Between the United States and Canada on East Coast Fishery Resources (and Appendices), Washington, D.C., March 1980.

Marketing

The population of New England and the entire eastern seaboard constitutes a large, stable (though somewhat price-sensitive) market for high-quality fish, mostly supplied from domestic landings. The fish markets in Boston and New York are especially important in meeting this demand, and the fish auctions at the Boston market tend to set the price for fish throughout New England. A concentration of fish brokers in the Boston area acts as middlemen between fishermen, processors, wholesalers, importers and exporters.

Boston is the distribution centre for scallops, lobster, groundfish, and processed products to the entire United States and to export markets. However, there is no accessible data base with which to analyse distributional patterns within the United States, much less to keep track of the origin and destination of a particular fish. For such products as frozen fillets and steaks, fish sticks, and fish portions which pass through the Boston market and/or New England processing plants, the larger buyers are fast-food chains, institutions, food wholesalers, and supermarket chains. Actual consumption, therefore, is spread over a wide geographical area. For example, cod landed by a Newfoundland fisherman may be sold to a Nova Scotia company, imported as frozen blocks and slabs via a Boston broker, processed into fish sticks and portions in Gloucester, stored in a New England warehouse, sold to a food wholesaler in Chicago, exported to a supermarket chain in Toronto, and purchased and consumed by a customer in Alberta.

Cold storage facilities play an important role in the marketing of fish, enabling companies to buy at a good price when fish are available and sell at a later time when the price has improved. High interest rates in the early 1980s raised the costs of storage and put pressure on companies to reduce their holdings. This effort was, in turn, foiled by the downturn in the economy in 1981 which resulted in a sharp decrease in demand, particularly for frozen fish sticks and fish portions, causing an undesirable increase in holdings.

Product substitutability in the market-place has a negative impact on fish marketing in New England. The consumer, caught in a price squeeze after about 1980, ate less fish at restaurants and became more price-conscious in the supermarket. Many restaurants in the fast- food fish chains closed their doors. The price of poultry, pork, and beef in the supermarkets dropped (New Englanders paid $0.49 a pound for their Grade A Thanksgiving turkey in 1981), while the price of fish continued to rise, with fish fillets typically retailing at over $2.00 a pound and up. This price pattern resulted in part from higher fuel costs and related fleet operating expenses. By late 1981, the retail price index for poultry and pork was well below that for fish, and the indices for beef and fish were about equal.[6]

Market analysts were projecting in 1983 that the market for high-quality fresh fish would remain strong, but that the market for frozen processed products such as fish sticks and fish portions would continue to decline. Although storage holdings were subsequently reduced, the impact of the market decline rapidly backed up through the system. This recent experience comes at a time when groundfish stocks on Georges Bank and off Newfoundland are expected to recover, so that catches may also be expected to increase in the future. Fishermen relying on sales to the processors can thus expect increasing difficulty in marketing, with competition driving the price down. While the premium market for fresh fish at first resisted the decline, that market has recently seen increased competition attracted by the higher prices paid.

Canada's Atlantic Coast Fishing Industry

The Atlantic coast fishing industry also has been important throughout Canada's recorded history. The Grand Banks cod fishery attracted European fishing vessels even before the period of European settlement in North America began, and it was a key factor in coastal settlement patterns, particularly in Newfoundland. In the Maritime Provinces, in Newfoundland, and in the Gaspé and Magdalen Islands of Quebec, the fishery has always played an important role in employment and as a way of life. The value of the fishery to the small coastal communities throughout the region cannot be overemphasized.

The inshore fishery, typified by small boats and a seasonal operation, has not been regarded as an economically efficient industry, but it has been an important source of income for 1,300 communities and 36,000 fishermen (1978 estimates).[7] Faced with increased competition from foreign fleets in the 1960s and 1970s which took as much as 90 per cent of the northern cod stocks off northeastern Newfoundland, Canada also began to develop a more efficient and competitive offshore fleet. Whereas the inshore fleet had always been owner operated, the high capital investment requirements for the offshore vessels meant that they were company owned.

The collapse of the cod stocks through the early to mid-1970s led to disaster for the Atlantic groundfish industry in 1974, and large federal subsidies were required to keep the industry in operation. Overfishing by foreign fleets also led to intense political pressure within Canada and resulted in the declaration of a 200-NM fisheries zone which came into force January 1, 1977. Since then, the fishery resources have been relatively well managed, but the fishing industry has not. Although a general recovery of groundfish stocks has occurred, the push and pull between the inshore and offshore fisheries, exacerbated by inconsistent and often illogical policies of the federal government, have resulted in an industry that again teeters on the brink of economic collapse.

Despite these problems, Canada's Atlantic coast fishing industry does have long-term, inherent strengths. The nominal catch in the ICNAF convention area, most of which is now under

Canadian jurisdiction, averaged over 4 million tonnes during the ten-year period from 1966 to 1975, and substantial recovery from current lower stock levels is almost a certainty. Even with present market problems, projected shortages of world protein over the long term should result in an increased demand for fish products.

The Atlantic coast fishery is by far the largest and most important in Canada, with a nominal catch of 1.2 million tonnes in 1982 and a landed value of $589 million. This represented 88 per cent of the volume and 71 per cent of the value of marine fish landings in Canada. In 1982, Canada's Atlantic coast fleet landed 61 per cent of the value for the entire Atlantic Canada New England region. The Pacific region had a nominal catch of about 160,000 tonnes, with a landed value of $240 million.[8] This high value-to-catch ratio is largely due to higher profit margins associated with the salmon fishery on the west coast. Canada's freshwater fisheries accounted for 58,000 tonnes, worth $59 million.[9]

Regional Aspects of Canada's Atlantic Coast Fishery

As shown in Table 6.5, Nova Scotia is the leading province in fishing when measured by the value of fish *landings*, with 44.3 per cent of the total landed value for Canada's Atlantic coast in 1982. Table 6.5 also gives the total value of all fish *products* for each province in 1981 (total value includes landed value), and shows that Nova Scotia has only a marginal lead over Newfoundland. Newfoundland's dependence on the northern cod stock, as compared to the more diversified fishery in Nova Scotia, resulted in a larger proportional increase in value added by processing. The value of processed groundfish products is approximately five times the landed value, while shellfish products are only double the price paid at the wharf.

The provinces show a wide variation in the proportion of different species of fish landed. Table 6.6 contains data for combinations of important species and species groupings. Newfoundland, Nova Scotia, and Quebec are highly dependent on groundfish landings, while Prince Edward Island and New Brunswick focus on shellfish. Nova Scotia not only has the largest fishery by value, but it also has the most diversified fishery, with significant volumes of scallops and lobster supplementing the groundfish catch.

Structure of Canada's Atlantic Coast Fishing Industry

The traditional analysis of Canada's Atlantic coast fishery classifies vessels as either inshore or offshore. The inshore sector tends to be labour intensive, operates primarily close to shore on a seasonal basis, uses small vessels from a large number of ports, and predominantly catches either lobster or cod. In 1978, over 28,000 inshore vessels were operating along the Atlantic coast, and they were valued at approximately $70 million and crewed by 36,000 fishermen.[10] The offshore sector is capital intensive, uses large vessels from just a few ports, and fishes in relatively distant waters within the 200-NM fishing zone on nearly a year-round basis, predominantly for groundfish, herring, and scallops. In 1978, there were over 500 offshore vessels valued at approximately $175 million and crewed by 5,000 fishermen.[11] By 1982, the number of inshore vessels remained about the same but the value had increased to $185 million, while the number of offshore vessels (including the midshore vessels) had increased to 2,583 valued at $656 million.

This new classification, midshore vessels, was introduced in recent years and consists of vessels between 45 and 99 feet in length. The use of the inshore, midshore, and offshore classification provides a more detailed analysis of the Atlantic groundfish industry which is shown in Table 6.7 (this analysis does not include the herring and scallop fleets).[12] According to the table, the inshore fleet takes 26.7 per cent of the groundfish catch with 90.7 per cent of the vessels, the midshore fleet 30.6 per cent of the catch with 8.6 per cent of the vessels, and the offshore fleet 42.7 per cent of the catch with only 0.7 per cent of the vessels. The fish-catching capability of the midshore and, especially, the offshore fleets has caused great dissension within the ranks of fishermen and, in some cases, has created successful political pressure by the more numerous inshore fishermen to restrict access of larger vessels to particular areas such as the Gulf of St. Lawrence.

The ownership of Atlantic coast fishing vessels is an important factor in the tension between fleet sectors. In 1979, 99.8 per cent of the inshore fleet vessels and 88.2 per cent of the midshore fleet vessels were individually owned. The offshore fleet, however, was 100 per cent owned by large companies,[13] and 92 per cent of the offshore groundfish fleet was owned by just four companies: National Sea Products Ltd., H.B. Nickerson and Sons Ltd., The Lake Group, and Fishery Products Ltd. These four were recently restructured into two companies (this reorganization is described shortly). Many of the inshore-offshore issues are articulated in terms of independent owners versus large corporations.

These large companies and approximately eight smaller ones are vertically integrated into the processing industry which

Table 6.5: Atlantic Coast Fishery: Provincial Shares of Landings (1982) and Products (1981)

	1982 Landings Value ($ millions)	%	1981 Fish Products Value ($ millions)	%
Nova Scotia	259.4	44.3	484.2	36.6
Newfoundland	173.0	29.6	457.8	34.7
New Brunswick	67.4	11.5	239.8	18.1
Quebec	50.0	8.5	84.6	6.4
Prince Edward Island	35.8	6.1	55.4	4.2
Total	585.6	100.0	1,321.8	100.0

Source: Canadian Department of Fisheries and Oceans, unpublished data, 1983.

Table 6.6: Atlantic Coast Fishery, 1982: Per cent Provincial Landed Values by Species and Groups

	Nfld.	N.S.	P.E.I.	N.B.	Que.	Total
Groundfish	76.6	47.9	14.0	12.0	42.7	49.7
Pelagic fish	8.6	7.7	6.1	12.3	6.4	8.3
Lobster	5.6	19.3	63.7	33.2	15.6	19.3
Scallops	0.5	21.2	2.9	4.8	0.6	10.3
Other M & C	8.2	3.0	6.8	33.7	34.7	11.0
Miscellaneous	0.5	0.9	6.5	4.0		1.4
Total	100.0	100.0	100.0	100.0	100.0	100.0

Source: Canadian Department of Fisheries and Oceans, unpublished data, 1983.

consists of about 600 processing plants located throughout the region's fishing communities. Most of the plants owned by the smaller firms are also small, and since they operate only on a seasonal basis they are not capital efficient. Thus, the large companies dominate the processing sector as well as the harvesting sector. Not only are these companies vertically integrated, but they are also horizontally integrated through branch processing plants and, to a lesser degree, forward integrated into the New England market-place. This dominant role of the large, integrated companies in the Atlantic fishing industry sharply contrasts with the structure of the New England fishing industry.

Table 6.7:   **Characteristics of Canada's Atlantic Groundfish Fleet, 1982**

	Inshore[a]	Midshore[a]	Offshore
Number in fleet	22,240	2,115	157
Per cent of fleet	90.7	8.6	0.7
Per cent of catch	26.7	30.6	42.7
Average catch (tonnes)	9.9	118.7	2,230.9

a   Definitions vary for inshore/midshore criteria: for the Maritimes, 25.5 gross tonnes; for Newfoundland, 35 feet; for Quebec, 45 feet.

Source: Canadian Department of Fisheries and Oceans, unpublished data, 1983.

Because the large processing companies also purchase supplies from the inshore fishermen, in addition to those from their own vessels, they command about 79 per cent of the groundfish production and an estimated 85 per cent of the frozen fillets and blocks. The degree of market dominance has a substantial influence on the price paid to fishermen throughout eastern Canada.

This influence has also been a large factor in the development of a number of fishermen's unions, cooperatives, federations, and associations in eastern Canada. Currently, the strongest and most influential is the United Food and Commercial Workers Local Fishermen's Union, formerly called the Newfoundland Fishermen, Food and Allied Workers Union. This union is the bargaining agent for fishermen, trawlermen, and plant workers in Newfoundland, and, recently, it also established a presence in Nova Scotia. In New Brunswick, many fishermen are represented by the Maritime Fishermen's Union, while in Nova Scotia numerous fisheries associations have organized under the umbrella of the Eastern Fishermen's Federation.

Although the large companies are a dominant force in the industry, they are also the sector that has experienced the most dramatic difficulties in the 1980s. Government subsidies and encouragement in the late 1970s led to a rapid expansion of the Atlantic coast fishing fleet and processing sector in anticipation of a bonanza for the fishing industry as a result of the 200-NM limit. But the bonanza did not occur. Instead, the industry was caught in a price squeeze with poor market projections, high inventories, rising fuel costs, overcapitalization, and high interest rates on its debts. The four largest companies became heavily indebted to the banks and both the federal and provincial governments, leading to talk of foreclosure with two or more large companies on the verge of bankruptcy. In 1982, the companies reportedly required $257 million in additional subsidies to avoid collapse.[14]

There was every reason to question whether or not the existing structure of the industry could or should be maintained. In response to the crisis, Ottawa appointed in January 1982 a task force on the Atlantic fisheries, chaired by Michael Kirby. It was asked to return with recommendations on how to achieve and maintain a viable Atlantic fishing industry, while considering the overall economic and social development of the Atlantic Provinces.

Following the release of the task force report in February 1983, restructure of the large processing/harvesting companies was given priority. Complex negotiations ensued, involving the companies, the banks, and both levels of government. In September 1983, Ottawa and Newfoundland signed an agreement to merge Fishery Products, The Lake Group, John Penney and Sons, the various H.B. Nickerson and Sons assets in the province, and a number of other smaller companies into a new "supercompany," Fishery Products International. The new company also gained ownership of the Nickerson scallop fleet in Nova Scotia in order to diversify its operations.

The federal government injected $75.3 million in equity into the new company, while the government of Newfoundland and the Bank of Nova Scotia converted $31.5 million and $44.1 million, respectively, in debt to equity.[15] This arrangement gave Ottawa controlling interest with 60 per cent of the shares of the new company, followed by Newfoundland with 25 per cent, the Bank of Nova Scotia with 12 per cent, and the employees with 3 per cent.   Both governments agreed to sell off their shares to private enterprise as soon as it is deemed feasible.

Negotiations in Nova Scotia involved National Sea Products and its parent company, H.B. Nickerson. Initially, it seemed that Ottawa would insist on an arrangement similar to that in Newfoundland, involving a merger of the two companies with the federal government becoming the major shareholder. Industry officials and the Nova Scotia government, however, were reluctant to accept this solution, and the final agreement left control of the new company, still called National Sea Products, with the private sector.

In this 1984 agreement, National Sea Products received the remaining assets of H.B. Nickerson which had been acquired by the federal government and the Bank of Nova Scotia the previous year. The federal government injected $10 million in new equity into the company and agreed to pay the bank $70 million over five years for release of the Nickerson debt. The government of Nova Scotia converted $25 million of the debt owed by the two companies to equity and agreed to postpone payment for five years of the remaining loans of about $25 million.[16] The private sector group that represented the minority shareholders was able to increase their shares from 44 per cent to 66 per cent by investing $20 million, thus gaining control of the company.

The Quebec industry did not escape the financial problems experienced in the Atlantic Provinces. The Pêcheries Unis du Québec (PUQ) cooperative declared bankruptcy on January 3, 1984, when its former affiliate, Madelipeche (85 per cent owned by the Quebec government), declared its intent to seize PUQ assets to offset debts owed. In 1979, plants owned by the PUQ processed over 43 million pounds of fish with sales totalling $48 million. In February 1984, the federal government bought the bankrupt PUQ out of receivership for $15 million with the added intention of injecting a further $6 million in equity to revitalize the plants.[17] In June 1984, the federal government and Le Mouvement Desjardin announced the investment of $30.5 million in the newly incorporated Pêcheries Cartier — created to manage the PUQ assets – making it the largest processing firm in Quebec.[18]

It remains to be seen how economically viable these new companies will be. National Sea Products is still reporting losses, while Fisheries Products International recently received a further $25 million from the federal and provincial governments and the Bank of Nova Scotia for operating expenses and to "ice-strengthen" some of its trawlers for the northern cod fishery. At the same time, smaller companies have also been experiencing economic difficulties and are looking to the government for assistance.

Marketing

The domestic market for fish in Canada, which is small in comparison to the volume of production, consumed only 24 per cent of all the fish harvested in Canada in 1978.[19] Domestic consumption has been increasing, however, particularly in institutions and restaurants. (It is estimated that only 30 per cent of consumption takes place within the home.[20]) As much as 40 per cent of the volume of fish consumed in Canada is actually imported, and, although some of the imports are products not readily available in Canada such as tuna, it is obvious that more effective marketing and distribution of fish within Canada would result in higher domestic sales. Industry, the provincial governments, and the federal government have been promoting Canada's fishery products to increase consumer awareness, but not to the same extent as other commodities such as dairy products.

In 1979, only 22 per cent of the value of Atlantic groundfish production was marketed within Canada, while 69 per cent was exported to the United States and 9 per cent to other export markets.[21] Since the United States is the predominant market for almost all product forms, the prime concern of Canada's fishing industry has been to maintain its share of US markets. In this regard, the larger companies have had a marketing edge over smaller suppliers because they can guarantee continuity of supply to large buyers, and because they have a wider range of products, economies of scale in their integrated operations, and more sophisticated marketing techniques.[22] The smaller suppliers are not as well organized, are not as well tuned in to market opportunities, and are more reliant on Boston brokers.

The 1981-1982 downturn in the economy and the decreased demand for fish in the United States, combined with a rapidly increasing production of groundfish in the Atlantic coast region, created nothing less than a marketing crisis for Canada in the early 1980s. In 1978, the federal government considered establishment of a single-desk marketing agency, but this was resisted by the processing companies who reacted by establishing the Canadian Association of Fish Exporters. Although this association has a mandate to develop new markets, it has acted more as a supplier of market intelligence to its members than as a direct marketing agency. Thus, the federal government is currently taking a harder look at establishing a single- desk marketing agency. The large processing companies are still not enthusiastic about the idea, however, because it would remove their flexibility and competitive advantage over small suppliers, but they may have to go along with it. Expanded markets and an improvement in product prices in both the United States and Canada are necessary to ensure the economic viability of the industry. The only safe observation that can be made at the moment on the structure of this industry is that it is characterized by tremendous uncertainty.

Canadian-US Fisheries Management

As neighbours, Canada and the United States share the fisheries resources of Georges Bank and the Gulf of Maine, and have a common interest in the management of transboundary stocks. As fishermen competing for the same fish and for the same dollar from the same consumer, the Canadian and American fishermen are concerned about any regulatory advantage that the other might have in catching and selling fish. For both reasons, an understanding of fisheries relations between New England and the Atlantic Provinces requires a knowledge of their separate fisheries management systems.

Canada and the United States have similar objectives in managing their marine fisheries resources and their respective fishing industries. Both systems are aimed at achieving the optimum social and economic benefits for those involved in the industry and the nation as a whole, while preserving fisheries resources over the long term. There are, however, important differences in the administrative frameworks and processes for achieving these goals. These are primarily associated with the areas of management jurisdiction, management responsibilities, and the processes whereby plans and policies are defined and implemented.

Jurisdiction

In Canada, jurisdiction over the management of marine fisheries rests solely with the federal government. This authority is derived from Section 91(12) of the British North America Act of 1867, which gives the federal government the exclusive right to legislate with respect to "Sea Coast and Inland Fisheries." The exception to this had been Quebec, which was delegated the administrative control of its marine fisheries by a federal-provincial agreement in 1922. In 1981, however, the federal government reclaimed its authority over marine fisheries for vessels greater than thirty-five feet and in 1983 for those less than thirty-five feet. Authority is manifested largely through the right to license fishing vessels. This issue remains a contentious one between these two governments, and Quebec is in the process of attempting to retain control, especially over the fixed-gear fisheries.

In the United States, jurisdiction is divided between federal and state governments. Each coastal state has the authority over fisheries resources within the territorial sea, which is 3 NM for all New England states. The area beyond the territorial sea, extending to the 200 NM limit, constitutes the fishery conservation zone which falls under the jurisdiction of the federal government. State authority over fisheries management within the territorial sea was reinstated by Congress through the 1953 passage of the Submerged Lands Act, while federal authority over management in the fishery conservation zone was established when the US Congress passed the Magnuson Fishery Conservation and Management Act of 1976.

The management of transboundary stocks in the United States is complicated by this jurisdictional split. Although regional management plans are being developed under the Magnuson Act, Section 306 maintains that state authority over fisheries management will not be diminished within the territorial sea. However, it also provides that the federal government, through the secretary of commerce, can override state authority if state regulations or lack of regulations hinder effective fisheries management within the fishery conservation zone. Thus, both interstate and federal-state conflicts can result in complicated negotiations to resolve jurisdictional problems associated with transboundary stocks and delay or prevent the achievement of a comprehensive domestic fishery policy.

It can be argued that the Canadian situation is more advantageous in terms of developing an overall management strategy. Exclusive federal jurisdiction over the regulation of fisheries can help prevent the potential problems of uncoordinated regulation and national goals in the fishery. Problems relating to migratory stocks within Canadian waters can be avoided when each fish stock is managed as a unit, although political considerations can still play a role in setting catch levels and allocations.

Administrative Responsibilities

In examining the administrative frameworks in Canada and the United States, the section on the US framework will be primarily limited to the delegated authority under the Magnuson Act which "parallels but does not replace the state management authority."[23]   Under Section 302 of the Act, eight regional councils were established to work in a coordinated effort with the National Marine Fisheries Service of the National Oceanic and Atmospheric Administration (NOAA), which in turn is an agency of the Department of Commerce.   The New England regional council includes the states of Maine, New Hampshire, Massachusetts, Rhode Island, and Connecticut. Section 302 also specifies the composition and the duties and responsibilities of a council. The major responsibilities of the New England council are to:

- develop fishery management plans and amendments to them
- review and revise assessments of optimum yield
- specify total allowable levels of foreign fishing and review applications by foreign nations for permits to fish in the fishery conservation zone
- submit periodic and prescribed reports to the secretary of commerce
- ensure input by the public to the development of fishery management plans
- undertake any other activities necessary to carry out the provisions of the Fishery Conservation and Management Act.[24]

At the present time, the New England council has two plans in operation, one for scallops and an interim one for groundfish. A draft Northeast Multi-Species Plan was recently submitted to the secretary of commerce for review. An important aspect of these plans is that they must be in accord with national standards set forth by Congress in the Magnuson Act under Section 301. To be implemented, each plan must be approved by the secretary of commerce, who then issues the necessary regulations required to carry out the plan. If the council fails to formulate its own regional plan, the secretary may do so if it is deemed necessary.

In Canada, management responsibilities stem primarily from the Fisheries Act, which covers domestic fisheries, and the Coastal Fisheries Protection Act, which deals with foreign fishing in Canadian waters. Both of these acts fall under the administration of the federal Department of Fisheries and Oceans.

The major point to be noted here is the difference in authority of the minister of fisheries and oceans and the secretary of commerce with respect to domestic fisheries. Although management plans in the United States must be amended if the secretary so desires before granting approval, controlling fishing effort by limiting entry, a major management tool, can only be "initiated and proposed by the regional councils."[25] On the other hand, "the Federal Fisheries Act gives the minister extraordinary influence, including discretionary power over a wide range of activities. His licensing authority (a form of limiting entry) enables him, in effect, to control the flow of raw material."[26]

Two further points deal with the questions of discretionary authority and the political reality of exercising authority. The Magnuson Act is more explicit as to what the secretary of commerce and the regional councils *shall* do, but this is not the case with the Fisheries Act in Canada. It has been noted that:

> Like many other federal statutes, the Fisheries Act is characterized by extremely frequent recourse to cabinet and ministerial discretion. The truth is that the Governor- in-Council (the Cabinet), the Minister of Fisheries, and through him the senior administrators of Fisheries Canada have wide discretionary powers in most areas of fishery administration.[27]

A Canadian fisheries policy report of 1976 states: "Implicit in the new orientation is more direct intervention by government in controlling the use of fishery resources, from the water to the table...."[28] It appears that this attitude will also prevail in the 1980s. A discussion paper prepared by the Department of Fisheries and Oceans in 1981 states that one of the strategic objectives of the department is "the best use of fisheries resources through a variety of measures affecting when, where, how and by whom these resources are harvested, processed and marketed to obtain optimal social-economic benefits."[29]

In the United States, there appears to be some doubt as to the breakdown in authority and responsibility between NOAA, acting within the Department of Commerce, and the New England council, as well as between the state and federal entities. In the first case, a report on the implementation of the Magnuson Act in 1980 declares:

> On several occasions the New England Fishery Management Council has taken exception to administrative procedures and regulations adopted by NOAA and determined by the Agency to be applicable to the activities of the Regional Fishery Management Councils.[30]

In the second case, it still remains to be seen whether vessels registered in a specific state can be regulated by that state when fishing outside state waters. The problem will be especially important if state regulations do not coincide with federal regulations in fishery management plans.

Decision-Making Processes

An important component of any management regime is the question of who has input into the decision-making process, especially the development of fisheries management plans. In the United States, under Section 302 of the Magnuson Act the regional councils are ensured a high degree of input into the development of plans. The councils, which comprise a wide array of interests, vary in composition from region to region. According to one study:

> The main reason for the divergence of expertise from council to council is that the type of membership on each council varies considerably. Some councils have more environmentalists than others; some have more commercial fishermen; some have more processors; some have more sport fishermen. For example, in the New England Council, the interests of the processors are more heavily represented than in other councils. . . .[31]

It is important to realize that although the secretary of commerce appoints the voting members of the councils, they are chosen from a list of candidates compiled by the governors of the states in each region.[32] In this sense, it can be interpreted as a balancing scheme whereby federal and state interests are represented.

Public involvement is ensured in the United States as public hearings are mandatory at various stages in the planning process. A council must hold these hearings prior to final completion of a management plan and for any amendments to a plan. Once the plan has been approved by the secretary of commerce, it must be published in the *Federal Register*. At this time, the secretary may hold another hearing within forty-five days of notification. This period also allows receipt of written comments on the plan. It is only after these steps that the secretary can promulgate the regulations necessary to implement the plan. A potentially important result of these public hearings and of having fishermen represented on the councils is that it could provide "intangibles associated with increased self esteem, belongingness, and self-actualization."[33] Because of this input, plans may tend to be self-enforced with the input-response loop and the whole fishery management system being reinforced.[34]

Unlike the US system, the Canadian system for developing a management plan is not enshrined in legislation. In past years the government has often been accused of not adequately involving all sectors of the industry in the establishment of plans. Snow points out that "[t]he public interest, like all other interests, at every stage of the management process in the Canadian system is left to be considered or ignored by the Minister of Fisheries . . . and all those who act in his name."[35]

In recent years, with the establishment of numerous consultative committees, it appears that some degree of optimism is warranted about industry input into the management process. A good example is the formulation of the Atlantic Groundfish Management Plan, in which the Department of Fisheries and Oceans is relying more heavily upon a structured process in arriving at total allowable catches, their allocation, and associated regulations. In using an established process for the development of recent plans, the government appears to be setting a precedent for a structured and integrated process which may be politically difficult to deviate from in future years. According to 1981 policy paper:

> The department intends to strengthen the consultation mechanism in the resource management process for Atlantic fisheries to provide a streamlined decision-making system with particular reference to annual discussion of TAC's, allocations and regulations for all fisheries.[36]

In terms of bilateral relations, Canada and the United States do not have a formal channel of communications for specifically addressing fisheries management issues. In light of the recent boundary settlement the Department of Fisheries and

Oceans has established the Gulf of Maine Advisory Committee, but its role, unlike that of the New England regional council, is to advise the minister and not to establish policy. At the federal level, a formal connection exists between the US Department of State and the Canadian Department of External Affairs, with informal contacts between the Canadian Department of Fisheries and Oceans and the US National Marine Fisheries Service and the New England regional council. For example, in March 1985 representatives of the Department of Fisheries and Oceans made a presentation to the New England council outlining the Canadian groundfish management system. At the provincial/state level, the New England governors and the eastern Canadian premiers have established a bilateral working group composed of representatives from both sides to examine and discuss the economic development features of fisheries.[37]

Regulations

Fishery plans in both countries can incorporate standard management tools such as catch quotas, area closures, seasonal closures, mesh size, gear restrictions, size limitations, and limited entry. Although all of these tools can be used, only certain ones are deemed appropriate for individual fisheries. A prime example of differences between the fisheries management systems of the two countries revolves around the question of using limited entry as a management tool. In management plans prepared by the New England council for both groundfish and scallops, limited entry is not used to control fishing. On the other hand, limited entry via licensing schemes is currently a major thrust of Canadian fisheries policy. The Department of Fisheries and Oceans views licensing as a means of control, primarily in response to the poor economic state of a fishery[38] — that is, the generally perceived notion that there are too many fishermen harvesting a finite resource, leading to decreased economic returns for all participants.

This difference in the use of a management tool has been a contentious point with respect to the scallop fishery on Georges Bank. While the number of Canadian scallop licences has not increased since 1973, an increasing number of US boats have been fishing for scallops in this area, leading to accusations by Canadians that this fishery is being seriously overfished by US fishermen. It may be difficult, however, to incorporate limited entry in the New England zone because of National Standard 4 which requires "fair and equitable" allocations between residents of different states. Thus, the limited entry concept is clearly not supported by New England fishermen. Of interest, nevertheless, is that Massachusetts recently implemented limited entry by banning vessels over 90 feet from fishing in state waters. Concern has been expressed that this may be a dangerous precedent for other New England areas.[39]

Another difference between Canada and the United States is the method of setting total allowable catch levels. Prior to the incorporation of social and economic criteria into determining total allowable catches, the biological basis for the levels must be formulated. The United States is currently using maximum sustainable yield (MSY) as its basis, while Canada is using what is known as $F_{0.1}$. MSY is the point on a yield curve where fishing at this level would produce the greatest physical yield on a long-term basis. $F_{0.1}$ is defined as "the level of fishing mortality at which the increase in yield (marginal yield) by adding one more unit of fishing effort is 10 per cent of the increase in yield by adding the same unit of effort in a lightly exploited stock."[40] This point is somewhat below the MSY level and is estimated to yield 80-90 per cent of the MSY yield over the long term. It should be noted that while the New England regional council does not set quotas based on total allowable catches, the MSY level is used as the basis for formulating other regulations such as mesh size and minimum fish size to optimize catches near or at this level.

It must also be remembered that this difference in approach may not in the end be a significant difference once the social, economic, and political inputs have been incorporated into determining optimal yields. There is no guarantee that optimal levels will coincide with either the MSY level for the United States or the $F_{0.1}$ level for Canada.

Conclusion

The fisheries management systems of both the United States and Canada seek to optimize net social and economic benefits for their respective fishing industries. However, as has been shown, the two systems are quite different in the means used to achieve this result. The key features of the Canadian system are the authority and discretionary powers of the minister of fisheries and oceans and his officials in managing fisheries. The American system is both less arbitrary and less flexible, but it features a more democratic and shared approach to fisheries management. The United States has chosen to follow a legislated framework which provides greater assurance of industry involvement. Although in practice the Canadian system parallels the US system to a certain extent in this area, it is continually subject to change depending upon the political climate of the fishing industry and the will of the minister.

Tri-regional Fish Trade

The positions of Canada and the United States in the fish catching and fish trading nations of the world are summarized in Table 6.8. Based on data from the Food and Agriculture Organization (FAO) of the United Nations, this table shows the 1981 volume of fish caught (in millions of tonnes), and the 1981 value of fish traded (in millions of US dollars).

Table 6.8: Summary of World Fisheries, 1981: Production, Exports, and Imports

	1981 Production (million tonnes)		1981 Exports (million $ US)		1981 Imports (million $ US)	
1	Japan	10.7	Canada	1,267.3	Japan	3,736.8
2	USSR	9.5	USA	1,142.0	USA	2,988.2
3	China	4.6	Norway	1,001.7	France	1,050.9
4	USA	3.8	Denmark	940.4	U.K.	977.1
5	Chile	3.4	Japan	863.2	F.R.G.	818.9
6	Peru	2.8	S. Korea	834.9	Italy	720.2
7	Norway	2.6	Iceland	712.6	Spain	479.3
8	India	2.4	Mexico	538.5	Hong Kong	361.5
9	S. Korea	2.4	Netherlands	511.6	Belgium	347.7
10	Indonesia	1.9	Spain	436.1	Netherlands	330.5
11	Denmark	1.8	Thailand	358.3	Denmark	304.8
12	Philippines	1.7	Chile	337.2	Canada	298.7
13	Thailand	1.7	China	324.6	Sweden	269.9
14	Mexico	1.6	U.K.	318.4	Nigeria	239.8
15	N. Korea	1.5	France	304.0	Switzerland	162.1
16	Iceland	1.4	F.R.G.	280.9	Singapore	162.1
17	Canada	1.4	Australia	268.3	Australia	161.8
Total World		74.8		15,382.0		15,958.8

Source: Food and Agriculture Organization of the UN, *Yearbook of Fishery Statistics, 1981* (Rome: FAO, 1982).

Although Canada ranked seventeenth in the world in terms of the volume of fish caught, it is the world's leading exporter of fish with sales of 1.27 billion US dollars in 1981. Although Canada also shows up as the world's twelfth leading importer of fish — a surprising fact to some observers — it still had a favourable balance of trade in fish of approximately 968 million US dollars in 1981.

The United States ranks fourth among the world's fishing fleets, catching 3.8 million tonnes in 1981, almost three times the Canadian catch. For both exports and imports, the United States ranks second in the world behind Canada and Japan, respectively. This equal ranking in fish trade masks the fact that the US dollar values of exports and imports are quite different, with imports close to $3 billion and exports just over $1 billion, leaving an unfavourable US trade balance in fish of almost $2 billion in 1981.

Canada and the United States conduct a large volume of trade with each other in fish and fishery products. Using different sets of data from each country, Tables 6.9 and 6.10 show that the United States is Canada's leading trading partner for both exports and imports of fish, while Canada is the leading source of US fish imports and ranks second to Japan as a market for US exports.

The data from Tables 6.8 and 6.9 indicate a 51 per cent increase in the value of total US fish imports from 1981 to 1982, while US exports decreased by 7 per cent. Thus, the US unfavourable trade balance in fish of $1.8 billion in 1981 almost doubled in 1982 to $3.5 billion, accounting for about 10 per cent of the total US trade deficit. This dramatic increase underlines the fact that the US policy of achieving self-sufficiency is not meeting with short-term success, despite advantages gained by the 200-NM fishing zone. The United States imports a significant volume of fish from a large number of countries so that, although it is the leading source of fish, Canada only supplies 18 per cent of the total. With $813.7 million in imports from Canada and $122.5 million in exports to Canada, the United States had a $691 million fish trade deficit with Canada in 1982.

The 1982 Canadian data emphasize the high export market concentration of Canadian fish: 56 per cent go to the United States, 23 per cent to Western Europe, and 15 per cent to Japan. As noted later in this chapter, the US market concentration is even higher for Canada's Atlantic coast fish. Similarly, Canada buys 59 per cent of her fish imports from the United States, with the remainder coming from a large number of countries.

Table 6.9:   US Foreign Trade in Fishery Products, 1982

	Exports			Imports		
To	Value ($ millions)	%	From	Value ($ millions)	%
Japan	620.2	58.6	Canada	813.7	18.0
Canada	122.5	11.6	Italy	512.1	11.3
France	52.9	4.9	Mexico	413.7	9.1
All other	263.3	25.3	All other	2,784.1	61.6
Total	1,058.9	100.0	Total	4,523.6	100.0

Source: US Department of Commerce, *Fisheries of the United States, 1983,* Current Fishery Statistics No. 8320, April 1984.

Table 6.10: Canadian Foreign Trade in Fishery Products, 1982

	Exports			Imports		
To	Value ($ millions)	%	From	Value ($ millions)	%
United States	879.6	55.6	United States	207.5	59.0
Europe	369.8	23.3	Europe	23.2	6.6
Japan	236.3	14.9	Japan	22.8	6.5
All other	97.6	6.2	All other	98.3	27.9
Total	1,583.3	100.0	Total	351.8	100.0

Source: Statistics Canada, Exports and Imports by Country, 1982.

Canada-US Fish Trade

Table 6.11 summarizes the fish trade in terms of value between Canada and the United States for 1978-1982 using Canadian data. During this period Canadian exports to the United States increased from $542.4 to $879.9 million, or 62.2 per cent. Canadian imports from the United States increased from $140.1 to $207.8 million over the same period, for an increase of 48.3 per cent. The overall result was a significant increase in Canada's favour of 67 per cent in the balance of trade in fish.

Table 6.11:   Canada-US Fish Trade (Million $ Canadian), 1978-1982

	Exports to US	Imports from US	Balance of Trade
1978	542.4	140.1	+ 402.3
1979	599.1	181.7	+ 417.4
1980	663.5	233.0	+ 430.5
1981	799.2	225.4	+ 573.8
1982	879.9	207.8	+ 672.1

Source: Statistics Canada, *Exports and Imports by Country, 1982.*

The general picture, when volumes as well as values are considered, is one in which Canada exports a large volume of an unprocessed and relatively cheap fish product to the United States, and buys back a small volume of relatively expensive fish. This is due in part to a strong demand in Canada for certain types of shellfish (shrimp, king-crab legs, rock lobster tails, etc.) that the domestic fishery cannot supply, and in part to tariffs.

US tariff duties on unprocessed fresh or frozen fish imports are quite small, from 0 to 2 per cent. For processed secondary products, however, such as fish sticks and portions, tariffs range from 10 to 15 per cent. Thus, Canada exports very little processed groundfish to the United States, but sends high volumes of frozen blocks and fillets to processing firms in New England. Some of the processed fish then returns to Canada through major food wholesalers. Aside from groundfish, Canadian exports to the

United States are dominated by scallops and lobster from the Atlantic coast, and salmon from the Pacific coast.

Table 6.12 breaks down Canada's 1982 fish exports to the United States by five commodity groups. The fillets or blocks group, consisting almost entirely of a frozen product, accounted for 52.1 per cent of the total value. The "other" group, which includes fresh or frozen scallops and lobster, accounted for 29.3 per cent of the total, leaving 18.6 per cent for the remaining three groups.

In Canada, fishermen often talk about the price of fish in Boston. This is not just a colloquial expression or a reflection of past colonial ties; it is an apt comment on linkages between the Canadian and American fishing industries. Table 6.12 also shows the destination of Canada's fish exports to the United States, and the fact that 70.3 per cent of the $879.9 million total goes to New England. Massachusetts, Connecticut, and Rhode Island receive 63.3 per cent of the total, and Massachusetts undoubtedly takes the majority, so that the Greater Boston area probably handles about 50 per cent of all fish exported to the United States from Canada. Thus, the price of fish in Boston plays a highly significant role in determining the price paid to Canadian fishermen at Canadian wharves.

Table 6.12:   **Canadian Fish Exports to United States ($ Millions), by Destination, 1982**

Commodity	Maine, N.H., Vt.	Mass., Conn., R.I.	Other US	Total US
Fish, whole or dressed	4.1	32.7	66.8	103.6
Fish, fillets or blocks	20.5	351.5	86.4	458.4
Fish, preserved	1.0	14.8	32.5	48.3
Fish, canned	1.7	0.5	9.8	12.0
Other, including shellfish	34.7	157.3	65.6	257.6
Total	62.0	556.8	261.1	879.9

Source: Statistics Canada, *Domestic Exports to US, 1982*.

Trade in Fisheries-Related Products

Aside from trade in fish and related food products, there is also a substantial international trade in fishing equipment such as nets, winches, navigational devices, and vessels. Although there generally has been little information available on this aspect of the fishing industry, a 1981 study of industrial development in Canada's Atlantic fishery provides considerable insight.[41]

Table 6.13 traces Canadian imports of fisheries-related products from 1975 to 1982 and shows an upswing in imports following 1977 and the concomitant expansion of the industry. The United States supplies about 65 per cent of total imports to the Canadian market, with the remainder scattered among the fishing/industrial nations of the world. Many of these products enter Canada duty-free, supplied through well- established relationships with foreign firms. Although Canadian policy is to increase research and development and to stimulate fisheries-related industry, some products such as polytwines are not supplied domestically. However, Canada had a trade surplus of fisheries-related products in 1982 with imports of $914.6 million and exports of $1,041.8 million. This was achieved in part through a decline in imports from 1981 to 1982, reflecting the economic crisis facing the industry.

Table 6.13:   Canadian Imports of Fisheries-Related Products ($ Millions), Selected Years, 1975-1982

Origin	1975	1977	1979	1981	1982
United States	355.9	366.1	527.0	720.0	639.1
Other world	183.0	214.9	285.4	308.7	275.5
Total	538.9	581.0	812.4	1,028.7	914.6

Source: Statistics Canada (as reported in David J. Patton, *Industrial Development and the Canadian Atlantic Fishery* [Ottawa: Canadian Institute for Public Policy, 1981]).

The Patton study estimates that the Atlantic fishery comprises approximately 70 per cent of the total Canadian market for fisheries-related products.[42]   Applying that percentage to the $639 million in products imported from the United States would allocate about $447 million in American fisheries-related products to the Atlantic fishery in 1982. Although data on US origins of these products are not available, there is no doubt that a large proportion comes from New England.

Atlantic Provinces Fish Exports to New England

Selling fish to Boston is such an integral part of the fishery in Atlantic Canada that many fishermen scarcely recognize that they are in the export business. Their broker just happens to live in Boston. When a small company in southwest Nova Scotia has fish to sell, a telephone call is placed to the broker and a truck arrives to pick up the fish and deliver them to the United States. The role of New Englanders as the middlemen and the processors of Canadian fish is accepted without question by the majority of fishermen in Atlantic Canada.

Fish exports from the Atlantic Provinces to the United States comprised 80.3 per cent of the value of all Canadian fish exports to the United States in 1982. In turn, 82.5 per cent of the Atlantic Provinces share went to New England at an export value of $582.9 million. Table 6.14 shows that $525.9 million of fish went to the census subdivision headed by Massachusetts.

By far the largest commodity group of exports in Table 6.14 is fish fillets or blocks. A high concentration of these shipments is destined for Massachusetts, where the fish are processed and redistributed. The "other" commodity group, primarily consisting of fresh or frozen scallops and lobster, also has a high concentration of shipments to Massachusetts. While exports to Maine are not insignificant, they account for only 8.1 per cent of Atlantic Canada's exports to the United States. The preserved and canned commodity groups have broader-destination markets as they do not require further processing.

Table 6.15 gives a province-by-province breakdown of the origin of regional fish exports to the United States and uses a more detailed class of commodity groups. Unfortunately, this data set is not available for destination regions within the United States, although we have already determined that 82.5 per cent goes to New England. Frozen fillets is the leader in this export class of commodities, followed by fresh or frozen shellfish and by frozen blocks and slabs. One interesting point is that, despite the proximity of New England to Atlantic Canada, historically very

Table 6.14: **Atlantic Provinces Fish Exports to United States ($ Millions), by Destination, 1982**

Commodity	Maine, N.H., Vt.	Mass., Conn., R.I.	Other US	Total US
Fish, whole or dressed	4.0	31.1	6.3	41.4
Fish, fillets or blocks	16.3	336.2	39.0	391.5
Fish, preserved	0.6	12.0	23.3	35.9
Fish, canned	1.7	0.5	8.2	10.4
Other, including shellfish	34.4	146.1	46.5	227.0
Total	57.0	525.9	123.3	706.2

Source: Statistics Canada, Cat. No. 65-003 (*Exports by Countries, 1982*).

Table 6.15: **Atlantic Provinces Fish Exports to United States ($ Millions), by Province of Lading, 1982)**

Commodity	Nfld.	N.S.	P.E.I.	N.B.	Total
Fresh fish, whole or dressed	1.2	20.7	0.3	4.1	26.3
Frozen fish whole or dressed	8.9	3.6	0.4	2.2	15.1
Fish fillets, fresh	5.7	15.4	0.8	0.4	22.3
Fresh fillets, frozen	157.1	83.4	8.9	13.2	262.6
Blocks and slabs, frozen	72.7	26.5	0.2	7.0	106.4
Smoked, salted, pickled, canned	4.9	25.3	0.5	15.7	46.4
Shellfish, fresh or frozen	21.7	103.9	12.4	88.4	226.4
Other fish and fish products		0.2		0.1	0.3
Total	272.1	279.1	23.4	131.2	705.8

Source: Statistics Canada, Domestic Exports by Province of Lading, 1982.

little fresh fish has been exported, although this is rapidly changing and is seen as a significant factor in US countervailing requests, described in a later section. Combining the first five commodity groups of Table 6.15 (all whole or dressed fish, all fillets, and all blocks or slabs), we find that only 11.2 per cent of the total export value is in fresh fish; 88.8 per cent is frozen.

The province-by-province variations are important Newfoundland exports only 2.8 per cent of the first five commodity groups as fresh fish and has a high dependence on the export of frozen blocks and slabs and frozen fillets. On the other hand, Nova Scotia exports 24.1 per cent of the first five commodity groups as fresh fish and also exports a high value of shellfish, resulting in a broader-based and more stable fishing industry. New Brunswick is not a major exporter of fresh or frozen groundfish, but relies on shellfish and herring exports. P.E.I.'s share of the export market is much smaller, with frozen fillets and lobster being the leading exports to the United States.

Quebec Fish Exports to New England

The total value of fish exports from Quebec was $100.9 million in 1982, compared with $1,026.4 million from the Atlantic Provinces. Unlike the other provinces, Quebec does not have a strong dependence on American markets. Only 54.6 per cent of its exports go to the United States; others go to the United Kingdom, West Germany, and France. Table 6.16 shows that this is particularly true for the shellfish and smoked, salted, pickled, canned commodity groups, while 73.6 per cent of fish in the first five commodity groups are exported to the United States.

According to Table 6.17, Quebec fish exports to New England follow a similar pattern to those from Atlantic Canada with Massachusetts as the primary destination. Within the United States, 59.6 per cent of Quebec fish exports go to New England and 21 per cent to the census subdivision headed by New York, a geographically logical trading partner for Quebec.

Atlantic Provinces Fish Imports from the United States

Fish imported by the Atlantic Provinces fall into two categories: use by the processing sector and direct consumption. The former is such a small volume of trade that data are not kept on the origin of shipments within the United States. The latter involves a combination of: (1) fish imported directly by the Atlantic Provinces (on which data are available), and (2) fish imported by food wholesalers in Ontario or Quebec and distributed to supermarket chains throughout the Atlantic Region (on which data are not available).

Table 6.16:   Quebec Laden Exports ($ Millions), 1982

Export Class	Exports to US	Total Exports	US as % of Total Exports
Fresh fish, whole or dressed	1.3	1.7	71.5
Frozen fish, whole or dressed	1.2	7.4	16.4
Fish fillets, fresh	2.1	2.2	95.3
Fish fillets, frozen	13.5	15.1	89.3
Blocks and slabs, frozen	7.3	8.1	90.2
Smoked, salted, pickled, canned	11.4	19.2	59.7
Shellfish, fresh or frozen	18.4	46.8	39.3
Other fish and fish products	-	0.4	-
Total:	55.2	100.9	54.7

Source: Statistics Canada, *Domestic Exports by Province of Lading, 1982*.

Table 6.17:   Quebec Fish Exports to United States ($ Millions), by Destination, 1982

Commodity	Maine, N.H., Vt.	Mass., Conn., R.I.	Other US	Total US
Fish, whole or dressed		0.6	1.9	2.5
Fish, fillets or blocks	4.1	14.5	4.3	22.9
Fish, preserved	0.3	2.8	8.3	11.4
Fish, canned				
Other (including shellfish)	0.2	10.4	7.8	18.4
Total	4.6	28.3	22.3	55.2

Source: Statistics Canada, Cat. No. 65-003 (*Exports by Countries, 1982*).

With the above limitations in mind, Table 6.18 summarizes all fish imported by the Atlantic Provinces in 1982. Total imports were $42.5 million, with 41.4 per cent of that value coming from the United States. The leading imports were tuna (fresh or frozen), lobster (fresh or frozen), and shrimp (fresh or frozen). This would seem to indicate that Atlantic Provinces processors occasionally import products that are available locally, presumably because they can get better prices or better quality or because of seasonal factors.

Table 6.18:   Atlantic   Provinces   Laden   Imports ($ Millions), 1982

Import Class	Imports from US	Total Imports	US as & of Total Imports
Fish, fresh, frozen or cured	8.8	25.6	34.4
Fish, canned		1.3	
Shellfish, fresh or frozen	7.4	7.8	94.9
Shellfish, canned	0.3	5.5	5.5
Other	1.1	2.3	47.8
Total	17.6	42.5	41.4

Source: Statistics Canada, *Domestic Imports by Country, 1982.*

Quebec Fish Imports from the United States

Quebec imported $86.4 million in fish during 1980, considerably more than the Atlantic Provinces, with 54 per cent coming from the United States (see Table 6.19). The leading imports were lobster (fresh or frozen), shrimp (fresh or frozen), frozen blocks, seafish (fresh or frozen), and canned tuna. Most of these would appear destined for Montreal restaurants or supermarkets.

Table 6.19: **Quebec Laden Imports ($ Millions), 1982**

Import Class	Imports from US	Total Imports	US as & of Total Imports
Fish, fresh, frozen, or cured	17.9	20.5	87.2
Fish, canned	1.0	7.5	13.3
Shellfish, fresh or frozen	22.3	48.4	46.1
Shellfish, canned	5.1	9.4	54.0
Other	0.3	0.5	59.6
Total	46.6	86.4	54.0

Source: Statistics Canada, *Domestic Imports by Country, 1982.*

Atlantic Provinces Fish Trade with Quebec

No data are available on fish trade between these two regions. Thus, the best one can do is to speculate about the likely movement from the resource-catching sector to the consumer. First, it is assumed that the trade is primarily from the Atlantic coast to the relatively populated St. Lawrence Valley. Second, it is assumed that Quebec, with 26 per cent of Canada's population, accounts for a similar proportion of domestic fish consumption. With 24 per cent of Canada's catch consumed domestically, and using the 1982 landed value of $585.6 million for the Atlantic coast (including Quebec), approximately $35 million may have been shipped to Quebec.

Bilateral Fisheries Issues

Bilateral fisheries issues between Canada and the United States of direct relevance to the New England and Atlantic coast fisheries fall into two broad categories: resource management issues and economic issues. The first category reflects a situation in which two countries share the fisheries resources of the Gulf of Maine-Georges Bank area, with many fish stocks spanning the new US-Canadian boundary. The second category reflects the frequent competition between fishermen on both sides of the border for the same market—fishermen who are quite sensitive about any comparative advantage that fishermen from the other country may have in the market-place. Thus, such topics as vertical integration, economic impact of regulations, government subsidies, dollar exchange rates, tariff rates, and fish/market access all become political issues.

Resource Management Issues

Although the International Court of Justice handed down on October 12, 1984 its binding decision on the US-Canadian boundary on Georges Bank, a joint management scheme for the transboundary stocks is still needed. The problems that might be encountered in formulating an acceptable solution are reflected in the past difficulties associated with the now-defunct East Coast Fisheries Agreement.

With the introduction of 200-NM fishing zones for both countries in 1977 and the resulting impending demise of the International Commission for Northwest Atlantic Fisheries, it was recognized that some form of joint management regime was required for the Gulf of Maine-Georges Bank area. At the same time, with the maritime boundary in dispute because of overlapping 100-NM zones, some fishermen became concerned about the impact that an adverse boundary settlement could have on their fishing operations. Thus, in this way the fisheries dispute and the boundary dispute became linked.

The United States appointed Lloyd Cutler to head its negotiating team, while Canada appointed Ambassador Marcel Cadieux. Both negotiators relied heavily on consultations with their respective fisheries advisory groups.[43] Negotiations were successfully concluded early in 1979 and the formal signing of two documents took place: a treaty to delimit the maritime boundary in the Gulf of Maine area and an agreement of east coast fishery resources. The documents were linked in that both documents had to be ratified by both countries, or there was no agreement. The documents were structured so that the fisheries agreement would come into force before sending the boundary dispute to the International Court (or to third-party arbitration). In this way the eventual boundary settlement would have little effect on quota allocations or on the management regime.

Given a parliamentary system and the prior Cabinet approval of Cadieux's negotiating position, ratification never presented a problem in Canada. The American system, however, requires that all such agreements must be approved by a two-thirds vote of the Senate, and it soon became apparent that the Senate Foreign Relations Committee was not in favour of ratification.

American fishermen had a number of reasons for not liking the proposed fisheries agreement: the management scheme was unnecessarily cumbersome and would undermine the New England regional council; US scallop allocations were felt to be too low; Canada would be managing scallop resources in undisputed US waters; groundfish allocations were too specific and by-catches would have to be thrown overboard; the boundary dispute should be settled before having a fisheries agreement; and the fisheries agreement should not be permanent.[44] The US fishermen formed a Fisheries Defense Committee which successfully lobbied against ratification.

President Reagan unilaterally withdrew the fisheries agreement from the Senate in 1981 and asked Canada to agree to send a de-linked boundary reference to the International Court. This provoked a bitter reaction from Canadian politicians and the fishing industry, but agreement on terms for the reference was reached late in the year.

The problems associated with separate management schemes were especially highlighted by the Georges Bank scallop fishery during the period when both sides were awaiting resolution of the boundary dispute. Georges Bank scallops are one of two important sea scallop stocks available to American fishermen, and they are the only sizeable stock available to Canadian fishermen. Traditionally, they were exploited only by New England fishermen, but Canadians began to participate in 1951. The Nova Scotia fleet rapidly expanded thereafter, dominating the fishery from 1965 through 1979, and taking a full 90 per cent of the catch in 1975. With scallop prices and stocks both high in the late 1970s, the New Bedford, Massachusetts fleet expanded and competition became intense.

The proposed fisheries agreement would have given Canada 73.35 per cent of all scallops on Georges Bank, including both the disputed area (about two-thirds of all Georges Bank scallops were in the disputed area) and undisputed US waters. The scuttling of the agreement left the latter scallops out of bounds to the Canadian fleet and led to increased competition in the disputed sector.

By 1980, the New Bedford fleet, augmented by mobile vessels from the Mid-Atlantic fleet, was taking at least 50 per cent of the Georges Bank catch, although Canada took about 74 per cent of the resource from the disputed zone. Nova Scotian fishermen vehemently opposed the increased American effort while awaiting ratification of the fisheries agreement, and charged the United States with poor management practices because the New England council had no scallop management plan. The main irritant was that the industry was tightly controlled by regulations in Canada, whereas the New England scallop fleet was virtually unregulated. (For example, entry to the scallop fishery is limited in Canada, voyages must be of twelve days or less, and scallop meats must average thirty-five or less per pound.)

By 1981, the stocks of larger scallops in the disputed area were depleted, but there was an abundant supply of small scallops (for which there is a consumer preference in New England). With the unregulated New England fleet still increasing its efforts, and with the Nova Scotian fleet having a difficult time catching its quotas at the regulated meat count (then forty per pound), political pressure was applied to ease regulations. And the scallop war was on, with both fleets mining the smaller scallops and threatening the future of the resource.

Late in 1981, the New England council completed its draft scallop management plan and submitted it to the secretary of commerce for approval. The plan does not limit entry, but it does include a thirty- five-meats-per-pound regulation for sea scallops similar to that used in Canada. The meat count regulation also applies to processors and food wholesalers, in part to ensure that imports of small sea scallops do not give the Canadian fishermen a competitive advantage in the market- place, although under a special agreement Canada can ship other small scallops to the United States if they are certified as not having been harvested on Georges Bank.

The meat count regulation, without a concurrent limited entry scheme, has not proven to be an effective management tool, however. Although the new boundary has ended the scallop war, giving Canada approximately 50-60 per cent of the scallops with the remainder available to the United States, damage to the stocks was extensive. Time and effective management are now required to increase harvests to the levels of previous years. While scallops are relatively sedentary on the Bank, the decline in stock biomass reflects the problems encountered when two countries harvest the same resource but under non-cooperative conditions. It also demonstrates the need for cooperative management of non-sedentary species such as lobster, herring, and groundfish.

Tariffs, Subsidies, and Countervailing Issues

In the early 1980s, the fishing industries of both New England and Atlantic Canada were caught in a price squeeze from a combination of high fuel costs, large inventories of frozen products, high interest rates, and poor markets. Given the competition for the same market, the respective industries were particularly sensitive to changes in economic conditions or policies that might result in comparative advantages to fishermen from the other country.

Currency levels are a case in point. The decline of the US and Canadian dollars between 1976 and 1981 (with respect to the Japanese yen, British pound, and German mark) increased the competitiveness of the fishing industries in both countries and contributed to their positions as leaders in exports of fishery products.[45] The US dollar has since risen in value relative to the Canadian dollar, giving the Canadian fishing industry an additional advantage in the US market-place.

Most of Canada's fish exports to the United States, as indicated above, are in processed or semi-processed form on which US tariffs are low, in the range of 0-2 per cent. For processed products such as fish sticks and fish portions, the tariffs range from 10 to 15 per cent and act as a serious impediment to export sales.[46] This explains why such a high volume of groundfish from Atlantic Canada, in the form of frozen fillets or frozen blocks, is shipped to New England for processing, and why it is cost-competitive. Since Canadian tariffs are low on all fish imports, part of this produce returns to Canada after processing in New England, and at a substantially higher price than the original exports. Canada's Atlantic coast industry would like to see tariffs reduced on processed groundfish entering the United States, while New England fishermen would like to see higher tariffs on all Canadian groundfish. In the meantime, the major beneficiaries of both tariffs and subsidies are the processors in New England (some of which are Canadian owned), who use cheap Canadian imports to bolster profit margins.

The Tokyo Round of GATT negotiations in 1979 resulted in general agreements on tariff reductions over an eight-year period which could ease some of the restrictions on Atlantic Canada fisheries exports to New England. Agreements on tariff concessions were reached on selected fish products, including the elimination of the US tariff quota on frozen fillets and the use of a single rate on all fish imports.[47] Critics argue, however, that this will not produce substantive changes because other factors (such as distance from primary markets) are also involved in decisions about where to locate processing plants. Moreover, possible countervailing action in the United States could offset the impact of the scheduled GATT decreases.

Subsidies to the Canadian fishing industry are a major issue in New England. Following the near collapse of the groundfish industry in 1974, Ottawa gave out about $250 million in subsidies to rescue the industry and introduced other subsidy programs that continue in effect to this day. This injection of large sums of money by the federal government was repeated in 1983-1984 when the major companies were restructured. Long-term federal subsidies include the Fishing Vessel Construction Assistance Program, Fishing Vessel Insurance Program, Fisheries Improvement Loans Program, Fisheries Prices Support Board, Newfoundland Bait Services, Shipbuilding Industry Assistance Program, Unemployment Insurance Benefits, Canada Manpower Training Program, Fisheries Development Program, Canadian Salt Fish Program, and provision of weather forecasting services and hydrographic charts. In addition, each provincial government provides a number of subsidy programs for shipbuilding and repairs, for defraying costs of gear, for the provision of ice and bait, for quality improvement, etc.[48]

While New England fishermen enjoy some similar subsidy benefits, there is no doubt that they are at a comparative disadvantage to their Canadian counterparts. A 1981 study of Canadian subsidies for lobster fishermen concluded that the impact of subsidized imports of Canadian lobsters has a significant effect in driving down prices paid to New England lobstermen.[49] This point has been made repeatedly by New England fishermen harvesting groundfish and scallops. US processors are said to use Canadian imports like a sledgehammer to drive down prices to US fishermen and to increase their own profit margins.[50]

All of the above periodically lead to pressure from US fishermen for countervailing measures. In 1978 following petitions from US fishermen, the US Tariff Commission held countervailing hearings involving over $200 million in Canadian fish exports that benefited from subsidies.[51] While the secretary of the treasury decided against countervailing duties, probably because of considerations for the impact that it might have on other Canada-US trade relations, the issue did not go away. With the Canadian government's decision to restructure the offshore sector and to take an equity position in the large companies in Newfoundland and Nova Scotia, American fishermen have once again called for countervailing duties.

This latest attempt at imposing countervailing duties formally commenced in November 1983 when the US trade representative, at the request of the New England fishing industry, asked the US International Trade Commission to undertake an investigation under Section 332 of the Tariff Act. The investigation began the following month for the purpose of gathering and presenting information on the competitive and economic factors affecting the performance of the Northeastern US groundfish and scallop industries in selected Northeastern US markets and to analyze these industries' competitive positions in these markets.[52]

Although the investigation included an examination of aspects of the Icelandic and Norwegian industries, its emphasis was on Canada. The Commission was asked to provide information on numerous aspects of the industry, including:

Government assistance to the fishing industries; fisheries resources and their management; production levels in harvesting and processing segments; volume of trade; industry integration; employment; product prices; financial structure of the harvesting and processing industries; the effects of exchange rates and tariff and non-tariff barriers on the flow of trade between the two countries; the importation of other types such as frozen fish blocks; and trade barriers of other potential Canadian export markets.[53]

The Trade Commission presented its report to President Reagan in December 1984. Some of the major findings of the report are reflected in the opinions expressed by US and Canadian fishing interests following its release. Both sides concentrated on different aspects of the report to justify their respective claims for or against proceeding with action to obtain countervailing duties. The US interests noted that the report confirmed that the Canadian industry is the beneficiary of much greater government assistance than is the US industry, that Canada's share of the lucrative fresh groundfish market (whole and fillets) has been increasing, that the ex-vessel price of Canadian fish is lower partly because of the concentrated buying power of the larger government-supported super companies, and that the United States has lost potential groundfish resources as a result of the International Court's boundary decision.[54] Canadian representatives, on the other hand, interpreted the report's findings on the problems encountered in the New England industry as being primarily due to "the general economic conditions in the US fishing industry: including rising costs, declining worker productivity and lesser resource availability."[55]

While the Canadian industry was expressing cautious optimism that countervailing duties would not be imposed, the North Atlantic Fisheries Task Force, a coalition representing all sectors of the New England fishing industry, decided to pursue the issue and file a countervailing duty case with the secretary of commerce and the International Trade Commission.[56] A decision is not expected until 1986 but, in the meantime, New England interests are suggesting that a trade-off could be arranged whereby they would regain access to that area of Georges Bank they lost by the boundary settlement in exchange for secure Canadian access to the New England market-place. Canadian authorities and the industry, however, are unwilling to agree to such a trade-off.

Only time will tell whether countervailing duties will be applied to Canadian fish entering the New England market, whether some form of arrangement will be reached allowing US fishermen to return to their traditional fishing areas on Georges Bank, and whether a new fisheries agreement will be negotiated between Canada and the United States to provide for cooperative management of the transboundary stocks. It is clear that the fishing industries of New England and the Atlantic coast of Canada will remain firmly linked. Whether that linkage is dominated by competitive pressures or by joint management of an immensely valuable resource will depend on the foresight and goodwill of participants in *both* countries.

Notes

1. US Department of State, Draft Environmental Impact Statement on the Agreement Between the United States and Canada on East Coast Fishery Resources (and Appendices), Washington, D.C., March 1980, pp. 132-146.

2. US Comptroller General, *The US Fishing Industry — Present Conditions and Future of Marine Fisheries* (Report to Congress), Vol. 1, Washington, D.C., 1976, p. 14.

3. US Department of Commerce, *Fisheries of the United States, 1983*, Current Fishery Statistics No. 8320, Washington, D.C., April 1984.

4. *Commercial Fisheries News*, Vol. 12, No. 8, April 1985.

5. Data from the Bureau of the Census, US Department of Commerce.

6. US Department of Commerce, *Food Fish Market Review*, Current Economic Analysis F-31, Washington, D.C., May 1981.

7. C.L. Mitchell, *Canada's Fishing Industry: A Sectoral Analysis* (Ottawa: Department of Fisheries and Oceans, 1980) p. 4.

8. Fisheries and Oceans Canada, *Annual Statistical Review of Canadian Fisheries*, Ottawa, 1982.

9. Fisheries and Oceans Canada, *Annual Statistical Review.*

10. Mitchell, *Canada's Fishing Industry*, p. 4.

11. Mitchell, *Canada's Fishing Industry*, p. 3.

12. Marvin Shaffer, *Structure, Behaviour and Performance of the Atlantic Groundfish Industry with Special Reference to the Quality Improvement Program*, Marvin Shaffer and Associates Ltd. for the Canadian Department of Fisheries and Oceans, 1981. (*Hereafter cited as Structure, Behaviour and Performance.*)

13. *Structure, Behaviour and Performance*, p. 58.

14.   *Sou'wester*, Vol. 15, No. 7, April 13, 1983.

15.   *Canadian Fishing Report*, Vol. 5, No. 10, October 1983.

16.   *Canadian Fishing Report*, Vol. 6, No. 2, February 1984.

17.   *Canadian Fishing Report*, February 1984.

18.   Canadian Department of Fisheries and Oceans, News Release, June 21, 1984.

19.   Mitchell, *Canada's Fishing Industry*, p. 50.

20.   Janet E. Forrest, The Atlantic Fishery: The Demand Side, unpublished ms. prepared for the Atlantic Provinces Economic Council, July 1980.

21.   *Structure, Behaviour and Performance*, p. 15.

22.   Forrest, *The Atlantic Fishery*, p. 7.

23.   Rodney A. Snow, Extended Fishery Jurisdiction in Canada and the United States, *Ocean Development and International Law Journal*, Vol. 5, No. 2/3 (1978).

24.   New England Fishery Management Council, brochure, no date.

25.   Snow, Extended Fishery Jurisdiction.

26.   Ernie P. Weeks, Key Issues Facing the East Coast Fisheries of Canada, Centre for Development Projects, Dalhousie University, December 1979.

27.   D.M. Johnston, The Administration of Canadian Fisheries, unpublished ms., Dalhousie University, 1978.

28.   Environment Canada, *Policy for Canada's Commercial Fisheries*, Fisheries and Marine Service, Ottawa, 1976.

29.   Fisheries and Oceans Canada, *Policy for Canada's Atlantic Fisheries in the 1980s*, Ottawa, 1981. (Hereafter cited as *Policy for Canada's Atlantic Fisheries*.)

30. US Department of Commerce, *Calendar Year 1980: Report on the Implementation of the Magnuson Fishery Conservation and Management Act of 1976*, National Marine Fisheries Service, National Oceanic and Atmospheric Administration, Washington, D.C., 1981. (Hereafter cited as *Calendar Year 1980*.)

31. Stephen Greene, *Washington: A Study of the US Fish Policy Process*, Centre for International Business Studies, Dalhousie University, 1978.

32. *Calendar Year 1980*.

33. Snow, Extended Fishery Jurisdiction.

34. Snow, Extended Fishery Jurisdiction.

35. Snow, Extended Fishery Jurisdiction.

36. *Policy for Canada's Atlantic Fisheries*.

37. New England Governors Conference, Inc., Background Paper on Fisheries Trade, prepared for the First Bilateral Symposium on New England-Canadian Affairs, Providence, Rhode Island, May 24-25, 1984.

38. *Policy for Canada's Atlantic Fisheries*.

39. *Commercial Fisheries News*.

40. *Policy for Canada's Atlantic Fisheries*.

41. Donald J. Patton, *Industrial Development and the Canadian Atlantic Fishery* (Ottawa: Canadian Institute for Public Policy, 1981).

42. Patton, *Industrial Development*.

43. For a detailed analysis, see Andre d'Entremont, The Canadian/American Advisory Groups for the Gulf of Maine Fishery Negotiations, unpublished ms., Dalhousie University, 1981.

44. Hal Mills, Georges Bank: The National Interest, *New Directions in Ocean Law, Policy and Management*, Vol. 1,

No. 2 (February 1981). Probably the most serious opposition arose because of its unbalanced stock allocations. The Canadian fishing industry, because it is more structured, integrated, and characterized by a stronger federal presence, was able to make its own internal trade-offs on groundfish for scallops. The relatively unstructured New England industry was not able to do so.

45.   Janet E. Forrest, Development of the East Coast Fishing Industry — Assessment of Canadian Government Policies, *Marine Policy*, Vol. 5, No. 4 (October 1981).

46.   *Structure, Behaviour and Performance, p. 82.*

47.   Forrest, Development of the East Coast Fishing Industry, p. 255.

48.   Subsidy programs are summarized in *Structure, Behaviour and Performance.*

49.   Nancy L. Hasselback, Joel B. Dirlam, and John M. Gates, Canadian Fisheries Policy — Canadian Lobster Imports and the New England Lobster Industry, *Marine Policy*, Vol. 5, No. 1 (January 1981).

50.   Greene, *Washington*, p. 26.

51.   Stephen Greene and Thomas Keating, Domestic Factors and Canada-US Fisheries Relations, unpublished ms., Dalhousie University, 1979.

52.   US International Trade Commission, *Conditions of Competition Affecting the Northeastern US Groundfish and Scallop Industries in Selected Markets*, USITC Publication 1622, Washington, D.C., December 1984.

53.   US International Trade Commission, *Conditions of Competition.*

54.   *National Fisherman*, February 1985.

55.   *Atlantic Fisherman*, Vol. 1, No. 15, January 4, 1985.

56.   *Commercial Fisheries News.*

Bibliography

Boeri, David and James Gibson. *Tell It Good-Bye Kiddo: Decline of the New England Offshore Fishery*. Camden, Maine: International Marine Publishers, 1976.

Donaldson, John and Giulio Pontecorvo. Economic Rationalization of Fisheries: The Problem of Conflicting National Interests on Georges Bank, *Ocean Development and International Law*. Vol. 8, No. 2 (1980).

Fisheries and Oceans Canada. *Resource Prospects for Canada's Atlantic Fisheries: 1981-1987*. Ottawa, 1981.

Guy, Stanton R. Nova Scotia Salt Dried Groundfish. Unpublished ms., Nova Scotia Department of Fisheries, February 1979.

Hollick, A.L. *US Foreign Policy and the Law of the Sea*. Princeton, N.J.: Princeton University Press, 1981.

LeBlanc, Michael. Fisheries Administration in Canada: A Synopsis, *Atlantic Fisheries and Coastal Communities: Fisheries Decision-Making Case Studies*, edited by Cynthia Lamson and Arthur J. Hanson. Halifax, Nova Scotia: Dalhousie Ocean Studies Programme, 1984.

MacDonald, R.D.S. Inshore Fishing Interests on the Atlantic Coast: Their Response to Extended Jurisdiction by Canada, *Marine Policy*. Vol. 3, No. 3 (1979).

MacKenzie, W.C. Rational Fishery Management in a Depressed Region: The Atlantic Groundfishery, *Journal of the Fisheries Research Board*. Vol. 36, No. 7 (July 1979).

McCarten, Bill and Janet E. Forrest. The Atlantic Fishery. Unpublished ms. prepared for the Atlantic Provinces Economic Council, 1981.

McDorman, P. Saunders and David VanderZwaag. The Gulf of Maine Boundary: Dropping Anchor or Setting a Course, *Marine Policy*. Forthcoming.

Mueller, Joe. *A Short-Run Economic Impact Analysis of the US-Canadian Agreement of East Coast Fishery Resources*. National

Marine Fisheries Service, National Oceanic and Atmospheric Administration, Washington, D.C., 1979.

NORDCO. *The Place of Northern Cod in Newfoundland's Development*, February 1981.

Pontecorvo, Giulio. Fishery Management and the General Welfare: Implications of the New Structure. Research Paper /157, Graduate School of Business, Columbia University, 1977.

Rhee, Sang-Myon. Equitable Solutions to the Maritime Boundary Dispute Between the United States and Canada in the Gulf of Maine, *American Journal of International Law*. Vol. 75 (1981).

Rieser, Alison, Nancy Ziegler, and Julie Douthit. *Status of Federal Fisheries Authority in the United States*. Marine Law Institute, University of Maine, 1981.

Scott, Anthony and Philip Neher (eds.). *The Public Regulation of Commercial Fisheries in Canada*. Ottawa: Economic Council of Canada, 1981.

Task Force on Atlantic Fisheries. *Navigating Troubled Waters: A New Policy for Atlantic Fisheries*. Ottawa: Supply and Services Canada, 1982.

US Department of Commerce, *Fisheries of the United States, 1980*. Current Fishery Statistics No. 8100, Washington, D.C., April 1981.

US Department of Commerce, *Shellfish Market Review*. Current Economic Analysis S-43, Washington, D.C., September 1981.

VanderZwaag, David. *The Fish Feud: The US and Canadian Boundary Dispute*. New York: Lexington Books, 1983.

Wang, E.G. Canada-United States Fisheries and Maritime Boundary Negotiations: Diplomacy in Deep Water, *Behind the Headlines*. Canadian Institute of International Affairs, Vol. 38/39, No. 2 (1981).

Weeks, Ernie and Leigh Mazany. *The Future of the Atlantic Fisheries*. Montreal: Institute for Research on Public Policy, 1983.

Winter, Ralph H. Unpublished ms. on Canadian-American fisheries relations, Acadia University, 1981.

Worthington, J.C. (ed.). *Worthington's Fish Market Report.* Vol. 1, No. 8 (November 30, 1981).

7: INTERREGIONAL INVESTMENT: PATTERNS AND POLICIES

W. D. Shipman

Investment across international boundaries is generally of three types: long-term direct investment, long- and short-term portfolio investment, and short-term changes in bank balances. Only long-term direct investment is considered here.[1] Changes in bank balances are normally the result of other types of international transactions (including investment) and can be disregarded for the purposes of this study. Portfolio investment can be of strategic importance, but tracing fractional ownership of securities to ultimate income recipients presents formidable difficulties. It is not unusual, for example, for Canadian provincial governments and government enterprises (e.g., Hydro-Quebec) to sell bonds on the New York market, with ultimate buyers spread across the country. It would be very difficult, and it would also probably serve no useful purpose, to attempt to calculate the proportion of each security issue held by beneficial owners in New England. Thus, portfolio investment — as that term is generally understood — is excluded from this study.

In general, the method used here in the case of direct investment is to examine first the macro data collected and synthesized by national agencies to see what, if any, regional flows can be identified. This examination is followed in each case by a discussion of micro information emanating from agencies, associations, and individual firms. While the method cannot do full justice to the extent of these cross-boundary flows, it may prove useful in explaining certain capital movements and even predicting trends.

US Investment in Canada

Starting from the general and moving toward the specific, Table 7.1 and Figures 7.1 and 7.2 present data on US direct investment in Canada for 1971, 1976, and 1981. About two-thirds of the total is in manufacturing and petroleum. While both of these categories increased in terms of book value, expressed in current dollars, over the decade, they clearly lagged in relative terms as

239

compared with trade, finance, and insurance. Investment in mining and smelting declined even in current dollars. Most of Canada's petroleum reserves, and hence US investment, are in the western provinces, although US-controlled refining and distribution capacity has been fairly important in the East. (The petroleum data reflect the substantial increase in book value of reserves as well as quantities.) The US manufacturing investment, on the other hand, is of much greater importance in

Table 7.1:   US Direct Investment in Canada (Million $ US): 1971, 1976, 1981

	1971		1976		1981	
	Amount	%	Amount	%	Amount	%
Mining and smelting	3,246	13.5	3,200	9.4	3,180	7.0
Petroleum	5,149	21.4	7,181	21.2	8,715	19.3
Manufacturing						
Food			1,433		1,932	
Chemicals			2,462		3,719	
Prim. & fab. metals			1,052		1,641	
Machinery			3,246		3,619	
Trans. equipment			2,965		3,847	
Other mfg.			4,807		5,055	
Total	10,590	43.9	15,965	47.0	19,812	43.9
Trade			2,145	6.3	4,162	9.2
Finance & insurance	5,121	21.2	3,785	11.2	6,945	15.4
Other industries			1,656	4.9	2,315	5.1
Total	24,106	100.0	33,932	100.0	45,129	99.9

Note: Direct investment is defined to equal the net book value of US direct investors' equity in, and outstanding loans to, Canadian affiliates in which a single US investor owns at least 10 per cent of the voting securities or the equivalent.

Source: Bureau of Economic Analysis, US Department of Commerce.

Figure 7.1

**Percentage distribution of applications for investment under Canada's
Foreign Investment Review Act, 1974-1981.
(Source: Canadian Foreign Investment Review Agency)**

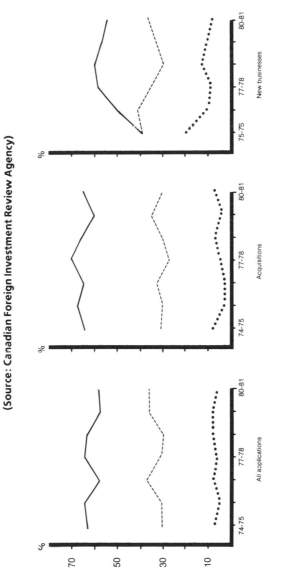

Figure 7.2

Percentage distribution of applications for investment in Canada by country of control and region, 1974-1979.

(Percentage)

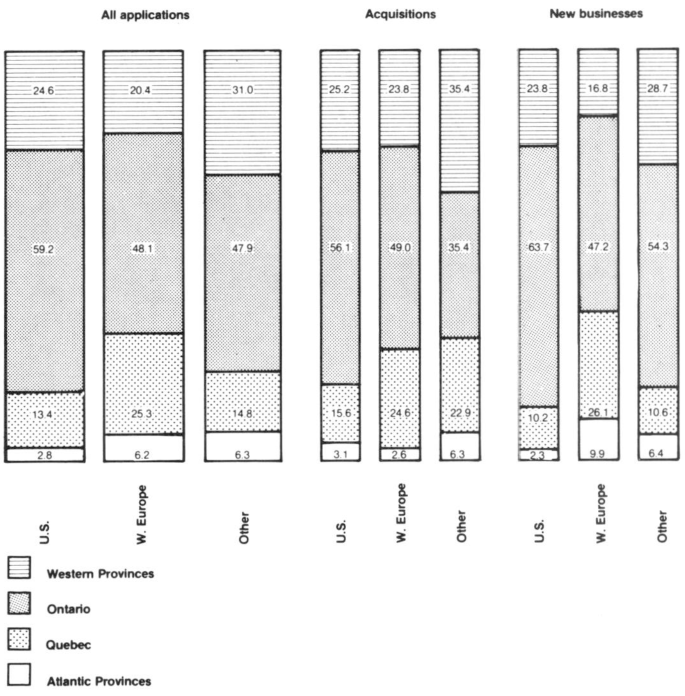

	All applications			Acquisitions			New businesses		
	U.S.	W. Europe	Other	U.S.	W. Europe	Other	U.S.	W. Europe	Other
Western Provinces	24.6	20.4	31.0	25.2	23.8	35.4	23.8	16.8	28.7
Ontario	59.2	48.1	47.9	56.1	49.0	35.4	63.7	47.2	54.3
Quebec	13.4	25.3	14.8	15.6	24.6	22.9	10.2	26.1	10.6
Atlantic Provinces	2.8	6.2	6.3	3.1	2.6	6.3	2.3	9.9	6.4

Western Provinces ▥ Ontario ▦ Quebec ▨ Atlantic Provinces ☐

or near the population centres of Quebec and Ontario than it is in Canada generally. Much of the growth in US investment in recent years reflects a liberalization of Canada's regulations in the financial sector, even as foreign investment was restrained in other fields.

Figures 7.1 and 7.2 trace US applications for investment in Canada from 1974 to 1981 (1979 for Figure 7.2). It is clear that US interest in acquiring or building facilities in Canada has been sustained at a higher level than has the interest of other countries. It is equally clear from Figure 7.2 that most of that interest has been centred in Ontario and the western provinces rather than in Quebec and the Atlantic Region. The latter areas accounted for only about 16 per cent of all US applications over the period 1974-1979; 1980-1982 data suggest an even smaller proportion.[2] Moreover, it will be seen in a moment that only a very small fraction of this investment came from New England.

US Investment in Eastern Canada

Probably the most fruitful attempts to measure the extent of US investment in eastern Canada have come from special studies by Statistics Canada[3] and the Foreign Investment Review Agency (FIRA).[4] Table 7.2 presents selected data from the first source. In terms of 1975 employment in firms having twenty or more employees, the US- controlled share varies from 17.7 per cent in Quebec down to 8.8 per cent in Prince Edward Island; the Atlantic Provinces average is 12.2 per cent, about midway between the extremes. To lend perspective, the comparable figure for Ontario is 29.5 per cent.

Table 7.3 presents data on value added by foreign-controlled firms in Canadian manufacturing industries from 1970 to 1980. These data, when compared with those in Table 7.2, suggest that the US position in manufacturing is considerably heavier than in Canadian industry generally. Approximately 30 per cent of manufacturing value added in Quebec is and was accounted for by US-controlled firms. The Quebec investment in turn accounted for slightly over 20 per cent of total US investment in Canadian manufacturing industries, as compared with 65 per cent in Ontario.

In the Atlantic Region, US-controlled firms contributed only 16-18 per cent of manufacturing value added, and US investors had allocated about 2 per cent of their total Canadian manufacturing investment to that region. It is worth noting (1) that the US *share* of value added in manufacturing appears to vary directly with the relative importance of manufacturing itself across the major Canadian regions, and (2) that the US

Table 7.2: **Employment by Canadian, US, and Other Controlled Enterprises in Quebec and the Atlantic Provinces, 1975**

	Canadian	United States	Other	Total
Quebec				
No. of enterprises	8,802	636	288	9,726
No. of employees	868,166	203,733	78,067	1,149,966
Per cent	75.5	17.7	6.8	100.0
Atlantic Provinces				
Newfoundland				
No. of enterprises	576	61	19	656
No. of employees	50,734	9,899	3,577	64,210
Per cent	79.0	15.4	5.6	100.0
Prince Edward Island				
No. of enterprises	187	31	5	223
No. of employees	9,079	884	77	10,040
Per cent	90.4	8.8	0.8	100.0
Nova Scotia				
No. of enterprises	1,051	130	55	1,236
No. of employees	89,187	13,654	10,788	113,629
Per cent	78.5	12.0	9.5	100.0
New Brunswick				
No. of enterprises	873	100	35	1,008
No. of employees	85,946	10,483	2,269	98,698
Per cent	87.1	10.6	2.3	100.0
Total of Atlantic Prov.				
No. of enterprises	2,687	322	114	3,123
No. of employees	234,946	34,920	16,711	286,577
Per cent	82.0	12.2	5.8	100.0

Note: This table is based on a study of establishments that are part of firms with twenty or more employees.

Source: Financial Flows and Multinational Enterprises Division, Statistics Canada.

share of value added decreased significantly in most of Canada (though possibly not in the Atlantic Provinces) during the 1970s. Finally, Table 7.3 confirms the wholly dominant position of the United States as compared with other sources of foreign direct investment in Canada, its proportion declining only moderately between 1970 (81 per cent) and 1980 (78 per cent).

Tables 7.4 through 7.6 use tax data to show the proportion of corporate *income* attributed to US-controlled enterprises, by region and province, for selected years from 1970 to 1981. The proportionate breakdown of corporate income by region for any given year (Table 7.4) indicates rough correspondence with employment and value added in the case of Quebec and the Atlantic Provinces. But the increasing quantity and (especially) profitability of US investment in western Canada, at least through 1980, tended to make the "eastern" share of total US-controlled corporate income shrink substantially during the 1970s. This is shown dramatically by the contrast between the less than 5 per cent growth rates for 1974-1978 in Ontario and Quebec versus 39 per cent in the western provinces. Most likely the decline in the pace and profitability of US investment between 1974 and 1978 reflected the business cycle as well as factors specific to particular industries and perhaps changes in government policy as well.[5] The 1981 data indicate a resumption in growth of US-attributed corporate income, with most regions' gains closely comparable except for Quebec, where growth was moderately below average, and for the Atlantic Provinces, where income grew much more rapidly, probably as a result of the impact of offshore oil and gas.

Table 7.5 shows annual data for corporate income attributed to US-controlled firms in each province, and indicates the US share of total corporate income in each case. Consistent with Table 7.4, the three-year interval 1978-1981 (1980 being the peak year) witnessed growth ranging from 40 per cent in Quebec to 55-65 per cent in the Maritimes and over 300 per cent in Newfoundland. Thus, growth in US-attributed corporate income by the end of the 1970s had recovered from the mid-1970s slack, but (except for Newfoundland) still did not match the years 1970-1974. In general, the US share in Quebec was remarkably stable over the entire period 1970-1981, declining only from 32 per cent to approximately 28.5 per cent. Within the Atlantic Provinces, except Newfoundland, the US share generally increased during the first half of the 1970s but declined thereafter; in Newfoundland the US share fell substantially over the period as a whole — until 1980. Nova Scotia was the only Atlantic province in which the US share of corporate income, after 1971, was as

Table 7.3: Value Added by US and Other Foreign (OF) Controlled Enterprises in Canadian Manufacturing Industries by Region, 1970-1980

Year	Atlantic Provinces[b]				Quebec				Ontario				Western Provinces				Canada[c]			
	$ Amt.[a]	% US	% OF	% CAN	$ Amt.[a]	% US	% OF	% CAN	$ Amt.[a]	% US	% OF	% CAN	$ Amt.[a]	% US	% OF	% CAN	$ Amt.[a]	% US	% OF	% CAN
1980[d]	2,994	16	18	66	19,174	28	11	61	34,811	46	9	46	13,006	23	10	67	69,985	35	10	55
1978	2,202	16	17	67	14,431	29	10	61	27,787	49	8	43	10,010	27	10	63	54,431	38	9	52
1976	1,649	20	15	65	11,223	30	11	59	22,144	50	8	41	7,536	27	10	63	42,553	40	10	51
1974	1,568	18	20	62	10,045	31	12	57	19,920	51	9	40	6,121	26	13	61	37,655	40	11	49
1972	913	18	18	64	7,020	30	11	59	14,000	52	9	39	4,048	28	12	60	25,982	41	10	49
1970	760	16	18	66	6,092	35	10	55	11,460	52	9	39	3,107	29	11	60	21,418	43	10	48

		Atlantic	Quebec	Ontario	Western	Canada
1980	US controlled	2.0	21.6	64.6	12.0	100.0
	Other foreign	7.6	29.8	44.2	18.4	100.0
	Canadian	5.1	30.4	41.6	22.8	100.0
1970	US controlled	1.3	23.4	65.4	9.9	100.0
	Other foreign	6.5	28.7	48.7	16.1	100.0
	Canadian	4.9	32.9	43.9	18.3	100.0

a   Expressed in Canadian dollars (millions).
b   Reflects estimated breakdown for Prince Edward Island.
c   Canadian total includes territories.
d   1980 data are preliminary.

Source: Statistics Canada, Cat. No. 31-401.

Table 7.4: Canadian Corporate Taxable Income ($ Millions) Attributed to US-Controlled Enterprises (Non-financial Industries) by Region, Selected Years, 1970-1981

	1970 Amount	%	1974 Amount	%	1978 Amount	%	1981 Amount	%
Atlantic Provinces	63.7	3.3	140.1	2.6	160.6	2.6	323.9	3.4
Quebec	391.9	20.5	889.2	16.8	929.9	14.9	1,304.3	14.3
Ontario	987.5	51.7	2,206.2	41.6	2,266.3	36.4	3,304.9	36.3
Western Provinces	467.1	24.5	2,061.8	38.9	2,866.5	46.1	4,209.4	46.1
Total Canada[a]	1,910.2	100.0	5,297.3	100.0	6,223.3	100.0	9,142.5	100.0
Percentage increases:								
Atlantic Provinces								
1970-74			119.9					
1974-78					14.6			
1978-81							101.7	
Quebec								
1970-74			126.9					
1974-78					4.6			
1978-81							40.3	
Ontario								
1970-74			123.4					
1974-78					2.7			
1978-81							45.8	
Western Provinces								
1970-74			341.4					
1974-78					39.0			
1978-81							46.8	
Canada, total								
1970-74			177.3					
1974-78					17.5			
1978-81							46.9	

a   Totals exclude territories.

Source: Statistics Canada, Business Finance Division and Cat. No. 61-210.

Table 7.5: Canadian Corporate Taxable Income ($ Millions) Attributed to US-Controlled Enterprises (Non-financial Industries) in Quebec and the Atlantic Provinces, 1970-1981

Year	Quebec Amount	%	New Brunswick Amount	%	Nova Scotia Amount	%	Prince Edward Island Amount	%	Newfoundland Amount	%
1970	391.9	32.1	15.3	20.4	27.5	27.3	1.0	10.5	19.9	35.3
1971	429.7	32.2	21.0	23.1	32.7	28.7	1.4	12.5	22.0	32.9
1972	488.7	32.0	29.4	29.2	40.4	32.4	2.6	21.9	12.9	19.5
1973	591.0	30.8	30.7	22.4	44.3	29.3	2.4	14.9	18.2	19.9
1974	889.2	31.7	43.1	21.6	72.6	32.8	4.5	19.8	19.9	17.2
1975	920.4	32.2	53.6	25.9	108.4	41.0	4.8	19.0	23.0	19.6
1976	845.7	29.8	42.2	22.3	87.6	37.6	3.1	13.4	22.3	20.5
1977	812.9	31.0	45.1	24.5	92.5	36.3	3.5	15.0	29.6	24.3
1978	929.9	29.5	42.1	21.5	89.5	28.8	3.7	12.6	25.3	15.4
1979	1,244.1	29.0	63.3	15.5	113.6	28.1	5.3	13.4	36.1	16.2
1980	1,460.6	29.3	70.6	14.6	166.0	32.1	6.5	14.6	48.9	18.8
1981	1,304.3	28.5	65.3	16.4	145.0	34.0	6.1	12.7	107.5	35.2

Note: Percentage figures show ratio of US to total corporate income in each province.

Source: Business Finance Division, Statistics Canada.

high as it was in Quebec. Again, within the Atlantic Provinces, Newfoundland shows a higher than average degree of US control when measured by share of employment (Table 7.2), but, except for 1981, a lower than average degree when measured by share of corporate income (Table 7.5). Throughout the period, Prince Edward Island evidences the lowest US share of both employment and corporate income, perhaps reflecting the greater emphasis on agriculture in that province and the relative lack of manufacturing and capital-intensive mineral extraction.

While the approaches and definitions underlying the several Canadian data sources do not permit close comparisons, it appears that US-controlled enterprises have a better profit performance than might be inferred from employment data alone. The profit attribution data could in turn reflect a number of things such as differences in scale of enterprise, capital intensity, innovation activity, market control, etc. On the other hand, the Canadian studies exaggerate the extent of US control by omitting data for smaller corporations and proprietorships. It seems likely that small business has a much larger proportion of local ownership and control than is true in large enterprises. Conclusions drawn from data of the kind presented above should be qualified accordingly.

Some additional light is shed on this subject by considering the industrial breakdown of US-controlled corporate income in eastern Canada (Table 7.6). During the decade 1972-1981, US-controlled enterprises accounted for between 42 and 46 per cent of corporate income in Quebec's manufacturing sector; this compares with between 29 and 35 per cent of value added (Table 7.3). In several other sectors, there appear to be large year-to-year fluctuations in the US share; the share in mining, for example, was very high in 1975 (79 per cent), approximately twice the 1972 figure. Such fluctuations no doubt reflect acquisition activity and other factors in addition to profitability *per se*. Utilities and wholesale and retail trade show a lower and declining trend, perhaps reflecting the expansion of Canadian-owned firms, including, in the utility sector, government enterprises. US control of Quebec service enterprises (or at least their profits) has been somewhat more stable as well as fairly high (28-33 per cent). The heterogeneous character of this sector makes generalization difficult, but the high and stable share must reflect in part the position of hotel, motel, leasing, and restaurant chains having US parents. Considering the overall US role in Quebec, it appears that gains in some sectors have been offset by declines in others, so that the proportion of total corporate income accounted for by US-controlled enterprises declined only slightly between 1972 and 1981.

The industrial breakdown shown for the Atlantic Provinces in Table 7.6 reveals both the dominant position of US-controlled firms in manufacturing and mining, and a distinct tendency for the US share, after declining in all sectors during the mid-1970s, to increase in a number of sectors after 1978. Looking at the 1970s as a whole, however, mining and services are probably the only sectors in which the US position has been strengthened. Examination of data for individual provinces within the Atlantic Region, although not detailed here, confirms this conclusion. It also shows that New Brunswick is the only Atlantic province in which US-controlled firms do not dominate the mining industries. In manufacturing, the US share of corporate income during the 1970s averaged between 30 and 40 per cent in Prince Edward Island and Newfoundland, but over 40 per cent in New Brunswick and more than 50 per cent in Nova Scotia.[6]

This perspective can be enhanced by considering once again the position of the eastern provinces in the context of changes in overall US investment in Canada. Both Figure 7.2 and Table 7.4 suggest that the bulk of the new direct investment (absolute dollars) is going into Ontario and (increasingly) the western provinces. Between 1970 and 1974, corporate taxable income attributed to US-controlled enterprises grew by 127 per cent in Quebec and 119 per cent in the Atlantic Provinces; the figure for all of Canada was 177 per cent, reflecting mainly the burgeoning US role in the West. Between 1974 and 1978, the same *relative* pattern is evident despite the dramatic slow-down in the growth of corporate income. After 1978, the growth pattern stabilizes, except for above-average growth in the Atlantic Provinces as a result of offshore ventures.

New England Investment in Eastern Canada

When one attempts to narrow the focus to New England investment in Quebec and the Atlantic Provinces, the problem of obtaining usable data is greatly intensified. Neither Washington nor Ottawa sources reveal the regional *origin* of cross-boundary investment. While it is reasonable to assume that many, perhaps most, of these flows originate in the head offices of multinational companies and financial markets centred in New York, Toronto, and Montreal, there seems to be no easy way to assemble the relevant data. Indeed, there is some question as to how relevant such information regarding origin would be. If General Motors makes an investment in Quebec, for example, should that

Table 7.6: Taxable Income ($ Millions) Attributed to US-Controlled Enterprises (Non-financial Industries) in Quebec and the Atlantic Provinces, by Industrial Sector, Selected Years, 1972-1981

	1972 Amount	1972 %	1975 Amount	1975 %	1978 Amount	1978 %	1981 Amount	1981 %
Quebec								
Agric., forestry, fishing	(D)	(D)	0.1	1.4	(D)	(D)	(D)	(D)
Mining	15.1	39.1	72.2	79.3	78.9	74.3	69.7	56.6
Manufacturing	353.8	45.4	655.7	46.3	637.7	42.8	975.2	42.1
Construction	6.4	7.8	5.8	2.7	(D)	(D)	(D)	(D)
Utilities	18.4	15.4	14.7	7.4	17.7	5.9	31.0	6.6
Wholesale trade	45.4	17.9	67.0	15.6	63.3	14.3	82.8	13.1
Retail trade	19.6	13.1	31.2	11.4	23.6	8.4	27.1	7.1
Services	26.1[a]	27.8[a]	73.6	32.5	81.4	28.9	112.4	27.5
Total	488.7	32.0	920.4	32.2	929.9	29.5	1,304.3	28.5
Atlantic Provinces								
Agric., forestry, fishing	(D)	(D)	0.5	6.9	1.2[c]		(D)	(D)
Mining	4.5[d]	68.0	12.1	78.6	15.6	77.2	99.9	81.0
Manufacturing	49.1	47.3	143.3	51.3	111.2	39.5	181.5	34.4
Construction	2.0[b]		3.2	5.3	2.0[c]		(D)	(D)
Utilities	(D)	(D)	1.4	3.5	3.6	3.1	1.5	0.9
Wholesale trade	12.1	23.7	6.9	8.4	4.9	6.5	7.6	8.8
Retail trade	11.9	20.2	17.6	19.3	13.3	13.7	23.3	19.8
Services	3.0	17.3	8.7	22.8	10.1	20.4	(D)	(D)
Total	85.3	28.1	193.8	31.6	160.6	22.9	323.9	27.5

[a] 1971 data: [b] 1973 data: [c] 1977 data: [d] estimated by author.

(D) = Data suppressed to prevent disclosure.

Source: Business Finance Division, Statistics Canada.

investment be traced to New York (corporate financial headquarters), to Michigan (centre of operations and management), or to Delaware (the state of incorporation)? More to the present point, should General Electric, whose corporate headquarters is in a Connecticut suburb of New York City, be regarded as a New England company when it comes to tracing US direct investment in Canada?

Clearly, the type of company apt to invest abroad is also likely to have plants and other properties in more than one state (or province). About the best that could be hoped for are data on Canadian investment by US firms having *both* their head offices and their operations base in New England. As indicated above, such information is not normally collected, or at least identified, by the official agencies.

It is possible, however, to show by way of example some of the kinds of direct investment that have taken place. Table 7.7 contains a partial list of New England-based firms having direct investments in Quebec, the Atlantic Provinces, or both as of 1980. The range of industries is wide, and most of the large firms have chosen the Montreal area, as opposed to other parts of Quebec or the Atlantic Provinces, as the location of their Canadian affiliate. As might be expected, New England is well represented in eastern Canada by affiliates engaged in some traditional industries (shoe and textile machinery, packaging, engineering) and also by a few of the newer, high-technology firms (aircraft engines, control devices, computers, electronics). It is believed, however, that in recent years these firms have mostly chosen to locate in the Metropolitan Toronto or Ottawa areas in preference to the eastern provinces.

It is plausible to conjecture that New England investment in eastern Canada is not of overwhelming importance as compared with overall US investment in those provinces. It is known that within the manufacturing sector the larger US paper companies have Quebec or New Brunswick subsidiaries; most of the parent companies would not qualify as New England-based, however. Within the services sector, most of the large US hotel, restaurant, transportation, communication, and recreation companies having investments in the eastern provinces are headquartered in other parts of the country (Sheraton and Sonesta being two exceptions). While a number of major US manufacturing firms having at least nominal headquarters in New England do have subsidiaries in Quebec or the Atlantic Provinces (e.g., Combustion Engineering, Dennison Manufacturing, Textron, Gillette, United Technologies), Table 7.7 suggests that the list is not a long one. Moreover, it appears that there was very modest interest in Quebec-Atlantic Provinces acquisitions or new businesses by New England-based firms during 1979 (Table 7.8).[7]

This view of the general distribution of investment by US firms in Canada, and changes therein, is corroborated by a number of other studies. One in particular has a bearing on the eastern Canada and New England roles just discussed. Brian Lorch undertook a study of foreign take-overs of Canadian firms in the period 1967-1976 and found both the "targets" and the domiciles of acquiring firms to be spatially very concentrated.[8] Quebec, and particularly the Greater Montreal area, were, next to Toronto and southwestern Ontario, by far the most important locations of the acquired firms. Montreal and Quebec accounted for 153 foreign take-overs, Toronto and Southwestern Ontario for 279, the Atlantic Provinces for 10, and the rest of Canada for 137 (total: 579). Of these Canadian acquisitions, 447 were made by US firms, but only 29 by New England-based firms.[9] This study also sheds light on the pattern of domestic (internal Canadian) acquisitions. In Quebec, gains in control more than offset losses (181 versus 160), whereas in the Atlantic Provinces the proportion was reversed (31 versus 41).[10] The latter figures reflect the increasing dominance of Toronto and possibly Montreal firms in the acquisition game.

It may be concluded that, on the whole, direct investment positions of New England firms in eastern Canada continue to be significant only in a few areas such as aircraft engines, electronic and control devices, computers, selected consumer goods, forest products, and hotel-restaurant chains. By far the greater part of this investment is in Quebec, and the headquarters of parent firms tend to be in either Connecticut or Massachusetts.[11] The recent rate of growth of such investment does not appear to be as high as in other parts of Canada. Indeed, it is quite clear that *neither* New England nor eastern Canada is where the action is. While the metropolitan areas of Montreal, Boston, and Halifax all continue to exhibit substantial economic growth, and while some rural areas, especially in New England, appear to be reviving, their respective regions have not regarded each other as primary target areas for either marketing or new investment. New England does have a number of growth industries, especially in the high-technology fields. As these industries have expanded into Canadian markets in recent years, their Canadian base has been located west of Quebec in most cases. Of overwhelming importance is the obvious greater population concentration and market growth in those areas.

Table 7.7:   Leading New England Direct Investments in Quebec and Atlantic Provinces, 1980

New England Parent Company or Subsidiary and Location	Quebec-Atlantic Provinces Affiliate	Location of Affiliate	Approximate # of Employees
American Biltrite, Inc. (Cambridge, Mass.)	American Biltrite (Canada), Ltd. Amtico Flooring (Canada), Ltd.	Sherbrooke, Quebec Sherbrooke, Quebec	565
American Optical Co.--sub. Warner-Lambert (Southbridge, Mass.)	American Optical Co.Canada, Ltd.	Montreal, Quebec	
Coleco Industries, Inc. (Hartford, Conn.)	Coleco Canada, Ltd. Herlicon Metals Superior Industries	Montreal, Quebec Montreal, Quebec St. Laurent, Quebec	505
Combustion Engineering, Inc. (Stamford, Conn.)	C-E Canada, Ltd.	Sherbrooke, Quebec Moncton, N.B.	660 48
Compo Industries, Inc. (Waltham, Mass.)	Compo Industries of Canada Ltd.	Montreal, Quebec	8
Dennison Manufacturing Co. (Waltham, Mass.)	Dennison Manufacturing Canada, Ltd.	Montreal, Quebec	125
Dunham-Bush, Inc. (W. Hartford, Conn.) E G & G, Inc. (Wellesley, Mass.)	Dunham-Bush of Canada, Ltd. Duplan Dyeing Co., Ltd. Radionics, Ltd.	Montreal, Quebec Valleyfield, Quebec Montreal, Quebec	
The Foxboro Company (Foxboro, Mass.)	Foxboro Canada, Inc.	LaSalle (Montreal), Quebec	475
The Gillette Company (Boston, Mass.)	Gillette Canada, Inc.	Montreal, Quebec	479
Gorton Division of General Mills (Gloucester, Mass.)	Gorton-Pew, Ltd.	New Brunswick Magdalen Islands	200
Grinnell Corporation (Providence, R.I.)	Grinnell Sales, Ltd.	Montreal, Quebec	51
John Hancock Mutual Life Insurance Co. (Boston, Mass.)	Maritime Life Assurance Co.	Halifax, Nova Scotia	
Hasbro Industries, Inc. (Pawtucket, R.I.)	Hasbro Industries (Canada), Ltd.	Longueuil, Quebec	115

Table 7.7: Continued

New England Parent Company or Subsidiary and Location	Quebec-Atlantic Provinces Affiliate	Location of Affiliate	Approximate # of Employees
Ludlow Corporation (Needham, Mass.)	Ludlow Canada, Ltd.	Montreal, Quebec	7
New England Nuclear Corp. (Boston, Mass.)	NEN Canada, Ltd.	Dorval Quebec	
Ocean Spray Cranberries, Inc. (Hanson, Mass.)	Ocean Spray Cranberries, Inc.	Saint Johns, Quebec	
Reece Corporation (Waltham, Mass.)	Reece Machinery Co., Ltd.	Montreal, Quebec	8
Royal Typewriter Co., Inc.	Royal Typewriter Co., Ltd.	Montreal, Quebec	
Sheraton Corporation (Boston, Mass.)	Sheraton Hotels--various properties	Montreal, Quebec	
Simonds Saw and Steel Co. (Fitchburg, Mass.)	Simonds Canada Abrasive Co., Ltd. Simonds Canada--Wallace Murray	Montreal, Quebec	
Sonesta Int'l. Hotels Corp. (Boston, Mass.)	Quebec Sonesta Corp.	Montreal, Quebec	
Textron, Inc. (Providence, R.I.)	Textron Canada, Ltd.	Pointe Claire, Quebec	280
Union Mutual Life Insurance Co. (Portland, Maine)	Union Mutual LifeInsurance Co.	Montreal, Quebec	
United Technologies Corp. (Hartford, Conn.)	Pratt & Whitney Canada, Inc.	Longueuil, Quebec	6573

Sources: Moody's Investors Service.
World Trade Academy Press.
Canadian Consulate, Boston, Mass.
Company Reports.

Table 7.8: New England-Based Firms Investing in Quebec or the Maritimes (FIRA Cases, 1979)

	Canadian Business Enterprise	Status
Acquisitions		
R.L. Martin and F.J. Wezniak, Mass.	Industrial Cab, Ltd. McAdam, N.B. (manufacture of cab enclosures) for heavy industrial equipment)	Allowed April 1979
D.E. Gompers, *et al.*, Hampton, N.H.	Braemar Lodge, Ltd. Yarmouth, N.S. (resort hotel and lodge)	Allowed April 1979
New Business		
J. Roy, Inc., Montreal (controlled by Romeo J. Roy, Inc., Upper Frenchville, Maine)	J. Roy, Inc. Edmonton, N.B. (wholesale plumbing and heating supplies)	Allowed March 1979
Slalom Skicare, Inc. Newport, Vt.	Slalom Sports Canada, Ltd. Rock Island, Quebec (sportswear)	Allowed February 1979
Ewing Technical Design, Inc. West Hartford, Conn.	Ewing Desseins Corp. Montreal, Quebec (aerospace engineering)	December 1979

(Total new and acquired assets = $1,187,000)

Note: New England includes the states of Maine, New Hampshire, Vermont, Massachusetts, Rhode Island, and Connecticut.

Source: Canadian Foreign Investment Review Agency.

Canadian Investment in the United States

Table 7.9 shows estimates of Canadian direct investment in the United States, by principal type of activity, for 1971, 1976, and 1981. Manufacturing investment at the end of 1981 accounted for $3.5 billion, approximately one-third of the total of $9.9 billion.[12] That $9.9 billion, it should be noted, is approximately 22 per cent of the comparable $45.1 billion of US direct investment in Canada (Table 7.1). Between 1971 and 1981, total direct investment increased about three times, measured in current dollars, but the manufacturing share decreased markedly, from 61 per cent to 36 per cent. The flattening out of manufacturing investment in absolute terms after 1976 (actually after 1979) apparently results in large part from a shift in ownership patterns as a result of mergers and acquisitions in 1980-1981; refined data would unquestionably show a more sustained increase. In any event, the more rapidly growing sectors since 1976 appear to be finance, real estate, and "other."

While Canada continues to be a major investor in the United States, its relative position is (1) far less significant than is the corresponding US position in Canada, and (2) obscured by the increasing use by Canadian investors of wholly owned, offshore subsidiaries which in turn control US investments. On the first point, in the early 1970s the United States accounted for about 80 per cent of total foreign direct investment in Canada.[13] The figure in 1984 remained close to 78 per cent. This compares with an apparent Canadian position in the United States of approximately 11 per cent, which has shrunk from roughly 27 per cent in 1961. The comparison, moreover, should be seen in the context of foreigners in general owning a much larger share of Canadian industrial investment than is true in the United States.[14]

Regarding the second point, direct foreign investment in the United States is conventionally measured by the domestic affiliate's first foreign parent. It is known, however, that a number of such first-level entities, particularly in recent years, have in fact been holding companies set up in such places as the Netherlands Antilles for tax and other advantages, whose beneficial owners are in fact Canadian investors. Consequently, the data in Table 7.10 and the figure of 11 per cent mentioned above undoubtedly understate the actual extent of direct investment by Canadians in the United States. The true figure may be in excess of $11 billion or even $12 billion, judging by the difference between Canadian assets data reported by country of foreign parent and by country of ultimate beneficial owner, as was done in the 1980 Benchmark Survey (see note 12).

Table 7.9: Canadian Direct Investment in the United States (Million $ US): 1971, 1976, 1981

	1971 Amount	%	1976 Amount	%	1981 Amount	%
Petroleum	207	6.2	676	11.4	1,387	14.0
Manufacturing						
Food			(D)		64	
Chemicals			(D)		171	
Metals			532		1,132	
Machinery			994		1,137	
Other			910		1,015	
Total, mfg.a	2,025	60.7	3,386	57.3	3,519	35.6
Trade			710	12.0	1,306	13.2
Finance	305	9.1	176	3.0	425	4.3
Insurance			246	42.0	393	4.0
Real estate			119	2.0	960	9.7
Other	802	24.0	594	10.0	1,894	19.2
Total	3,339	100.0	5,907	100.0	9,883	100.0

Note: Direct investment is defined as the net book value of Canadian direct investors' equity in, and net outstanding loans to, their US properties and affiliates.

a Manufacturing data for these years are of doubtful comparability given the large shifts made likely by arbitrary ownership criteria and changes in the location of "parent" companies (see text).

(D) = Data suppressed to prevent disclosure.

Source: Bureau of Economic Analysis, US Department of Commerce.

Canadian direct investment in the United States is widely dispersed, with virtually every state hosting one or more affiliates of Canadian corporations. A relatively few states, nevertheless, seem to account for a large proportion of the total.

Table 7.10: Foreign Direct Investment in the United States (Million $ US): 1971, 1976, 1981

Country	1971	1976	1981
Canada	3,339	5,907	9,883
United Kingdom	4,438	5,802	15,576
Netherlands	2,225	6,255	23,105
Germany	771	2,097	7,242
France	315	1,570	4,975
Switzerland	1,537	2,295	4,314
Japan		1,178	6,993
Middle East		201	3,592
Israel		(81)	(118)
Other		(119)	(3,474)
All others		5,465	11,349
Total	12,625	30,770	87,029

Source: Bureau of Economic Analysis, US Department of Commerce.

While a wholly adequate breakdown by states does not exist, Table 7.11 contains evidence indicating that New York and California are the leading hosts regarding employment, and Texas and California regarding number of affiliates and gross investment.[15] Traditionally, individual Canadians have had numerous real estate holdings in New England vacation areas such as Cape Cod and the southern coast of Maine, where eastern Canadians have sought sunshine and sea air during the summer months. Since World War II, however, the desire to escape the Canadian winter, combined with higher incomes and a somewhat older population, has led to the shift of such investment more toward Florida, Arizona, and California. Canadian industrial investment, once concentrated fairly heavily in the northern tier of states, has likewise been shifting toward the Sun Belt in

Table 7.11: Number of Affiliates, Number of Employees, Land, and Assets of Canadian Firms in New England and Selected Other States, 1980

	Number of Affiliates		Number of Employees	Acres of Land Owned (thousands)	Gross Value of Prop., Plant, Equip. ($ millions)	
	Total	Mgf. Only			Total	Mgf. Only
Maine	31	10	6,775	(D)	341	(D)
New Hampshire	21	10	2,602	1	54	29
Vermont	30	8	1,511	16	75	(D)
Massachusetts	59	21	6,030	1	121	73
Rhode Island	12	4	492		9	8
Connecticut	36	13	2,344	1	68	34
New England	189	66	19,754*	(D)	668	344
United States	1,103	221	290,018	2,692	23,141	5,774
N.Eng./US(%)	17.1	29.9	6.8		2.9	6.0
States having largest Canadian presence:						
New York	164	62	21,456	(D)	1,121	396
Illinois	105	39	16,758	5	712	311
Michigan	77	22	16,030	64	1,580	255
Minnesota	68	20	14,260	230	1,864	279
Florida	173	26	7,789	35	999	85
Texas	279	25	16,277	107	2,550	253
California	202	43	25,621	93	2,665	590

(D) = Data suppressed to prevent disclosure.

Source: US Department of Commerce, *Foreign Direct Investment in the United States, 1980, 1983.*

recent years. The US Department of Commerce reports that Canadian corporate investments during the period 1974-1978 were placed in thirty-five states, and that the leading recipients were New York, Florida, California, and Texas.[16] Florida's Canadian investment in this five-year period was roughly equal to that of New York, and Canada is now the largest foreign investor in Florida.

Canadian Investment in New England

New England has for many years been the recipient of Canadian direct investment — commercial, industrial, services, and transport, as well as individual vacation properties. Some of this investment was in the forest industry along or near New England's northern boundary and thus was essentially a geographic extension of similar Canadian industries. A limited number of wholesale and retail trade organizations have been either wholly or partly owned by Canadian firms, in some cases specializing in the distribution of Canadian products (e.g., winter sports gear, axes, saws, and related woods equipment). And some Canadian banking and insurance firms have had at least minor investments in New England since the early years of the century. Finally, the two principal Canadian railroads, Canadian National and Canadian Pacific, own subsidiary lines extending the Canadian network into New England. A picture of Canadian investment in the region drawn about 1970 would have emphasized these historical patterns and relationships.

Some suggestion of the present extent and variety of Canadian direct investment in New England is provided by recent surveys undertaken by the US Bureau of the Census. Tables 7.12 and 7.13 summarize data applicable to thirty-six Canadian-owned (10 per cent or more of voting stock) firms operating 128 establishments in New England during 1978.[17] (The questionnaire used by the Bureau of the Census was mailed to multi-establishment firms with fifty or more employees and to a third of the remaining smaller firms.) Within this group manufacturing accounted for 18 out of the 36 firms (50 per cent), 33 out of 128 establishments (26 per cent), and 7,023 out of 9,071 total employees (77 per cent). Other important sectors were wholesale and retail trade and services (Table 7.12). (Some firms owned establishments in more than one industrial sector.) When the data are broken down by state (Table 7.13), it appears that Massachusetts and Connecticut are the primary locations for firms and establishments (regardless of size), but that employment is concentrated in these states as well as Maine and New Hampshire. Interestingly, when these data are broken

Table 7.12: Characteristics of Establishments of Canadian-Owned US Firms Operating in New England, by Industry, 1978

Industry	Firms	Establishments	Employment for Week Including March 12	Payroll ($ thousands) First Quarter	Annual
Agriculture	1	1	(D)	(D)	(D)
Mining	2	2	(D)	(D)	(D)
Construction					
Manufacturing	18	33	7,023	2,614	93,530
Transportation, communication, & public utilities	2	6	(D)	(D)	(D)
Wholesale trade	13	53	717	3,025	12,838
Retail trade	2	24	(D)	(D)	(D)
Finance, insurance, and real estate	2	2	(D)	(D)	(D)
Services	5	7	143	256	1,198
Total New England	36	128	9,071	28,368	118,477

Note: The data exclude roughly two-thirds of firms having fewer than fifty employees.

(D) = Data suppressed to prevent disclosure.

Source: Bureau of the Census, US Department of Commerce.

down by *per cent* of Canadian ownership (not shown in the tables), it turns out that firms that are *majority* Canadian-owned accounted for 83 per cent and 75 per cent, respectively, of all the firms and establishments surveyed.

Table 7.13: Characteristics of Establishments of Canadian-Owned US Firms Operating in New England, by State, 1978

State	Firms	Establish- ments	Employment for Week Including March 12	Payroll ($ thousands) First Quarter	Annual
Maine	10	19	2,833	9,113	38,498
New Hampshire	8	14	1,698	6,234	26,396
Vermont	3	3	(D)	(D)	(D)
Massachusetts	22	43	2,045	5,900	24,506
Rhode Island	5	7	(D)	(D)	(D)
Connecticut	19	42	1,763	4,837	19,955
Total New England	36	128	9,071	28,368	118,477

Note: The data exclude roughly two-thirds of firms having fewer than fifty employees.

(D) = Data suppressed to prevent disclosure.

Source: Bureau of the Census, US Department of Commerce.

While inferences drawn from data in several of the preceding tables must be qualified by problems of non-comparability, offshore ownership, etc., it appears that Canadian direct investment in New England is only on the order of 3-5 per cent of US investment in eastern Canada. Deleting Quebec from the latter raises the ratio to perhaps 30-40 per cent.

The pace and extent of Canadian investment in New England appears to have increased during the 1970s, though not at the rate characteristic of some other regions of the United States. A number of major Canadian companies representing the manufacturing, insurance, and financial service sectors have recently established or acquired full- scale subsidiaries in New England. Indeed, the "acquisition game" seems to have been played at least as vigorously by Canadians as any other national group. On the other hand, the leading Canadian commercial and real estate developers, such as Oxford Development, Olympia and York, and Cadillac Fairview, have to a large extent bypassed New England in their expansion southward.[18] It might be said, therefore, that new Canadian investment in the United States, while having some significant impact on New England, has followed the general movement of US investment activity toward the southern and western states. At the same time, it should be noted that any recent expansion into New England has had the effect of greatly increasing the diversity of Canadian investment there; a broader geographic distribution of Canadian investment sources has thus been accompanied by a more varied portfolio of regional activities.

Eastern Canadian Investment in New England

When the range of investment activity is narrowed to exclude Canadian investors outside of Quebec and the Atlantic Provinces, data collected at the national level become of limited relevance. Again, the conceptual problem arises as to whether the location of the head office of a multi-plant corporation says anything important about interregional investment flows. Much of Canadian direct investment in New England originates in either Montreal or Toronto. But should a company such as Canadian Pacific, for example, headquartered in Montreal, be regarded as a Quebec company and hence an instrument of Quebec-New England capital movement? The problem is compounded by the recent tendency of many large Canadian companies to change head-quarters cities — to move from Montreal, for example, to Toronto or points west.

Keeping in mind the somewhat ambiguous character of this regional flow identification, it is possible to list examples of major investments in New England by Canadian concerns which are, or have until recently been, identified with the Greater Montreal area or with urban centres in the Atlantic Provinces. Some of the leading examples are shown in Table 7.14, together with the location of the New England affiliate and some fragmentary employment data. Many of the company names suggest the general type of activity in which the subsidiary is engaged. Obviously, they have little in common aside from their interest in New England. Much of the investment reflects traditional activities or linkages (e.g., railroads, paper-making, marine products). But it is also true that some recent investment activity reflects the move toward conglomerate organization and the expansion of services activity.

Table 7.14: Leading Quebec and Atlantic Provinces Direct Investments in New England, 1980

Canadian Parent Company or Subsidiary	New England Affiliate or Property	New England Location	Approx. No. of Employees
Bell Canada, Ltd.			
Northern Telecom	Northern Telecom	Waltham, Mass.	
	Northern Electronics	Concord, N.H.	
Bombardier, Inc.[a]	Bombardier, Inc.	Barre, Vt.	
Canadian National RR	Grand Trunk RR	Maine, N.H., Vt.	
	Central Vermont RR		
Canadian Pacific, Ltd.			
Canadian Pacific RR			
Canadian Pacific Enterprises	Corenco Corp.	Tewksberry, Mass.	
Dominion Bridge	AMCA International	Hanover, N.H.	
	Amtel, Inc.	Providence, R.I.	
	Engineer Fasteners	New Bedford, Mass.	
	Fenn Mgf.	Newington, Conn.	
Fishery Products, Ltd.	Fishery Products, Inc.	Danvers, Mass.	150
Fraser, Ltd.	Fraser Paper	Madawaska, Maine	
Gamebridge Ltd.	Gamebridge	Swanton, Vt.	
Genstar, Ltd.	Flintkote Co.	Stamford, Conn.	65
H.B. Clyde Lake, Ltd.	Caribou Fisheries	Gloucester, Mass.	
	Caribou Food Ind.	Boston, Mass.	
National Sea Products, Ltd.	National Sea Products	Rockland, Maine	
Neill and Gunter, Ltd.	Neill and Gunter	Falmouth, Maine	50
A.B. Nickerson & Sons, Ltd.	Commodore Foods	Lowell, Mass.	
Noranda Mines, Ltd.			
Noranda Metals Industries	Noranda Metals Industries	Newtown, Conn.	30
Pedigree			
Chadon Mgf.	Pedigree USA	St. Albans, Vt.	30
Preci-Tools, Ltd.	Preci-Mgf.	Winooski, Vt.	50
Sun Life Assurance of Canada	Sun Life Assurance	Wellesley, Mass.	1,100
George Weston, Ltd.			
Eddy Paper Co.	Eastern Fine Paper	Brewer, Maine	

[a]   Established in 1981.

Source: Office of Foreign Investment in the United States, US Department of Commerce.

Policy Issues

Most of the policy issues surrounding foreign investment are concerned with possible impacts and with existing or threatened impediments to the free flow of capital, particularly direct investment. During most of the nineteenth and twentieth centuries, foreign investment was welcomed, even promoted, by both Canada and the United States. The reasoning was based essentially on free market principles and the acknowledgement that investment, from whatever source, was necessary for economic growth. Since both Canada and the United States had large, undeveloped natural resources and yet were limited in their ability to generate domestic investment, it was only natural to look overseas, that is, to Europe, for assistance.

The United States grew out of this investment dependency stage earlier than Canada. By the 1920s the United States had become a net creditor and possessed an internal market that was both large and growing rapidly. While both countries had, after 1860, utilized high tariffs to promote industrial growth, the nature and scale of the US domestic market was such that it both generated and absorbed a high level of industrial investment. The smaller scale and slower development of the Canadian economy, on the other hand, led to protracted dependency, which was intensified by US investors seeking new outlets and a favoured position inside the Canadian tariff wall. The result was the emergence in the twentieth century of Canada's so-called "branch plant" economy.

For better or for worse, Canada's industrial development in the twentieth century has been powerfully shaped by US investment, both portfolio and direct. It was pointed out earlier that the US portion of foreign direct investment in Canada was something like 80 per cent in the 1970s and only slightly less in 1981. US direct investment as a portion of *total* foreign investment (direct and portfolio) increased from about 26 per cent in 1930 to 49 per cent in 1967, but it has since declined to perhaps 30-35 per cent due to Canadian acquisitions in the resource industries and large increases in portfolio investment, especially in utilities.[19] Moreover, foreign investment in general has been a substantially higher fraction of total investment in Canada than in any other industrialized country, in 1970 approaching 60 per cent in manufacturing, 65 per cent in mining and smelting, and approximately 95 per cent in petroleum.[20] (Comparable figures for 1982-1983, however, had decreased to 49 per cent in manufacturing, 43 per cent in mining and smelting, and 45 per cent in oil and gas.) Thus, while Canadians have achieved a high rate of economic growth and now enjoy real incomes comparable to those of other advanced industrial nations, their economy has been subject to a degree of outside control that is unique among such nations. Most of that control rests with US firms.

It is not surprising that the Canadian economy has come to be seen, by both Canadians and others, as a sort of northern extension of the US economy. Indeed, the tariff wall is one of the few remaining obstacles to the several Canadian provinces occupying the same *economic* position as a number of northern states within the United States. And the tariff wall is gradually being lowered. One plausible result of tariff reduction, dampened no doubt by the prevalence of "buy Canadian" directives and other non-tariff barriers at both the federal and provincial levels, will be the increased flow of manufactured goods northward, perhaps even to the point where the value of that flow will equal the value of Canadian natural resources (including energy) moving southward. A related but less obvious result may be a reduction in US direct manufacturing investment in Canada, as less than optimum scale branch plants give way before a general reorganization and rationalization of the North American economy.[21] That would most likely apply, however, only to the manufacturing sector. Since US tariffs are not significant deterrents to the import of most raw materials, Canada's occupation by US firms in the natural resource industries might continue even in an increasingly free trade environment.

It is in this context of continuing US dominance in Canadian energy and raw materials industries that Canada's moves in the early 1970s to control foreign investment must be seen. An integral part of that context is, of course, the political environment engendered by Canadian awareness that the country's natural resources are, to a considerable extent, controlled by outsiders and, in particular, by large US firms. It is hardly surprising that policies at both the federal and provincial levels have responded to these political, as well as economic, realities.

Thus, a number of provincial governments have expanded their public sectors well beyond the limits existing at the end of World War II, at least partly because certain basic utilities and resource industries were seen to be largely foreign owned and beyond public control. Under the influence of post-1960 Liberal Party philosophy (and prodded by the New Democratic Party), the federal government began, through FIRA, to exercise control over new investment and acquisitions by non-Canadian firms.[22] Finally, the 1980 National Energy Program called for, and apparently achieved, substantial increases in Canadian ownership in the oil and gas industries.

It should be noted that expansion of already existing Canadian affiliates was not covered by FIRA except in instances where such expansion was unrelated to the existing business(es) of those affiliates. Since most increases in foreign investment have been financed via the subsidiary route — possibly as much as 90 per cent — it is easy to exaggerate the impact of FIRA. On the other hand, above FIRA was an informal, federal-provincial "megaprojects committee" established to review major resource projects valued at more than $100 million. The committee's membership has varied from time to time and has apparently preferred the "jaw-boning" technique to any predetermined set of rules in making certain that Canadian suppliers are given opportunities to bid on contracts and that Canadian workers are hired to the extent feasible.

This general policy has had some interesting fall-out regarding interregional investment in the Northeast. The Quebec government took a position critical of FIRA, partly because the latter was thought to be ineffective, and partly because the agency applied federal criteria to situations in which provincial and federal objectives may not have coincided.[23] Nor did the province approve of the case-by-case approach, or the loophole for expansion of existing affiliates. Rather, it favoured adoption of an investment code in which certain sectors are thrown open to foreign investment and others are not and similar criteria are applied to the other provinces as well as to other nations.[24]

Probably Quebec's primary interest is in shifting somewhat its existing comparative advantage toward high-technology areas and away from forest products and energy. Some progress has clearly been made in this respect — for example, in the transportation equipment industries and in engineering services[25] — but it remains to be seen whether such a shift can be accomplished on any significant scale. The earlier discussion suggested that the preponderant part of US investment in the communications, electronic, and computer industries was going to Ontario or points west, primarily as a result of perceived limitations of the Quebec market.

Nova Scotia is another case in point. The government of Premier Buchanan has taken the position that "US foreign investment is fully welcome; we want it, and want as much as we can possibly get."[26] This position probably reflects both a conservative political party's distaste for any but the most essential forms of government intervention in the market-place, as well as the Maritimes' great need for new investment to overcome lower rates of growth and high dependence on federal transfer payments. Nova Scotia was one of the first provinces to oppose FIRA, in part because of fear that the mere existence of such a screening agency might well discourage foreign investors.[27] Also, to the extent that FIRA guidelines favoured existing as opposed to entirely new investment (the loophole exempting existing affiliates), it was difficult for less industrialized provinces such as the Maritimes to attract the kind of foreign investment they most wanted.[28] Whether the recent abolition of FIRA and the creation of Investment Canada will lead to significant increases in foreign investment in Atlantic Canada remains to be seen.

With the possible exception of Newfoundland, It does not appear that the Canadian National Energy Program had any significant impact on interregional energy investment *in the Northeast*. While New England utilities might have been willing to invest in the development of Quebec hydro resources or New Brunswick nuclear resources, those provinces apparently did not require, or desire, US participation except through purchase contracts and via the indirect (portfolio) route. Only if the Fundy tidal project reaches the point of economic feasibility might what remains of the energy program's "Canadianization" rules present an obstacle, and even here it is likely that a provincial corporation would be the logical owner and undertaker.

The possibility that FIRA and the energy "Canadianization" program had a dampening effect on other types of US investment in Quebec and the Atlantic Provinces cannot be dismissed lightly, however. While there would seem to be no adequate means of measuring the impact, since the usual measure of relying on percentage of "reviewable" applications approved does not touch the problem of would-be investors who do not choose to run the gauntlet, this author's own conversations with US business people suggest the effect was by no means negligible.[29] In the case of major energy projects, where New England's needs and interests are obvious, it is hard to believe that a Canadian screening procedure or ownership criterion would discourage the necessary efforts by the states themselves. But, for every such energy proposal there must be 20, or 50, or 100 manufacturing, retailing, or service industry opportunities in which the prospective gain to the investor, faced with alternative investment possibilities outside of Canada, might not have been worth the effort.[30]

This would seem to be especially true in Quebec and the Atlantic Provinces, where federal guidelines ignored or simply compounded other, less obvious obstacles to US investment. Quebec clearly faces a problem convincing US, including New

England, firms (1) that it, and not Ontario, or Alberta, or British Columbia, is an appropriate place to service the Canadian market, and (2) that its insistence on French as the primary language of business will not interfere with or raise the cost of US operations in that province. (Where investment implies family relocation, the education law, despite some escape clauses, has been still another obstacle.) The Atlantic Provinces, on the other hand, have the problem of convincing US investors that their location and their lower per capita income and rates of growth do not offset any market- or resource-related advantages of locating there.

When we turn to policy issues involving Canadian investment in the United States, the question until recently might have been: What issues? The United States has welcomed foreign investment throughout most of its history as a way of promoting growth, and since World War II as a means of offsetting heavy unilateral transfers and an unfavourable balance on current account. It has only been since about 1970 that serious questions have been raised about foreign ownership, related mainly to the purchase of American farm land and other real estate by Japanese or OPEC investors.[31] The congressional response to this concern was to pass legislation in 1976 calling for the monitoring of foreign investment and in 1978 requiring foreign investors in agricultural land to file reports with the Department of Agriculture.

The US Office of Foreign Investment, established within the Department of Commerce in 1975, presently observes and collects data on foreign direct investment and advises and informs the Congress when necessary. This office attempts to record new Canadian (and other) direct investment in the United States, relying on such diverse sources as the Securities and Exchange Commission, Moody's, Dun and Bradstreet, and newspaper and trade journal articles reporting significant new investments and acquisitions.[32] However, with few exceptions neither it nor the government can generally, under existing legislation, exercise control over that investment.[33] Nor does it appear that there is much likelihood of its doing so, despite the increasing pace of such investment in recent years and unhappiness in certain US circles, including the Congress, about the restrictive Canadian measures discussed above.[34]

There are probably three major reasons for the open policy regarding Canadian investment. One is the somewhat doctrinaire stance the United States has taken concerning open (world) markets generally. Even before the Reagan Administration the United States had made it clear that it favoured minimal controls on foreign investment on the grounds that such controls inevitably restrict international trade and thus (in its view) retard world economic growth generally. While it was recognized that developing nations might try to influence the form and direction of development, restraints on investment were thought to be, at best, a clumsy method of control. With the advent of the Reagan Administration, the US position became a good deal more doctrinaire, and hardly a week passed without some Washington official making pronouncements about the beneficial effects of the free flow of capital, both domestically and internationally. Thus, the United States was, and is, hardly in a position to place impediments in the path of Canadian investment when its message to the rest of the world is to eliminate such impediments.

Another major reason why the United States is not likely to introduce controls on Canadian investment is that such investment is in fact miniscule relative to that of domestic corporations and individuals. Unlike the situation in Canada where US investors control perhaps 40 per cent of the manufacturing sector and, until very recently, a larger fraction still of several natural resource sectors (as discussed above), Canadian control of US manufacturing industries has been almost insignificant—not more than 2 per cent in 1979.[35] It is negligible in most other areas as well. The only exception appears to be real estate holdings for commercial and individual vacation purposes. In that area, Canadian ownership is now a significant factor in the Florida real estate market and in certain other southern states, as well as in Maine and Massachusetts. Moreover, through the activities of a handful of real estate development firms, Canadians are responsible for a number of the newest and largest commercial (shopping, office, apartment) complexes in major US cities. The glamorous character of and general publicity surrounding these projects no doubt accounts for the image increasingly held in the United States of the Canadians moving in. In fact, Canada's share of US commercial real estate is still probably much less than 1 per cent. Despite the publicity given to certain Canadian take-overs, or attempted take-overs, of US industrial firms in recent years, it seems doubtful that such activities, even if successful, would have much effect on the overall percentages. In any event, concerns about Canadian investment have usually been allayed when it is made clear how relatively modest Canadian ownership is in the whole picture.[36] The investment roles that each country plays in the other are so different that, once they are understood, Canadian foreign investment policies could hardly justify investment retaliation by the United States.

A final and most basic reason for believing the United States will and should continue its open market policy is the benefit derived from Canadian investment. Where such investment takes place in US markets, it is generally because the enterprises in question are able to produce a better product, or pursue a more effective development strategy, or produce at a lower price, or some combination of these. In other words, Canadian investment, particularly where it involves the establishment of a new firm or plant, typically leads to increased employment, and to new and healthy competition whose benefits are shared with American consumers. This type of benefit, while difficult to measure, is, after all, the principal *raison d'être* for free trade and free capital movement.

It is understandable that US producers object to Canadian intrusion into their industries and markets. The political response to such an intrusion, moreover, is almost certain to focus rather narrowly on the competitive impact on established producers. But the reality of the public benefits from heightened competition, whether in the form of new products or lower prices or both, should not be denied simply because they are widely diffused or difficult to measure. It is probably too much to expect the entry of large Canadian firms (especially when it is via the acquisitions route) to lower the prices in American markets dominated by a few large enterprises to begin with. Canadians, for historical and other reasons, are at least as prone to cartel behaviour as are their US counterparts. But, to the extent that the typical Canadian firm investing in the United States — whether in manufacturing, retailing, financial services, or real estate — represents new competition, the results for Americans can be highly beneficial and appear to be recognized by policy makers.

The single qualification to this argument stems from the possible existence of subsidies on the Canadian side. In such instances, while American consumers and new workers may well benefit, American producers (and their employees) are penalized, quite possibly to the extent that a political consensus would come down on the side of controls. This question is, of course, part of the larger issue concerning US trade policy in the face of the subsidized exports of its trading partners (Chapter 3), the welfare implications of which are considerably more complex than is suggested above. Thus, two types of questions must be answered in the investment policy area: Does the Canadian *affiliate* enjoy a home-sponsored subsidy? If it does, is it nevertheless desirable to welcome the investment?

The first question – whether or not Canadian firms investing in the United States are in fact subsidized by their government to an extent that enables their subsidiaries to undersell domestic producers – is very difficult to answer. While it is usually possible to identify particular sources of subsidy, it is frequently impossible to determine whether subsidies are a sufficient reason for the affiliate's success in US markets. Lacking hard evidence, good performance by a Canadian- owned firm can obviously be as readily attributed to a better product, or to superior management or marketing skills, as to the existence of a subsidy. Apparently a detailed study of each individual situation is the only way one can determine the reasons for a successful operation. This individual approach is in fact employed by the US International Trade Commission in determining (1) whether dumping of export products has occurred, and (2) whether US producers have suffered injury as a result.

The term "subsidy" itself is difficult to define. If a Canadian firm benefits from lower income taxes, or from a government injection of new equity or guarantee of its debt, or from a government-established procedure and incentives for retiring high-cost, parent company plant or for consolidating smaller firms into larger ones, does this signify that a subsidy exists? It is well known that government has traditionally played a larger role in Canadian industry than in US industry. (The same holds true for Western Europe.) And it is at least debatable whether such intervention has in general resulted in lower costs or greater efficiency. Without doubt it has done so in specific cases. But, if a subsidy is construed in these broad terms, it would be necessary to examine every investng firm to determine whether its taxes (actually, those of its US subsidiary), or cost of capital, or other expenses approximate some (probably ill-defined) average market rate or level. It is not at all easy to see how some of these sources of subsidy can be distinguished from lower factor costs generally. Consequently, it is probably not good policy to set up obstacles to foreign investment simply because there is reason to believe the foreign parent enjoys certain cost advantages attributable to public policies in the home country. It may be very difficult to determine whether or to what extent the US affiliate shares any such cost advantage. Moreover, such a US policy would seem to deny the fact that all industrial nations attempt to promote exports and live, so to speak, in glass houses, the United States being no exception.

The second question remains to be answered. Even if a subsidy on the Canadian side can be identified, and if it can be shown that the investing firm's favourable market position in the United States is or would be attributable to that subsidy, does this justify restraining or otherwise interfering with the investment? While there is always the possibility that domestic firms might be damaged or even eliminated, after which the foreign (Canadian) firm would be free to raise its price, such arguments should be viewed skeptically – they are about as old as competition itself. One could just as easily argue that the competition provided by foreign entry, or the threat thereof, is likely to be sustained wherever barriers to entry (domestic as well as foreign) are low or moderate. Furthermore, if the Canadian federal or provincial governments choose to tax their citizens in order to underwrite foreign investment, one could argue that US consumers should welcome the effort. They, after all, are the prime beneficiaries.

This, of course, overlooks the political and economic costs of weakening, or perhaps displacing, domestic producers whose costs are not subsidized, or not subsidized as much. After many years of wrangling over these matters in the areas of merchandise and commodity trade, most countries appear now to subscribe to rules against dumping, at least in its more extreme forms. The rules can be pernicious – for example, when they are applied against imports whose prices fully reflect long-run marginal costs. (Some would say even short-run marginal costs, reflecting high plant utilization.) But the political consensus against dumping is strong, and one would think that US and Canadian negotiators could, if pressed, agree on a set of criteria for deciding in advance whether a given type of investment was in fact subsidized to an objectionable degree.[37]

On the whole, it appears that New England, along with the rest of the United States, gains a good deal from Canadian investment and should continue to be receptive to such investment. Canadian investment does not, in fact, control any important sector of the New England economy. Even if it did, the proper policy response would be no clearer than it is in Canada. Indeed, New England, with its own mature and – aside from a limited number of high-technology industries--somewhat slower-growing economy, is in much the same relative position as the eastern provinces. National policy limiting or restraining foreign investment would almost certainly work against the region's own interest.

Notes

1. Direct investment usually implies legal ownership and control of real assets. For statistical purposes the assets may be owned directly, or ownership-control may take the form of security holdings where the home country investor holds a "substantial" or controlling portion of the equity in the host country asset. Portfolio investment would then include security holdings where this minimum equity criterion is not met.

2. Canadian Foreign Investment Review Agency, *Annual Report 1981-82*, Ottawa, 1983.

3. See Statistics Canada, Financial Flows and Multinational Enterprises Division, *Employment by Domestic and Foreign Controlled Enterprises in Canada: A Provincial Analysis*, Ottawa, 1980. Also see *Domestic and Foreign Control of Manufacturing, Mining, and Logging Establishments in Canada*, various issues, 1969-1970.

4. Canadian Foreign Investment Review Agency, *Indicators of Foreign Control of Non-financial Industries by Province*, FIRA Papers No. 3, Ottawa, 1978. This study was in turn based largely on data assembled under the Corporations and Labour Unions Returns Act (CALURA) by the Business Finance Division of Statistics Canada. The establishment of FIRA followed publication of the so-called Gray Report. See Government of Canada, *Foreign Direct Investment in Canada* (Ottawa: Information Canada, 1972), which also contains valuable data. (Hereafter cited as *Foreign Direct Investment in Canada*.)

5. While some investment shifts might logically be attributed to the creation of FIRA in 1974 and to the growth of political and cultural barriers in Quebec after 1976, conclusive evidence is not generally available. The downward trend in US value added (Table 7.3) was clearly evident before FIRA took effect. See, on the FIRA question, Steven Globerman, *US Ownership of Firms in Canada* (Montreal: C.D. Howe, 1979) pp. 82-85. For a recent discussion of factors influencing the flow of foreign investment into Canada, see H.C. Byleveld, Foreign Investment in Canada: What's the Score? *The Canadian Business Review* (Summer 1982).

6.   Annual data for each province starting in 1970 are given in the Corporations and Labour Unions Returns Act. Part I, Corporations.

7.   FIRA data supplied by letter. Comparable information for years prior to 1979 is not available. This short list excludes expansion of existing subsidiaries, however.

8.   Brian J. Lorch, Mergers and Acquisitions and the Geographic Transfer of Corporate Control: Canada's Manufacturing Industry, in *Industrial Location and Regional Systems,* edited by J. Rees, G.J.D. Hewings, and H.A. Stafford (Brooklyn: J.F. Bergin, 1981) pp. 123-134.

9.   Lorch, Mergers and Acquisitions, p. 127.

10.   Lorch, Mergers and Acquisitions, p. 129.

11.   But see an interesting exception to this tendency discussed in the appendix to this chapter: a formerly Canadian firm with headquarters now in New Hampshire.

12.   Total assets controlled by Canadian investors probably exceeded $60 billion, as opposed to the $9.9 billion "investment position." See the report of the US Department of Commerce's Benchmark Survey, *Foreign Direct Investment in the United States, 1980* Washington, D.C., 1983. (Hereafter cited as the Benchmark Survey.)

13.   Globerman, *US Ownership,* Table 1. See also *Foreign Direct Investment in Canada, Tables 1-5.*

14.   Between 50 and 65 per cent of Canadian manufacturing investment is or was controlled by foreigners, depending on the measure used. See *Foreign Direct Investment in Canada,* Table 5, as well as Table 7.3 in this chapter.

15.   Data are from the 1980 Benchmark Survey. Also see J. Arpan and D. Ricks, *Directory of Foreign Manufactures in the United States,* 2nd edition (Atlanta: Georgia State University, 1979) Exhibit 3.

16. US International Trade Commission, *Canadian Direct Investment in the United States,* Washington, D.C., 1980, p. 16.

17. Data are from the US Bureau of the Census and are distilled from unpublished figures which, in summarized form, provide the basis for the Bureau's *Selected Characteristics of Foreign-Owned US Firms: 1978,* Washington, D.C., 1980.

18. Olympia and York have undertaken commercial development in the Greater Boston and Hartford areas, however, and both Montreal's Mondev and New Brunswick's Rocca groups have been active in shopping centre development in the New England states.

19. *Foreign Direct Investment in Canada,* Table 1. Also, Statistics Canada, Cat. No. 61-210, and personal correspondence.

20. *Foreign Direct Investment in Canada,* p. 1 (1967 data).

21. See, for example, paper given by R. Wonnacott before the Conference Board of Canada and reported in the Toronto *Globe and Mail,* September 27, 1979. See also Chapter 4 in this volume and the discussion of free trade impacts by the Wonnacotts and others in: Canada-United States Trade Policy Issues, *Canadian Public Policy,* Supplement VIII (October 1982).

22. For a good summary of foreign investment policies up to and including FIRA, see P. Morici, A.J.R. Smith, and S. Lea, *Canadian Industrial Policy* (Washington, D.C.: National Planning Association, 1982) pp. 36-45.

23. See Government of Quebec, *Challenges for Quebec — A Statement on Economic Policy,* Quebec, 1979, p. 47.

24. See B. Bonin, American Investments in Quebec, a paper prepared for a meeting of the Carnegie Endowment for International Peace, New York, June 5, 1981.

25. Quebec now exports both aircraft and aircraft engines, finished automobiles (as part of the General Motors assembly-distribution system), and rail passenger

equipment. It also has several of North America's largest engineering-design firms, partly as a result of its extensive hydro development experience.

26. See Buchanan's speech to the Canadian Society of New York as reported in *The Calgary Herald*, November 21, 1981, p. B 12.

27. See Globerman, *US Ownership*, Part II, Ch. 5.

28. See C. Green, *Canadian Industrial Organization and Policy* (Toronto: McGraw-Hill Ryerson, 1980) p. 310.

29. See, in this regard, J. LeMay, Public Policy in Canada: American Business Experiences, a paper presented at a conference of the Association for Canadian Studies in the United States, Rockland, Maine, September 1983. LeMay reports that among the US business firms interviewed a majority were "quite upset and angry about what happened to them during the FIRA application process and/or the loss of investment value from both FIRA and the National Energy Program."

30. While there is evidence that FIRA relaxed its criteria in some degree as a result of the 1982-1983 recession (and perhaps also as a result of US congressional moves toward legislation defining FIRA activity as an "unfair trade practice," with the consequent penalties), it is not clear that the response of US firms greatly changed because of this.

31. Arpan and Ricks, *Directory of Foreign Manufactures*, p. xi.

32. US Department of Commerce, *Foreign Direct Investment in the United States (1974-76)*, Washington, D.C., 1977, pp. 1-2.

33. Existing legislation permits the government to alter the terms of access to federally owned lands, and this authority could be used to bar Canadian prospecting and exploration firms from receiving leases in areas with promising mineral resources.

34. This is not to say that the United States will eschew new forms of protection against Canadian imports, however, if

it is convinced that such imports are "subsidized" — an issue discussed later in this chapter and in Chapter 3.

35.   Estimate from the US Department of Commerce. Canadian direct investment in specific industries or subindustries may, of course, exceed this level.

36.   Recent debates centring on the "reciprocity" issue suggest that the concern may be rising, however.

37.   Member countries of OECD (Organization for Economic Cooperation and Development), including Canada and the United States, have in fact agreed to certain limitations on export credits.

APPENDIX: SPECIFIC EXAMPLES OF INTERREGIONAL INVESTMENT[1]

New England Investment in Eastern Canada
Pratt & Whitney Canada, Inc.

Pratt & Whitney Canada (P&WC) is a Canadian subsidiary of United Technologies, based in Hartford, Connecticut. Located in Longueuil, Quebec (across the St. Lawrence River from Montreal), the subsidiary dates from 1928 when it was established as a Canadian sales and servicing unit for aircraft engines manufactured by the Pratt & Whitney division of the former United Aircraft Corporation of Hartford. The 1950s witnessed movement of this subsidiary into manufacturing itself, so that by 1960 all of Pratt & Whitney's piston engines were being produced in Canada. An engineering department had also been established by 1960, by which time total employment had reached about 2,300. Subsequent growth of P&WC has centred on the design, development, and manufacture of gas turbine engines for the civil aviation market (small and mid-sized aircraft) and for marine and stationary applications — for example, electric utility generation at remote locations. With approximately 8,500 employees in 1981, this company is presently this largest manufacturing employer in the Greater Montreal area, and has the second largest research and development budget in Canada's private manufacturing sector (after Bell Canada).

The relationship between the parent company and its Canadian subsidiary continues to be complementary, with an advantageous division of labour in manufacturing, sales, and engineering. As a Canadian company with a largely Canadian board of directors and engineering staff, P&WC has benefited from financial assistance provided under programs of the Canadian federal government to advance the country's research and development effort. Having, in addition, access to the considerable scientific and engineering strengths of the parent company (which, with General Electric and Rolls Royce, holds a

281

dominant position in the world aircraft engine market), P&WC
has unusual leverage in its own field of smaller gas turbine
applications.

The company experienced very strong growth during the
1970s, but its performance since 1980 has been adversely affected
by the slow-down in economic activity, particularly as evidenced
by a slump in the civil aviation market. (The latter reflected
curtailment of US general aviation following the air-controllers
strike, as well as a recession-induced reduction in the use of
corporate and private aircraft.) But the gradual diversification of
markets for gas turbines, together with renewed growth in
military procurement, both US and Canadian, argues for P&WC
continuing its leading role among Canadian industrial firms
during the 1980s.

P&WC is unlike many Canadian affiliates of US
manufacturing companies in that it has a world product mandate
and is essentially producing for that market. Specialization
within the company, in other words, has been carried to the point
where the Canadian market is largely, though not entirely,
incidental to the purposes of the subsidiary. Approximately 80
per cent of production is for export, with three-fourths of this
going to the United States.

P&WC thus fits in well with the Canadian federal
government's objective of creating sources of export strength in
high-technology industries. This, of course, is also an objective of
the Quebec government, and P&WC has been an important
source of demand for Quebec-trained engineers and technicians.
Most technical recruitment is now from within the province
itself. At the same time, P&WC has also developed its Toronto
office to the point that roughly 25 per cent of the engineering
work is done there.

The Montreal manufacturing location is regarded as
satisfactory given the nature of the product and the location of
many components and materials suppliers in the northeastern
United States. Customers are distributed widely but with some
concentration in the Midwest and Southwest, along with
expanding markets in Europe.

The Gillette Company

Gillette is a well-established multinational firm based in Boston
with an important affiliate, Gillette of Canada, Ltd., located in
Montreal. The Canadian affiliate dates back to 1906 when it, like
so many other Canadian subsidiaries of US manufacturers, was
established to serve the Canadian market behind a then-
substantial tariff wall. The affiliate, which is 100 per cent owned

and has approximately 750 employees, manufactures most of the Gillette product line including razor blades (but not razors), toiletries and grooming aids, and writing instruments (Papermate). The Montreal facility, moreover, has undergone major expansion in recent years with a 50 per cent increase in manufacturing space in 1979 and substantial additions to office space in 1974 and 1981. The company estimates that its Canadian-produced lines average about 85 per cent Canadian content. Canadian products are differentiated from those sold in the United States primarily by labelling requirements in the respective countries and, to a lesser extent, by advertising programs. Almost all (over 95 per cent) of Gillette Canada's output is intended for the Canadian market; none enters the United States. Moreover, Gillette's share of the market for its traditional product lines is somewhat higher in Canada than in the United States.

While the company has relied on Montreal as its manufacturing and distribution centre for Canada, the acquisition of Liquid Paper Corp. by the US parent in 1979 brought Gillette Canada some manufacturing space in Toronto as well. Present plans are to locate the Canadian writing instruments business increasingly in Toronto, thus permitting the use of Montreal manufacturing space for expanding lines of toiletries and related items.

Apparently Gillette's product line is one in which there are only minor scale economies in production once a certain, and relatively low, threshold level of output has been achieved; the manufacturing technology is not particularly capital intensive. There is, consequently, much less specialization among manufacturing facilities between the United States and Canada than is the case in, say, transportation equipment (see Pratt and Whitney discussion). Nor are shipping costs of overriding importance; the Montreal location is not viewed as being disadvantageous from this standpoint even in the context of Canada's westward-shifting centre of gravity. Labour costs in manufacturing, on the other hand, are of considerable importance, as are income taxes, and the Montreal location is probably no longer optimal according to these criteria.

Quebec's moves toward more cultural independence and political autonomy had a gradual rather than dramatic impact on the company. Recruitment of younger people at non-French institutions for managerial tracks in Montreal was beginning to encounter some resistance in the mid-1970s; Ontario graduates, for example, were increasingly reluctant to accept Quebec positions. The company apparently overcame this problem, however, by looking for people with specific Quebec connections at the outset. (This is true both for academic recruitment and in business career markets generally.) While the managerial group in Montreal is predominantly bilingual, English has, up to the present, clearly been the "first" language for most of them. Thus, Gillette's position seems to be one of gradual accommodation to the modern realities of its Quebec location.

Maritime Life Assurance Co.

– owned by John Hancock Mutual Life (Boston)

Maritime Life, a mid-sized Canadian life insurance company, was founded in 1923 and is located in Halifax. Its primary market area through the 1950s was the Atlantic Region together with some business in the Caribbean. Moves to serve the (Canadian) national market were commenced in the 1960s and powerfully strengthened by infusion of new capital subsequent to acquisition by John Hancock in 1969. Prior to that date, the company's stock was largely in the hands of a small group of Maritime businessmen; in this respect Maritime differed from the larger Canadian life companies, most of which had adopted a mutual form of organization and were thus exempt from acquisition by stock purchase. While the capital infusion provided by Hancock was beneficial to Maritime's further expansion, the Halifax company in turn provided Hancock with a presence in the Canadian market and a reputation for rapid growth through non-conventional insurance services. In recent years, the company has ranked in the top twenty among Canadian life insurance firms, the exact position varying according to the measure employed (assets, premium income, insurance in force).

Maritime is known among Canadian insurers for having stressed innovative forms of life insurance and, in some cases, anticipating changes in market demand. Thus, the company moved early on into types of term insurance that provided greater coverage per premium dollar balanced by somewhat greater risk to the insured. "Reunderwritten term" policies, for example, provide such coverage, yet enable the company to require medical examinations prior to renewal. The growth of this and related types of insurance has far outpaced the general market, with the result that Maritime has had a satisfactory growth performance over a period in which life insurance companies have been hard-pressed to maintain their position among financial institutions generally.

From John Hancock's standpoint, the Canadian subsidiary apparently is meeting the geographic and product diversification objectives envisioned at the time of acquisition. Net income generated by the subsidiary, on the other hand, has been disappointing, a not-uncommon attribute of insurance companies these past few years. But the timing of the acquisition was probably fortuitous (for Hancock) in the sense that such a take-over might have faced tough opposition from FIRA a few years later.

The location of Maritime in Halifax does not appear to be a significant net disadvantage in servicing the Canadian market. While time spent in travel by management may exceed somewhat that of other Canadian life companies, and while the Atlantic time zone hardly facilitates telephone communications with western Canada, the general level of amenities (minus congestion) characteristic of Halifax, together with the opportunity to select superior people from the regional employment market, are thought to convey advantages that more than offset any disadvantage stemming from the down east location. Unlike most manufacturing and resource industries, insurance can be economically sold and serviced at great distances by taking advantage of a network of agents (independent agents in Maritime's case) held together by an effective communications system. The company thus provides a good example of a nationally oriented enterprise conducted from the Atlantic Region, as well as of an intercompany affiliation between that region and New England.

Arthur D. Little, Inc.

This company, which has its headquarters in Cambridge, Massachusetts, is a major provider of research and development, engineering, economic, and information services and does extensive business in management and professional consulting. In addition to subsidiaries in Europe, South America, and the Far East, an affiliate located in Toronto (Arthur D. Little of Canada, Ltd.) is responsible for a growing volume and variety of business services in Canada. The company conducts work for Canadian government agencies, Canadian commercial firms, Canadian subsidiaries of US firms, and American firms interested in Canadian markets and products. Payments for services may be made to the Canadian affiliate.

Arthur D. Little's Canadian business is increasing, although there are substantial year-to-year variations, depending on the timing of specific contracts. The company may conduct anywhere from ten to forty separate Canadian-oriented projects in a given year. While a substantial amount of business is still with clients in Quebec and the Atlantic Provinces, there has been a tendency for Ontario and especially the western provinces to account for an increasing portion of total contract volume. No one particular type of consulting service dominates the firm's Canadian activities. From time to time there have been discussions concerning affiliation with Canadian organizations conducting similar services.

Quebec and Atlantic Provinces Investment in New England
AMCA International
– (formerly Dominion Bridge)

Dominion Bridge was an old-line Canadian company with headquarters in Montreal, specializing in the fabrication of structural steel for use in buildings, bridges, dams, etc. In the late 1960s and early 1970s, the management re-examined corporate objectives and decided (1) that the company's product line was unduly narrow, was subject to cyclical variation, and did not lend itself to export; (2) that the Canadian economy was not growing as fast as others; and (3) that the political climate in both Quebec and Canada generally was not sufficiently supportive of private enterprise as evidenced by high taxes, rising labour costs, and increasing government intervention. Accordingly, the company sold off some of its Canadian plants and other assets and used the proceeds to start on the acquisitions route in the United States (which was seen as having better growth prospects and a more stable political environment) via its then US subsidiary, Dombrico, Inc. This subsidiary's name was later changed to AMCA International, and its head office was located in Hanover, New Hampshire. The mid-1970s witnessed the move of the executive offices to Hanover, and in 1981 AMCA itself was transformed into the parent company, with Dominion Bridge now the Canadian subsidiary.

Clearly, AMCA International is no ordinary Quebec or even Canadian investor in New England. Even by 1976 the company (Dominion) reported that Quebec itself was contributing no more than 4 per cent to net income from operations. The major operating subsidiaries increasingly were in the United States and overseas; however, there were only three such subsidiaries in New England around 1980 (see Table 7.14). The choice of Hanover as a headquarters site is attributed to that city's location about midway between Montreal, Boston, and New York; to its having a number of rural yet collegiate amenities (including access to an airport and a first-rate medical facility); and, of course, to New Hampshire's tax situation. That state presently has no income tax, making it an especially desirable location for corporate executives. Moreover, the state's relatively heavy reliance on property taxes has little impact on a set of executive suites. It is significant, nevertheless, that northern New England is seen as a feasible base of control for a company whose operations are increasingly international in scope. It is interesting, further, to note that this particular company is not a true conglomerate; all of its recently acquired subsidiaries continue to operate within the construction and engineering industries.

Fishery Products, Inc.[2]

This firm, located in Danvers, Massachusetts, is a wholly owned subsidiary of Fishery Products International, Ltd. in St. John's, Newfoundland. After having developed and sold a major processing firm in Cleveland, Fishery Products centred its attention on New England in the late 1960s. A Gloucester sales office was first enlarged, and then supplanted by a modern headquarters and processing plant in Danvers, opened in 1974. The parent company owns extensive trawling and processing facilities in Newfoundland, and is a major purchaser of fish from independent fishermen as well. Total sales are currently in excess of $110 million annually, of which the New England subsidiary accounts for more than three-fourths.

Most of the material going into the Danvers plant is in frozen block form and is trucked from Newfoundland. The structure of the US tariff is such as to work against the importation of processed fish (which are subject to duties of 8-15 per cent), whereas raw fish in block ice enter under only nominal rates (1-2 per cent). Somewhat over 60 per cent of the unprocessed fish arriving at the plant in either frozen blocks or frozen fillets is resold directly to restaurant and hotel chains and other large-scale users with their own processing facilities; the balance is processed at Danvers into a variety of packaged forms by the company and distributed widely throughout the United States. Total sales of the US subsidiary are in the neighbourhood of $90 million, and approximately 150 persons are now employed at the Danvers facility. According to 1980 data, the investment in this facility approaches $4 million.

The decision to locate the plant in New England was shaped by a number of factors, some of which are obvious, others less so. Given the weight loss in processing, there was great advantage in having basic processing facilities as close to the source of raw material as possible. Thus, the tariff structure, together with the availability of adequate trucking routes, argued for a location on or near the northeastern coast. The Greater Boston area has for many years been an important centre for fish processing and distribution, with numerous established traders and brokers feeding a national distribution network. Again, this is related to the historical proximity of sources of supply and to the weight loss and value added that accompanies processing. In general, trucking services to the south and west are good. Since the predominant movement of food products in the United States is from the west and south, service (and costs) for movement in the opposite direction have tended to reflect the imbalance, to the advantage of Northeast food processors. Finally, there is probably a traditional element at work; fish processing and the New England coast share an historic relationship. While the plant labour input does not, for the most part, involve high levels of skill or training, the pre-existence of a labour force familiar with and accustomed to the work of processing, together with financing sources familiar with the industry, no doubt helps to keep the industry where it is.

It is worth noting that Canadian entrance into the New England fish processing industry is characterized by large-scale firms as compared with the domestically owned portion of the industry. In a survey undertaken by the US General Accounting Office for the Congress in 1980, it was found that the five leading foreign-owned firms in the northeast region (four of which are Canadian) all had assets in excess of $10 million, while only one of the firms not foreign owned was of this size.[3] Indeed, the typical US fishing-fish processing firm surveyed was in the $1-5 million class. This same survey also found that, while there was no consensus as to the effects of foreign investment in fish processing in the northeastern states, about one-third of the domestic firms expressed fears about foreigners' abilities to control supplies, or markets, or both. Moreover, fully half of them argued for government measures to restrict or exclude foreign-owned firms from the US fish processing industry.[4] This view reflects in part the belief that Canadian and other foreign firms are in some sense subsidized, and hence represent unfair competition. Fishery Products, Inc. denies the existence of a subsidy in its own case. (The issue is discussed in Chapter 7.)

Sun Life Assurance Company of Canada

This company affords a good, though not typical, example of the Canadian role in New England related to both investment and services. Sun Life, the largest and one of the oldest of Canada's insurance companies, is organized on a mutual basis – that is, without stockholders. It carries on its business through an extensive network of company (non-independent) agents. Its headquarters has been traditionally located in Montreal, but the late 1970s saw a metamorphosis which placed the new international headquarters in Toronto, leaving the Canadian office in Montreal. Of immediate interest, however, is the development of a US headquarters in the Boston area.

Although the company has had policyholders in the United States since the late nineteenth century and for many years has had sales operatives working in various parts of the country, it was not until the late 1960s that a regional sales and service office was established in New England. This initial move was followed in 1973 by a decision to consolidate US servicing operations in one location, Wellesley, Massachusetts, where Sun Life now owns and partially occupies an office park complex. Employment in this location has grown from roughly 300 in late 1973 to 1,100 today. Over fifty sales offices are presently located in the United States, all coordinated through the Wellesley headquarters. US business has more than doubled in the past seven years, and US life insurance in force now exceeds $10 million. Essentially, the US and Canadian investment portfolios are managed separately and the former portfolio strongly emphasizes securities of US governments and corporations. Interestingly, all but a very small fraction of the company's real estate holdings and mortgages are outside of New England.

The company originally chose the Boston area as its US headquarters because a large number of policyholders were in the northeastern United States, because of the city's proximity to Montreal, and because of New England's strong position in the insurance industry. Given the nature of the product, transportation costs are not particularly important. Hence, there appears to be no significant disadvantage in servicing policies, claims, etc. throughout the United States from this location. While other Canadian insurance companies have recently established US headquarters in Denver and Atlanta, one suspects that amenities and tradition, as well as proximity, may have played a role in Sun Life's opting for a New England location. (A US "headquarters" is generally sought to comply with state insurance laws restricting foreign ownership.)

Bombardier, Inc.

This company's plant in Barre, Vermont was established in 1982, primarily to assemble mass transit vehicles ordered by US cities, including New York. The Vermont location provides proximity to the corporate headquarters in Montreal and to the principal mass transit division plants in Quebec. This move was also necessary for Bombardier to qualify for US sales under preferential "buy American" laws governing federal government support of mass transit capital projects. The intention is to assemble henceforth in Vermont all transit vehicles destined for US markets.

At one time limited to the manufacture of snowmobiles, the parent company (founded in 1942) has since the early 1970s diversified into various types of transportation equipment. Current annual sales are about $500 million. The company now manufactures locomotives, trucks, military vehicles, motorcycles, airplane landing gear, and (in Austria) engines and related precision parts. It appears, however, that the manufacture of mass transit equipment may experience the most rapid growth in coming years as an increasing number of the world's cities set about improving or replacing their transit systems.

The New York City contract, believed to be the largest single export contract ever awarded to a Canadian firm, calls for the delivery of 825 subway cars with an ultimate indexed value of approximately a billion dollars. Deliveries will extend from 1984 through 1987. While competitors claimed that Bombardier's bid was successful because of export financing subsidies provided by the Canadian government, US federal authorities investigating the claim found that other factors played dominant roles. The cars in question combine Japanese design technology with Canadian manufacturing expertise.

The location in Barre, Vermont is literally at the top of a mountain (now mostly excavated) of granite, that city's traditional product. A new plant has been built which will ultimately employ about 200 people, and finished equipment is routed down a precipitous rail line formerly used by mining engines. While the rationale for choosing a northern Vermont location is clear, it is equally clear that the plant owes its existence to US legislation specifying preference for US-manufactured equipment, one of several non-tariff barriers which exist on both sides of the boundary that are shaping increasingly the pattern of Canada-US trade.

Neill and Gunter, Ltd.

The New Brunswick firm of Neill and Gunter, Ltd. was established in 1965 to provide engineering and project management services primarily for the paper and forest products industries. Services include plant design and consulting on a variety of problems requiring structural, mechanical, and electrical engineering skills. In recent years, there has been some broadening in emphasis to include energy conservation techniques, design of hydroelectric and fish-handling facilities, and related areas. In 1979, this firm, together with H.G.

Moeltner and Associates, Ltd. (Ontario), formed a new entity, NGM International, to provide design and project management services to the rapidly expanding composition board industry. The new firm is thought to have a dominant share of this market.

In 1975, a US subsidiary, Neill and Gunter, Inc., was formed to better service the needs of New England clients, to gain visibility in US markets generally, and for other reasons discussed shortly. The subsidiary is located just outside of Portland, Maine. Also relevant was the belief that the optimum scale of an office providing personal engineering services and capable of attracting creative engineering talent was in the neighbourhood of fifty to seventy people. The home office in Fredericton had by then (1975) already expanded to approximately sixty-five. The Portland subsidiary has grown fairly rapidly, to the point where perhaps one-third of consolidated sales is now generated there. The parent firm also has branches in Nova Scotia and Newfoundland, and has, through its New England subsidiary, recently taken on projects in a number of southern and midwestern states. The company's overall growth rate since 1965 has been in the neighbourhood of 30 per cent, and the growth of its US business has been substantially higher.

This company is a good example of early and rapid growth in direct, cross-boundary services emanating from a Canadian city (in this case Fredericton), followed by establishment of a corporate entity in the host country which maintained and even enhanced the growth of sales while lessening the actual amount of international "services" traffic. Northern New England was a particularly fertile area for expansion, since the region's dominant paper and wood products industry relied largely on "imported" engineering services. A new, smaller firm offering advanced technology to an industry whose market was expanding, and locating in that industry's own front yard, so to speak, was thus able to capture a substantial share of this specialized business. It is entirely possible in these circumstances to see an absolute decline in actual cross-boundary services trade, and hence trade flows in the balance of payments, as the subsidiary takes on a major part of the growth.

The history of Neill and Gunter is in many respects similar to that of other Canadian consulting and management firms seeking to expand in US markets. Before the expansion has gone very far, one or more corporate subsidiaries are established which thereafter account for much of the development and work effort. For example, Shawinigan Group of Montreal, a successor to the former Quebec private power entity, now provides engineering services to US clients largely through an affiliate incorporated in California. Canadian real estate development firms, on the other hand, appear not to require the establishment of corporate affiliates to do business in the United States.

The Neill and Gunter example is different in one respect, however. Because Mr. Neill's engineering work for US clients had by 1974 expanded to the point where he was spending several days a week in the United States on a regular basis, immigration authorities acted to revoke his status as a business visitor. The Immigration and Naturalization Service's interim decision argued that Neill did not seek to enter the United States *temporarily*, in that he was not engaged in business as that term is used in the law, that he was extending his professional engineering practice to the United States, and that his services were "not performed as an incident to any international commercial activity, except to the extent that the performance of this service can, itself, be considered an international commercial activity."[5] Thus, since he was neither a business visitor nor an immigrant, he was to be excluded. While the decision might have been appealed successfully, Neill and Gunter had by that time (1975) a number of other reasons for preferring the subsidiary route. The decision revealed a fundamental weakness in a law which finds it difficult to recognize cross-boundary business and professional services as a form of commercial activity. It seems likely that the case helped to confirm the pattern of consulting and other services firms establishing subsidiaries in those countries in which they expect to do a significant amount of business.

Notes

1. Information in all cases comes primarily from company sources.

2. The following description antedates the 1984 restructuring of Canadian fish processors discussed in Chapter 6.

3. US General Accounting Office, *Foreign Investment in US Seafood Processing Industry Difficult to Assess*, Report B-202302 GA 1.13: CED 81-65, Washington, D.C., 1981, various appendix tables.

4. US General Accounting Office, *Foreign Investment*, Introduction.

5. US Immigration and Naturalization Service, *Matter of Neill in Exclusion Proceedings*, Interim Decision /2392, May 16, 1975.

8: TRI-REGIONAL ECONOMIC LINKAGES: OVERVIEW AND AGENDA

J. D. McNiven

The preceding chapters have explored some of the economic linkages among Quebec, Atlantic Canada, and New England. This chapter summarizes a few of the arguments already made and uses them as a basis for discussing the future policy agenda.

As the preceding chapters have shown, there is no question that north-south economic ties among Quebec, Atlantic Canada, and New England are being strengthened. Trade opportunities become ever more visible as regional economies expand, especially where geography, hence transportation cost, is favourable. Such opportunities reinforce the conventional Canadian wisdom that the tugs southward constitute the most serious threat to continued existence of an east-west Canada. Research has shown that trade linkages between other parts of Canada and the United States also demonstrate the direct north-south pull. British Columbia's trade tends to focus on the US West Coast, while Ontario's US trade is heavily oriented toward New York and Michigan.

The evolution of tariff reductions agreed to by signatories of the General Agreement on Tariffs and Trade and the ability of both the United States and Canada to avoid (up until now) excessive non-tariff barriers further support the growth of north-south trade. Within a few years the effective overall level of conventional tariffs may no longer be a significant obstacle to trade. This evolution has raised considerable debate in Canadian circles, reflecting concern about the presumed heavy influence that the United States, whose population and gross product are ten times those of Canada, will bring to bear on the Canadian economy. This concern extends to the northeast region where US manufacturing has been dominant, and where cross-border competition in forestry and food products has long been a fact of life. Managing this close and, to Canadians, preponderant relationship has been at the core of Canadian concerns for much of the period since Confederation in 1867.

The United States and, in this instance, New England see this evolution from a different perspective. Intensified economic linkages with Canada do not represent any kind of threat to the United States. Nor do they represent, outside of very limited areas in fishing, food, and forest processing, a serious threat to US industry or labour. Rather, the basic concern of Americans is the potential for instability in their northern neighbour and its impact on reliable supplies of raw materials, including energy. Canadians have learned to function effectively within their national ambiguity. To Americans, however, dependability must generally be equated to clarity of intent. Canada-US trade as a whole constitutes the largest bilateral exchange of goods and services in the world. If it is to remain so, Canadians and Americans alike must learn more about the pitfalls and possibilities associated with a closer relationship.

Understanding more about the relationship between eastern Canada and New England can contribute to the needs described above. The historic relationship discussed in Chapter 1 is one of the oldest on the North American continent. It spurred France and England onto conflicts in the 1600s and 1700s. Later, conflicts between England and the United States formed the present boundary. Today, the boundary falls in a rural zone between the urbanized belt of southern New England and a similar belt along the St. Lawrence. Trade flows in the greater northeast region have tended to be based on exports of manufactures from New England, reciprocated by exports of raw and semi-processed goods from Canada, together with a few finished manufactures reflecting traditional Quebec and Atlantic Provinces specializations (Chapter 3).

A number of factors have been changing which may act on this relationship. Changes in national policies, together with economic growth, have resulted in an almost similar quality of life in all parts of the three regions. Levels of education, social services, and suburban development (and its transport base), as well as new forms of economic activity in these regions, have all tended to converge so that neither intraregional, urban-rural, nor interregional Canadian-American disparities exist to the extent they once did (Chapters 1 and 2). Per capita incomes seem to be converging as those in southern New England move downward somewhat to American averages and eastern Canadian incomes, supplemented by federal equalization and transfer schemes, move upward. Only in migration patterns has there been an adverse change in recent decades. Whereas Canadians used to migrate from the eastern provinces into New England as much if not more than directly west, eastern Canadians today resemble

New Englanders in their propensity to migrate to the western areas of their respective countries. Cross-border movements of capital and services are increasing, whereas movements of labour are not, except for a continuing filtering of enterprising and/or older Canadians into the more congenial climates of the United States, and a trickle of Americans, mostly young, seeking a different natural or political environment in Canada.

The trading relationship between the regions has diversified as they have come closer together in socio-economic terms. Movements of raw and semi-processed goods still dominate trade to the south, while manufactures dominate trade to the north. However, the growth of multinational corporations, regional imbalances in energy supply and demand, and the increasing sophistication of eastern Canadian society have worked to inject new goods into the relationship. Movements of semi-raw and semi-processed materials related to forests and fish now occur on a south-to-north basis as corporations involved in their production in the rural belt take advantage of production and market locations regardless of the boundary. The same holds true for some manufactured goods, especially out of Quebec and into New England (Chapter 3).

Trade between Atlantic Canada and Quebec resembles in many ways that between eastern Canada as a whole and New England. It is dominated by a movement of processed materials from Quebec and of raw materials, including energy, from the Atlantic Region (including Labrador). Again, there are exceptions to this trend. As well, the sketchy data available suggest that the growth of trade between the two regions of Canada is slower than that of north-south trade, which brings one back to the concerns expressed at the beginning of this chapter.

A recurring question in Canada-US economic relations has concerned the possible effects of tariff elimination on both sides of the border – that is, a comprehensive free trade agreement. Apprehensions about such an agreement have been especially strong in Ontario and Quebec, where some manufacturers – including foreign branch plants – were thought to be unprepared for unfettered competition with US firms. Western Canada and the Atlantic Region have generally been more receptive. Analysis of the despecialization, scale, migration, and relocation effects of tariff removal (Chapter 4), however, shows that the consequences for *all* provinces are highly uncertain. This is true in part because of (1) the largely unpredictable responses of US corporations having (or contemplating) plants in Canada, (2) a possibly increased tendency for Canadian producers to invest in

US facilities, and (3) ongoing geographic shifts in the US market itself. Moreover, it is shown that under free trade Quebec might be more disadvantaged than Ontario, mainly due to differences in industry mix (and hence in the ability to realize scale economies). The Atlantic Region, while enjoying a reduction in the cost of manufactured goods, might not be able (1) to attract more finished processing of its raw materials, some of which is already in New England, or (2) to achieve free access to US markets for fish and forest products without giving up some intra- Canadian transfers which have the effect of lowering Atlantic production costs and thus giving the appearance of subsidies.

In addition to the free trade analysis, four types of economic linkages were considered in the previous chapters. Two — those dealing with fish and energy — concerned specific exports of raw or semi- processed goods from north to south. The other two — generalized trade flows (including services) and investment — reflected a more varied pattern, although research on services and (until the late 1970s) investment suggests a somewhat stronger south-to-north flow. Difficulties in measurement are immense in cross-boundary trade involving subnational regions; many of the interregional flow figures must, therefore, be taken as indicative rather than as definitive.

Energy linkages among the regions (Chapter 5), following curtailment of the northbound flow of crude oil through the Portland-Montreal pipeline, have been dominated by southbound electricity transmission and secondarily by trade in refined oil products. Movements of electricity could still grow considerably as evidenced by continuing negotiations. While differential resource costs argue strongly for such growth, institutional and political considerations, mainly though not exclusively on the US side, have been and will continue to be a dampening influence. Movements of such products as gasoline and fuel oil depend in large part upon the marketing and distribution strategies of companies within Canada and by occasional openings of the New England market to Canadian exports. The potential for natural gas movements from Nova Scotia to New England is large, but its realization may be some years off.

Trade in fish products (Chapter 6) presents a somewhat different situation than does that in energy. Whereas electricity, for instance, is a highly regulated commodity that is sold to New England producers/distributors by exporters having province-wide monopoly powers, fish products are generally exported by competitive Canadian concerns which are also in competition with New England fishermen. A third party in the United States, the processor, buys from both domestic and foreign sources. The number and variety of fish producers potentially leads to a more intensive conflict between people on both sides of the border. This situation is complicated by the different roles played by the respective governments in the Canadian and American fishery, and by the heavy dependency of Canadian producers on the New England market. Finally, while east coast Canadian production is four-fifths of the total Canadian fishery, it is but one-fourth the size of the overall (eastern, southern, western) American industry. Consequently, concerns about competition between Canadian and New England fish production tend to be seen in Washington as matters of regional rather than of national policy. In this context, the Canadian fishery may at times be viewed as an overly large and not too welcome appendage of the New England fishery. The Canadian product is welcome in American households and eating establishments, but possibly not if it displaces that of the domestic producer, and probably not if the displacement can be attributed to government subsidies on the Canadian side.

Business and professional services and the so-called high-technology product linkages are dominated by New England, while Canada (aside from a few aviation and telecommunications products, and certain engineering services) is left in a kind of catch-up position (Chapter 3). The early establishment of a growing technology complex around Boston led to its being the natural successor to declining textile and other manufacturing industries. Today, Quebec is faced with a similar situation with a large number of moribund and mature industries and is looking to the New England example as a way of making the transition from a nineteenth-century to a twentieth-century economy. Smaller efforts are being made by the Atlantic Provinces in this regard.

Investment flows (Chapter 7 and its Appendix) are the most difficult to interpret, partly because of the non-specific geographical character of many of the corporations involved and partly because of the difficulty in identifying the flows themselves. Few cross-border investments located entirely in the three regions under discussion are identifiable. Examples of resource processing investments exist, especially in the food and forest sectors. Atlantic Provinces fish processors have facilities in New England, while lumber and blueberry processors from both countries have cross-border investments. Insurance companies on either side of the boundary have affiliates in the other country (region). Canadian engineering and construction firms have opened offices in New England, while examples exist of a few New England high-technology manufacturers opening facilities in Quebec, and vice versa. Yet it must be noted that much of the investment originating on either side of the border tends toward locations throughout the host country rather than concentration within the tri-regional area.

In sum, the sectoral examples presented in the previous chapters indicate that the three regions are significant trading partners. There also appears to be room for expansion of these linkages both in the sectors discussed and in new product and service lines. Benefits range from needed future energy supplies for New England, to the possibility of rejuvenating Quebec's economy following New England's example, to enhanced market opportunities for Atlantic Canada resource products.

A Possible Agenda

First and foremost, trade development depends upon opportunities that are perceived and acted upon by the private sector. If opportunities do not exist, or if they are not perceived, an expansion of trade will not occur. Public sector bodies can act to either help or hinder the identification and exploitation of opportunities. They may help in a number of ways such as providing market information or altering the mix of front-end and subsequent costs of exporting, among others. The means whereby the public sector can hinder trade are many and need little elaboration here.

Most trade activity discussed in the previous chapters was related to that crossing the border. This trade is regulated by federal authorities in both countries. Regional trade considerations are generally given secondary priority to broader national objectives. Within the parameters of international regulation, however, a number of policy areas can be tied to provincial or state jurisdictions. Depending on the activity at this level, trade may be further helped or hampered.

The states and provinces in northeastern North America are uniquely positioned to affect trade policy relevant to their jurisdictions. They can act to pressure their respective federal governments and to coordinate their individual approaches to trade-related policies that come under their respective jurisdictions through the vehicle of the New England Governors and Eastern Canadian Premiers Conference.

The Conference consists of an annual meeting supplemented by the activity of a number of committees and supported by secretariats on either side of the border. It has considered trade issues frequently, and in 1983 it moved to create a committee of officials to explore economic and trade opportunities.

The impetus for this increased level of activity is clear. The volume of international trade in the Northeast is growing and, with it, both problems and opportunities. Some products, such as fish and potatoes, are intensely competitive across the boundary. Although the overall American market can absorb production from both sides of the border, the differences in administering production incentives, taxation regimes, and even input prices all serve to exacerbate problems between producers in times of oversupply or in specific competitive situations.

The volumes of trade are paralleled by the importance of this trade to each region in the area. About one-half of New England's trade with Canada is with its counterparts in the northeastern area. Atlantic Provinces trade with the United States follows a similar pattern, with about one-half of its exports to that country going to New England. Quebec, however, only sends about one-seventh of its American exports to New England. In spite of this differential, the Quebec government attaches considerable importance to its economic links with New England, in part because the effects of the Auto Pact with the United States may distort this province's future trade possibilities, and in part because Quebec perceives benefits from promoting increased contact with the technologically sophisticated New England region.

Because the stakes in this trading relationship are so significant, it is important that the three regions define their particular interests and communicate them to their partners. Relying on national mechanisms for bargaining these interests may lead to their being ignored or may create levels of conflict that only harm producers on both sides. Solutions that can be discussed and agreed to off the national agendas seem to offer more flexibility and to be easier to implement. The Conference could, for example, take the lead in working out a mutually acceptable definition of the word "subsidy" and establishing criteria of particular relevance for the northeastern region in determining whether or not a given import or export is subsidized.

One of the most critical trade policy areas requiring more attention is that of free trade, whether a general free trade agreement or sectoral free trade. Sectoral free trade would involve the elimination of trade barriers between Canada and the United States in specific types of goods and services, as opposed to more general free trade (Chapter 4). Proponents of this view point to the success of the Auto Pact, which has encouraged increased auto production, including parts, in Canada, while reserving a continuing large proportion of the Canadian market for American cars. The definition of new sectors for discussion is proceeding on the national level, while various economic interests are coming forward with differing priority lists. Whether these lists meet the needs of the northeastern part of the continent is not known, but it is doubtful. It is probable, as well, that sectoral agreements will be overtaken by moves toward a comprehensive Canada-US trade agreement.

Two especially sensitive sectors in which changes in trade policy would have an impact on the Northeast are energy and fisheries. Both are commodities for which Canadian exports to the United States must compete with local production. The energy trade has evolved quickly over the past few years. While attention has centred more on trade in electricity, the prospect of dedicated natural gas supplies from the Scotian Shelf adds a new dimension to this discussion. New sources of energy such as this or the power that could be derived from the tides of the Bay of Fundy require careful consideration of the overall energy trade mix of the next decade and beyond.

The trade in fisheries products presents a different sort of sectoral problem, although in some ways it resembles that faced by the forest products sector on both sides of the border in recent years. The method of administering already-established industries often tends to differ as a result of domestic pressures and political conditions. One example of this is, in the case of the forest industries on the west coast, the method of gaining revenue from publicly owned forest land. Canadian practice led to the assessment of stumpage fees that were related to the market value of the timber when harvested. American practice is based on a competitive auction system that forces bidders to try to guess future prices and returns when devising their bids. In a period of oversupply and low overall prices, the American system has proven to be less favourable to producers, and they have charged that the Canadian industry is being subsidized by the way in which Canadian stumpage fees are structured.

The fishery on the east coast faces similar problems. Canadian, as opposed to American, practice is conditioned by different constitutional and political methods and by a different problem in economic geography. The New England fishery is to some degree integrated into a rather heavily populated and economically diverse region, while the Canadian fishery is dispersed among widely scattered small communities where the alternatives to migration are almost nil were the fishery to fail. The lack of employment alternatives and the consequent threat to hundreds of small communities have resulted in organization of the industry into something akin to an old-fashioned telephone system, with large and small plants spread throughout the region. As it has in much of the Canadian telephone system, government involvement has gradually and irregularly crept into this industry.

The problem facing the three regions, as well as the two countries as a whole, is how to reconcile freer trade with the interests of specific industrial sectors in which administrative and economic circumstances differ widely across the border. Sometimes these problems cannot be reconciled, but often, with mutual understanding and a determination to devise a solution in which both sides gain, something can be worked out. The alternative is a confrontational process in which symbolic and short-term victories are pursued to the detriment of longer-term advantage.

It is a truism that action takes place on the margin. This underscores the need to consider from a public point of view those items and industries that are on paths of growth or decline in tri-regional trade. Often, these are not the core items of interregional trade, but they are nonetheless important. Since these items and industries are relatively numerous and constantly changing, a continual updating and research process is required.

Another area of potential concern is that of investment flows among the three regions. While these do not appear to be very large at this time, there is reason to believe that they may grow. Canadian (mainly national) concerns about the amount of American investment in the 1960s and 1970s led to barriers to investment being put in place. This attitude is now changing. As well, investment requires a perception that a region has the potential to allow the investment commitment to succeed. Over the past two decades, neither Canadians nor Americans have viewed the East as the most promising place to invest. Competition with the Sun Belt and the Canadian West may be less intense in the 1980s, however, while the vigour of the New England economy and the attractiveness of eastern Canadian locations may act to sustain, if not increase, cross-boundary investment. At this point, it may be appropriate to begin to promote aggressively the virtues of interregional investment, on the assumption that entrepreneurs in all three regions may be unaware of opportunities close to home as attractive as those in the South and the West.

Public policy should also begin to address comprehensively the problems of non-standardization in trade movements. Non-standardization refers here to different practices related to grading of food products, measurement systems, truck haulage weight limits and licensing freedom, and red tape in general. While many of these practices are nationally determined, others reflect provincial and state regulations. In either case, the provinces and states can play significant roles in developing and pushing for greater standardization in trade-related practices. Such steps would reduce costs and eliminate unintended trade barriers.

While trade barriers against goods have been altered as a result of the last round of GATT negotiations and restrictions on services appear to be relatively minor between the two countries, there are significant cross-border restrictions on labour mobility where outright migration is not involved. In the East, this has two manifestations. One relates to the ability of businessmen to move quickly and easily from one side of the border to the other. This problem is partly due to low levels of demand for air service, and is aggravated by route restrictions and regulation of air traffic and fares. The result is a level of service that hampers the growth of business ties among the three regions where these ties cross the border. The second restriction on labour mobility has its roots in attempts to protect local labour markets from outside competition. While this may make some political sense when applied to mature industries, its application to technologically sophisticated industries or other areas of activity where some type of skill transfer might assist in further economic development in the regions is regrettable. At some point in the near future the problem of labour mobility between Canada and the United States will have to be addressed if North American technological superiority is to be maintained and enhanced.

These and other policy concerns can best be addressed by a combination of further research, discussion, consultation, and initiatives by the public and private sectors of both countries. This last point may be most effectively pursued through wide support for the international business councils being formed on both sides of the border. The New England/Canada Business Council is three years old and an Atlantic Canada/New England Business Council has recently been formed. Bodies such as these can be of great assistance in influencing regional and national policy to promote stronger ties in northeastern North America.

Conclusion

Many of the points discussed in this chapter do not end in solid conclusions. The same can be said for much of the material in the previous chapters. Given the paucity of existing knowledge about interregional ties along and across the border, this should not be surprising. The fact that so little work has been done with respect to the regions along the northeast boundary, when it is this part of North America that is most active at political, and to some extent business, coordination, underlines Canada's tendency to take the dominance of historical north-south ties as given and the US tendency, even in border areas, to take Canada for granted. More work is needed if the full potential of interregional trade and investment across the northeast boundary is to be realized. It is hoped that this volume has helped to point the way in that direction.

THE MEMBERS OF THE INSTITUTE

Professor Kell Antoft
Institute of Public Affairs
Dalhousie University, Halifax
Marie-Andrée Bertrand
École de criminologie
Université de Montréal
Dr. Roger A. Blais
École Polytechnique de Montréal
George Cooper, Q.C.
McInnes, Cooper and Robertson, Halifax
James S. Cowan, Q.C.
Partner, Stewart, MacKeen & Covert
Halifax
V. Edward Daughney
President, First City Trust Company
Vancouver
Dr. Wendy Dobson
Executive Director, C.D. Howe Institute
Toronto
Marc Eliesen
Chairperson
Manitoba Energy Authority, Winnipeg
Emery Fanjoy
Secretary, Council of Maritime Premiers
Halifax
Dr. Allan K. Gillmore
Executive Director, Association of
Universities and Colleges of Canada, Ottawa
Dr. Donald Glendenning
President, Holland College, Charlottetown
Margaret C. Harris
Past President, The National Council of
Women of Canada, Saskatoon
Richard W. Johnston
President, Spencer Stuart & Associates
Toronto
Dr. Leon Katz, O.C.
Saskatoon
Terrence Mactaggart
Managing Director
Sound Linked Data Inc., Mississauga
Dr. John S. McCallum
Faculty of Administrative Studies
University of Manitoba, Winnipeg
Claude Morin
École nationale d'administration publique
Québec
Milan Nastich
Canadian General Investments Limited
Toronto
Professor William A. W. Neilson
Dean, Faculty of Law
University of Victoria
Roderick C. Nolan, P.Eng.
Executive Vice-President
Neill & Gunter Limited, Fredericton
Robert J. Olivero
United Nations Secretariat, New York
Maureen O'Neil
Co-ordinator, Status of Women Canada
Ottawa

Garnet T. Page, O.C.
Calgary
Dr. Gilles Paquet
Dean, Faculty of Administration
University of Ottawa
Dr. K. George Pedersen
President, University of Western Ontario
London
Professor Marilyn L. Pilkington
Osgoode Hall Law School, Toronto
Dr. David W. Slater
Ottawa
Dr. Stuart L. Smith
Chairman, Science Council of Canada
Ottawa
Eldon D. Thompson
President, Telesat, Vanier
Marc-Adélard Tremblay, O.C.
Departement d'anthropologie
Université Laval, Québec
Dr. Israel Unger
Department of Chemistry, University of
New Brunswick, Fredericton
Philip Vineberg, O.C., Q.C.
Phillips & Vineberg, Montreal
Dr. Norman Wagner
President, University of Calgary
Ida Wasacase, C.M.
Winnipeg
Dr. R. Sherman Weaver
Director, Alberta Environmental Centre
Vegreville
Dr. Blossom Wigdor
Director, Program in Gerontology
University of Toronto

Government Representatives
Herb Clarke, Newfoundland
Joseph H. Clarke, Nova Scotia
Michael Decter, Manitoba
Jim Dinning, Alberta
Hershell Ezrin, Ontario
Honourable Lowell Murray, Canada
John H. Parker, Northwest Territories
Henry Phillips, Prince Edward Island
Norman Riddell, Saskatchewan
Jean-K. Samson, Québec
Norman Spector, British Columbia
Eloise Spitzer, Yukon
Barry Toole, New Brunswick

INSTITUTE MANAGEMENT

Rod Dobell	President
Louis Vagianos	Special Assistant
Edgar Gallant	Fellow-in-Residence
Tom Kent	Fellow-in-Residence
Eric Kierans	Fellow-in-Residence
Jean-Luc Pepin	Fellow-in-Residence
Gordon Robertson	Fellow-in-Residence
Yvon Gasse	Director, Small and Medium-Sized Business Program
Barbara L. Hodgins	Director, Western Resources Program
Barry Lesser	Director, Regional Employment Opportunities Program
Frank Stone	A/Director, International Economics Program
Shirley Seward	Director, Co-ordination and Liaison
Parker Staples	Director, Financial Services & Treasurer
Donald Wilson	Director, Communications
Tom Kent	Editor, *Policy Options Politiques*

PUBLICATIONS AVAILABLE - MARCH 1986

Order Address: The Institute for Research on Public Policy
P.O. Box 3670 South
Halifax, Nova Scotia
B3J 3K6

Leroy O. Stone & Claude Marceau	*Canadian Population Trends and Public Policy Through the 1980s.* 1977 $4.00
Raymond Breton	*The Canadian Condition: A Guide to Research in Public Policy.* 1977 $2.95
Raymond Breton	*Une orientation de la recherche politique dans le contexte canadien.* 1977 $2.95
J.W. Rowley & W.T. Stanbury (eds.)	*Competition Policy in Canada: Stage II, Bill C-13.* 1978 $12.95
C.F. Smart & W.T. Stanbury (eds.)	*Studies on Crisis Management.* 1978 $9.95
W.T. Stanbury (ed.)	*Studies on Regulation in Canada.* 1978 $9.95
Michael Hudson	*Canada in the New Monetary Order: Borrow? Devalue? Restructure!* 1978 $6.95
David K. Foot (ed.)	*Public Employment and Compensation in Canada: Myths and Realities.* 1978 $10.95
Raymond Breton & Gail Grant Akian	*Urban Institutions and People of Indian Ancestry: Suggestions for Research.* 1979 $3.00
Thomas H. Atkinson	*Trends in Life Satisfaction Among Canadians,1968-1977.* 1979 $3.00
W.E. Cundiff & Mado Reid (eds.)	*Issues in Canadian/U.S. Transborder Computer Data Flows.* 1979 $6.50
Meyer W. Bucovetsky (ed.)	*Studies in Public Employment and Compensation in Canada.* 1979 $14.95
Richard French & André Béliveau	*The RCMP and the Management of National Security.* 1979 $6.95
Richard French & André Béliveau	*La GRC et la gestion de la sécurité nationale.* 1979 $6.95

311

G. Bruce Doern & Allan M. Maslove (eds.)	*The Public Evaluation of Government Spending.* 1979 $10.95
Leroy O. Stone & Michael J. MacLean	*Future Income Prospects for Canada's Senior Citizens.* 1979 $7.95
Richard M. Bird	*The Growth of Public Employment in Canada.* 1979 $12.95
Richard J. Schultz	*Federalism and the Regulatory Process.* 1979 $1.50
Richard J. Schultz	*Le fédéralisme et le processus de réglementation.* 1979 $1.50
Lionel D. Feldman & Katherine A. Graham	*Bargaining for Cities, Municipalities and Intergovernmental Relations: An Assessment.* 1979 $10.95
Elliot J. Feldman & Neil Nevitte (eds.)	*The Future of North America: Canada, the United States, and Quebec Nationalism.* 1979 $7.95
David R. Protheroe	*Imports and Politics: Trade Decision Making in Canada, 1968-1979.* 1980 $8.95
G. Bruce Doern	*Government Intervention in the Canadian Nuclear Industry.* 1980 $8.95
G. Bruce Doern & Robert W. Morrison (eds.)	*Canadian Nuclear Policies.* 1980 $14.95
Allan M. Maslove & Gene Swimmer	*Wage Controls in Canada: 1975-78: A Study of Public Decision Making.* 1980 $11.95
T. Gregory Kane	*Consumers and the Regulators: Intervention in the Federal Regulatory Process.* 1980 $10.95
Réjean Lachapelle & Jacques Henripin	*La situation démolinguistique au Canada: évolution passée et prospective.* 1980 $24.95
Albert Breton & Anthony Scott	*The Design of Federations.* 1980 $6.95
A.R. Bailey & D.G. Hull	*The Way Out: A More Revenue-Dependent Public Sector and How It Might Revitalize the Process of Governing.* 1980 $6.95
David R. Harvey	*Christmas Turkey or Prairie Vulture? An Economic Analysis of the Crow's Nest Pass Grain Rates.* 1980 $10.95
Donald G. Cartwright	*Official Language Populations in Canada: Patterns and Contacts.* 1980 $4.95
Richard M. Bird	*Taxing Corporations.* 1980 $6.95
Leroy O. Stone & Susan Fletcher	*A Profile of Canada's Older Population.* 1980 $7.95
Peter N. Nemetz (ed.)	*Resource Policy: International Perspectives.* 1980 $18.95
Keith A.J. Hay (ed.)	*Canadian Perspectives on Economic Relations With Japan.* 1980 $18.95
Dhiru Patel	*Dealing With Interracial Conflict: Policy Alternatives.* 1980 $5.95
Raymond Breton & Gail Grant	*La langue de travail au Québec : synthèse de la recherche sur la rencontre de deux langues.* 1981 $10.95

Diane Vanasse

L'évolution de la population scolaire du Québec. 1981 $12.95

David M. Cameron (ed.)

Regionalism and Supranationalism: Challenges and Alternatives to the Nation-State in Canada and Europe. 1981 $9.95

Heather Menzies

Women and the Chip: Case Studies of the Effects of Information on Employment in Canada. 1981 $8.95

H.V. Kroeker (ed.)

Sovereign People or Sovereign Governments. 1981 $12.95

Peter Aucoin (ed.)

The Politics and Management of Restraint in Government. 1981 $17.95

Nicole S. Morgan

Nowhere to Go? Possible Consequences of the Demographic Imbalance in Decision-Making Groups of the Federal Public Service. 1981 $8.95

Nicole S. Morgan

Où aller? Les conséquences prévisibles des déséquilibres démographiques chez les groupes de décision de la fonction publique fédérale. 1981 $8.95

Raymond Breton,
Jeffrey G. Reitz &
Victor F. Valentine

Les frontières culturelles et la cohésion du Canada. 1981 $18.95

Peter N. Nemetz (ed.)

Energy Crisis: Policy Response. 1981 $10.95

James Gillies

Where Business Fails. 1981 $9.95

Allan Tupper &
G. Bruce Doern (eds.)

Public Corporations and Public Policy in Canada. 1981 $16.95

Réjean Lachapelle &
Jacques Henripin

The Demolinguistic Situation in Canada: Past Trends and Future Prospects. 1982 $24.95

Irving Brecher

Canada's Competition Policy Revisited: Some New Thoughts on an Old Story. 1982 $3.00

Ian McAllister

Regional Development and the European Community: A Canadian Perspective. 1982 $13.95

Donald J. Daly

Canada in an Uncertain World Economic Environment. 1982 $3.00

W.T. Stanbury &
Fred Thompson

Regulatory Reform in Canada. 1982 $7.95

Robert J. Buchan,
C. Christopher Johnston,
T. Gregory Kane,
Barry Lesser,
Richard J. Schultz &
W.T. Stanbury

Telecommunications Regulation and the Constitution. 1982 $18.95

Rodney de C. Grey

United States Trade Policy Legislation: A Canadian View. 1982 $7.95

John Quinn &
Philip Slayton (eds.)

Non-Tariff Barriers After the Tokyo Round. 1982 $17.95

Stanley M. Beck &
Ivan Bernier (eds.)

Canada and the New Constitution: The Unfinished Agenda. 2 vols. 1983 $10.95 (set)

R. Brian Woodrow & Kenneth B. Woodside (eds.)	*The Introduction of Pay-TV in Canada: Issues and Implications.* 1983 $14.95
E.P. Weeks & L. Mazany	*The Future of the Atlantic Fisheries.* 1983 $5.00
Douglas D. Purvis (ed.), assisted by Frances Chambers	*The Canadian Balance of Payments: Perspectives and Policy Issues.* 1983 $24.95
Roy A. Matthews	*Canada and the "Little Dragons": An Analysis of Economic Developments in Hong Kong, Taiwan, and South Korea and the Challenge/Opportunity They Present for Canadian Interests in the 1980s.* 1983 $11.95
Charles Pearson & Gerry Salembier	*Trade, Employment, and Adjustment.* 1983 $5.00
Steven Globerman	*Cultural Regulation in Canada.* 1983 $11.95
F.R. Flatters & R.G. Lipsey	*Common Ground for the Canadian Common Market.* 1983 $5.00
Frank Bunn, assisted by U. Domb, D. Huntley, H. Mills, H. Silverstein	*Oceans from Space: Towards the Management of Our Coastal Zones.* 1983 $5.00
C.D. Shearing & P.C. Stenning	*Private Security and Private Justice: The Challenge of the 80s.* 1983 $5.00
Jacob Finkelman & Shirley B. Goldenberg	*Collective Bargaining in the Public Service: The Federal Experience in Canada.* 2 vols. 1983 $29.95 (set)
Gail Grant	*The Concrete Reserve: Corporate Programs for Indians in the Urban Work Place.* 1983 $5.00
Owen Adams & Russell Wilkins	*Healthfulness of Life.* 1983 $8.00
Yoshi Tsurumi with Rebecca R. Tsurumi	*Sogoshosha: Engines of Export-Based Growth.* (Revised Edition). 1984 $10.95
Raymond Breton & Gail Grant (eds.)	*The Dynamics of Government Programs for Urban Indians in the Prairie Provinces.* 1984 $19.95
Frank Stone	*Canada, The GATT and the International Trade System.* 1984 $15.00
Pierre Sauvé	*Private Bank Lending and Developing-Country Debt.* 1984 $10.00
Mark Thompson & Gene Swimmer	*Conflict or Compromise: The Future of Public Sector Industrial Relations.* 1984 $15.00
Samuel Wex	*Instead of FIRA: Autonomy for Canadian Subsidiaries?* 1984 $8.00
R.J. Wonnacott	*Selected New Developments in International Trade Theory.* 1984 $7.00
R.J. Wonnacott	*Aggressive US Reciprocity Evaluated with a New Analytical Approach to Trade Conflicts.* 1984 $8.00

Richard W. Wright	*Japanese Business in Canada: The Elusive Alliance.* 1984 $12.00
Paul K. Gorecki & W.T. Stanbury	*The Objectives of Canadian Competition Policy, 1888-1983.* 1984 $15.00
Michael Hart	*Some Thoughts on Canada-United States Sectoral Free Trade.* 1985 $7.00
J. Peter Meekison Roy J. Romanow & William D. Moull	*Origins and Meaning of Section 92A: The 1982 Constitutional Amendment on Resources.* 1985 $10.00
Conference Papers	*Canada and International Trade. Volume One: Major Issues of Canadian Trade Policy. Volume Two: Canada and the Pacific Rim.* 1985 $25.00 (set)
A.E. Safarian	*Foreign Direct Investment: A Survey of Canadian Research.* 1985 $8.00
Joseph R. D'Cruz & James D. Fleck	*Canada Can Compete! Strategic Management of the Canadian Industrial Portfolio.* 1985 $18.00
Barry Lesser & Louis Vagianos	*Computer Communications and the Mass Market in Canada.* 1985 $10.00
W.R. Hines	*Trade Policy Making in Canada: Are We Doing it Right?* 1985 $10.00
Bertrand Nadeau	*Britain's Entry into the European Economic Community and its Effect on Canada's Agricultural Exports.* 1985 $10.00
Paul B. Huber	*Promoting Timber Cropping: Policies Toward Non-Industrial Forest Owners in New Brunswick.* 1985 $10.00
Gordon Robertson	*Northern Provinces: A Mistaken Goal.* 1985 $8.00
Petr Hanel	*La technologie et les exportations canadiennes du matériel pour la filière bois-papier.* 1985 $20.00
Russel M. Wills, Steven Globerman & Peter J. Booth	*Software Policies for Growth and Export.* 1986 $15.00
Marc Malone	*Une place pour le Québec au Canada.* 1986 $20.00
A. R. Dobell & S. H. Mansbridge	*The Social Policy Process in Canada.* 1986 $8.00
William D. Shipman (ed.)	*Trade and Investment Across the Northeast Boundary: Quebec, the Atlantic Provinces, and New England.* 1986 $20.00